Sin, Grace an[...]

Volume I

Sin, Grace and Free Will

A Historical Survey of Christian Thought

Volume I

The Apostolic Fathers to Augustine

Matthew Knell

©
James Clarke & Co

James Clarke & Co
P.O. Box 60
Cambridge
CB1 2NT
United Kingdom

www.jamesclarke.co
publishing@jamesclarke.co

Hardback ISBN: 978 0 227 17606 1

Paperback ISBN: 978 0 227 17654 2

British Library Cataloguing in Publication Data
A record is available from the British Library

Copyright © Matthew Knell, 2017

First Published, 2017

Cover vector designed by Garry Killian of Freepik.

Quotations from *Against Eunomius* (tr. M. DelCogliano and A. Radde-Gallwitz). Washington, D.C.: Catholic University of America Press, 2011. Used by permission.

All rights reserved. No part of this edition may be reproduced, stored electronically or in any retrieval system, or transmitted in any form or by any means, electronic, mechanical, photocopying, recording, or otherwise, without prior written permission from the Publisher
(permissions@jamesclarke.co).

Contents

Acknowledgements | vii

Introduction | 1

1. Early Church Views | 5

2. Irenaeus | 27

3. Tertullian | 47

4. Origen | 70

5. The Greek Fathers on Sin | 98

6. The Greek Fathers on Grace | 129

7. The Greek Fathers on Free Will | 159

8. Early Augustine | 177

9. Late Augustine | 195

Epilogue: After Augustine | 239

Final Thoughts | 249

Bibliography | 251

Index | 258

For Nicola,
may grace always be at the centre of all that you are.

Acknowledgements

The first thanks must go to those writers featured in this book who have wrestled with the revelation of God in their own contexts and in the face of great challenges from culture and philosophy to teach others about the nature of Christian faith concerning sin, grace and free will. I hope that I have treated them honourably in these presentations of their thought and that this work will encourage the wider church, not only those engaged in theological study, to consider these themes from different perspectives to appreciate the riches that are available to us through this great heritage.

For this particular project, I would like to thank all those at the University of Notre Dame that have inspired the writing of these volumes, particularly all those students who have taken the class on sin, grace and free will as they have helped me to process various strands of thought. My thanks also go to the community of the London School of Theology for all the encouragement and support that I receive on a daily basis and especially to Professor Tony Lane for his insight and wise advice as this project developed. I must also thank my two short-term research assistants, George Ioannou and Jonah Knell, who helped work through some of the Apostolic Fathers.

Finally, I am grateful for the patience and love of my family who, given the ongoing work for volumes two and three, are still dealing with the effects of this large-scale research project and who teach me so much about grace through the life we share.

Introduction

I remember a discussion with some fellow students about life and the choices we make and being shocked when one of them, latching onto this concept of choice, declared that I was an Arminian. At the time, I thought it rather harsh, given that I had not at the time read Arminius' work, or the *Remonstrance* that his followers had compiled, and was not seeking to engage in a seventeenth-century theological discussion, let alone a recent, processed version.

Having now read these texts, and many others concerning the core issues in the four hundred years since the death of Jacob Arminius (1560-1609), I reflect that the appellation was not merely unfair in the context but rather fundamentally incorrect. 'Arminian' has become jargon used by Christians, largely without an understanding of the historical and the theological roots underpinning the concept; the result of which is often that division between individuals and communities increases because the deeply nuanced areas of belief are simplified from a spectrum of greys into a clear 'black and white' alternative.

As a historical theologian, the task of charting the development of beliefs across centuries of Christian thought in different areas of the world, in vastly different historical and cultural contexts, encourages humility in approaching the subject. When reading sources from various periods of Christian history, one recognises a devotion to God's revelation in Scripture, church and experience. Writers throughout history have displayed a Spirit-filled wisdom that seeks to process this in theological and philosophical terms, in a lived-out spirituality, which recognises current challenges, and in practical calls to holy and faithful witness in a broken world.

This does not mean that the Church today should blindly accept the teachings of any one writer in history; there are, however, wise voices that need to be included in our thinking, which support us and challenge us. When I find passages in historical texts that I struggle with, I try to recognise that instead of taking a judgemental attitude toward my brothers and sisters from the past, I should rather be aware that no one is complete in knowledge and lifestyle; I should question at which point these men and women would have had issues with my faith and life.

This approach creates a complexity to the Christian life; apparent absolutes of faith and thought are often challenged as one considers others who have engaged with these ideas in societies in which Christians have served throughout the history of the Church, these experiences mediated through different languages and systems of thought. There are understandable solutions available today in systematic works that clarify an area of belief for the reader; these books are immensely valuable for those who struggle with an issue, the answer to which is needed to confirm and strengthen them. However, there is a danger, if one is limited to these packaged solutions, that a box forms around how God reveals and relates in any given area, which prevents the majesty of God's dynamic interaction with creation from being understood. This can limit the wonder and worship (and often the confusing complexity) that results from the experience the Church has had of God through history. As a consequence, there is a need to go back to read the original writings of Christians, instead of relying on others to tell us what the texts might have said, to enrich our beliefs and our lives.

There is thus a general inspiration to present directly the thought of great Christian writers through history. In terms of the precise themes of this work – sin, grace and free will – the decision to write this book came from a course that I developed to teach for Notre Dame University at their global gateway in London. A key aspect of the course I created had to be the historical development of thought. The themes of sin, grace and free will seemed, in their inter-relationship, to offer a broad scope, which could engage the students in some interesting debates. While seeking to prepare the course structure and materials, however, it soon became clear that these areas of thought generally had not been dealt with over a broad span of history but were either focused on particular debates – Augustine and Pelagius, Calvinists and Arminians – or were presented systematically with references to particular points supporting the view expressed.

Throughout the course of my own studies and then my teaching, I had been aware of the richness of thought that exists and I resolved to encourage the students to engage directly with the primary sources. The issue this posed was that, given the time for reading assigned and the fact that thought on sin, grace and free will was often embedded in writing about wider topics, only a limited amount could be read, which often involved engaging with, at best, tangentially relevant material.

I therefore decided to create this reader on sin, grace and free will, through looking at the works of some of the most prominent theologians in the history of the church, extracting the relevant passages and organising them thematically to give focused access to the development of thought about these themes. The intention is twofold: firstly, as indicated above, to help readers to recognise the breadth and depth of thought in these areas by Christians from different backgrounds, working in different contexts, to guard against an over-simplification, which would say one point of view is 'right' and another is 'wrong'; and, secondly, to encourage people to go beyond the quotations provided here, back to the original texts that interest them to study their work in greater detail – to this end, each chapter ends with links to the primary sources. In addition, the quotations here come from the most easily accessible editions of the works, generally speaking, those that are freely available online, in order that those who wish to move from the thought here to the context of the original works will be able to recognise the quotation that they are working from. There are two main drawbacks from working this way: the lack of gender-neutral language and the use of some arcane terms, but the intention to encourage the reader beyond this work, to the original sources, is more important than seeking the latest editions available.

I have sought to include the most prominent theologians in this volume from the first thousand years of the Church but others will undoubtedly highlight omissions they consider worthy: St Jerome, Cyprian of Carthage, Ambrose of Milan, for example. A book of this size is necessarily limited in the number of sources with which it can engage; there will always be the regret that more could not be included. I decided to group the Greek Fathers together because there is a general unanimity of thought on these concepts. Augustine of Hippo has been divided into two chapters, early and late, since there are discernible changes in his thought on sin, grace and free will as he confronted different groups.

In terms of the three main subjects studied here, the aim is to present sin, grace and free will as the writers use these concepts, rather than comparing their ideas to any preconceived definition. For two of the three, there are areas that need highlighting in this regard. Grace has become tied, in certain traditions, closely with particular aspects of Christianity – salvation, sacraments, spiritual gifts – but no assumptions are made here about what grace entails. The use of grace in biblical texts is so varied that a definitive reduction of its application would seem counter-intuitive. Free will is another problematic term, particularly in the Latin tradition where there are two phrases (*libera voluntas*, free will, and *liberum arbitrium*, free choice), which are used, and often translated, as 'free will', although they can have very particular, nuanced differences. This work is not aimed at a postgraduate level at which an understanding of this is vitally important; therefore individual instances where one or other Latin word is used are not noted. As a basic introduction to the difference between the two, the will is the core motivation or value, whereas a choice is the realisation of the will in an action. A choice is therefore more contextually limited than the fundamental orientation of a person's will.

This volume begins with a chapter on the Early Church Fathers, some of whose writings were considered for inclusion in the New Testament (indeed, some were part of New Testament canons until the end of the fourth century). These writings, with the exception of Justin Martyr, were not systematic treatments of Christian thought but are included here to act as something of a bridge between the New Testament and the history of theology, showing how the concepts of sin, grace and free will were treated in the earliest writings. Following this, three key early theologians are studied in depth – Irenaeus, Tertullian and Origen – in which we see the development of theological thought, generally in response to perceived incorrect teachings from groups that were overly reliant on current philosophical or religious teachings but differed from that received from the Apostles. At this stage, the New Testament was still in the process of formation and thus the oral tradition maintained an authority alongside the written tradition until at least 200 CE.

After these three writers, the centre of theological thought was firmly rooted in the eastern part of the Roman Empire, written in Greek and largely aimed at clarifying the doctrine of God. The chapter looking at the Greek Fathers surveys a number of different writers from the late fourth to the early sixth centuries, who were largely agreed in their teaching on sin, grace and free will. The last of the Greek Fathers, John of Damascus, who wrote in the early eighth century, is also included here. Finally, the work of Augustine of Hippo is discussed in two chapters covering his early and late work. He is the most influential theologian in the history of the church because of his defining role in the development of western thought. The split is not simply down to chapter size limitations, but the transition in his thought across all three areas. This was influenced by his switch from confronting the thought of the Manicheans to the Pelagians and addressing the different bases of theology. The Epilogue looks briefly at two later works – the canons of the Council of Orange and the work of John Scottus Erigena – that demonstrate how the western church engaged with Augustine in the centuries between his death and the twelfth-century renaissance that saw the birth of the scholastic movement.

1.
Early Church Views

When starting this survey, there was the option to begin with Irenaeus of Lyon. As the next chapter shows, he wrote more systematic theology against a variety of Gnostic heresies. There are, however, some important church writers before Irenaeus who can provide a connection in our understanding of how the concepts of sin, grace and free will were approached between the New Testament writings and the development of more systematic thought.

This chapter will therefore look at these earliest Christian writers, in this case comprising a group known as the Apostolic Fathers – Clement of Rome, Ignatius of Antioch, Polycarp of Smyrna, the *Didache*, the *Epistle of Barnabas*, the *Shepherd of Hermas* – and the great early apologist, Justin Martyr. Since the New Testament canon was not formally agreed until the Council of Carthage in 419, there was great importance given to the Apostolic Tradition and the developing oral tradition. Given the significance of many authors presented in this chapter, these documents were key in helping the Early Church develop its understanding of God's revelation. A good example of how important these texts were is the *Shepherd of Hermas*, which was accepted as Scripture by Irenaeus, Clement of Alexandria and Origen, and included in *Codex Sinaiticus*, an important edition of the Bible from the fourth century.

1 Clement is a letter from the bishop of Rome that was written at the end of the first century to the church in Corinth, with many similarities in style to the letters of the New Testament. It was another early document included in some versions of the New Testament. The authority given to 1 Clement shows the respect that bishops of Rome were gaining in early Christianity. 2 Clement, meanwhile, does not seem to be related to 1 Clement in authorship or style, being a sermon of unknown origin that was retained by the church because of the importance of its teaching.

Although we know little of the life of Ignatius of Antioch, his seven letters are important because they are an important resource in our knowledge of the Early Church, being written shortly before he was martyred in Rome. Polycarp is much better known for his life of faithful service, being martyred at the age of eighty-six after widespread influence in the church in the second century. There is an account of Polycarp's martyrdom written by the church in Smyrna that is a remarkable read. On being challenged to renounce his faith to gain his freedom, Polycarp is reported to have replied, 'For eighty-six years I have been his servant, and he has done me no wrong. How can I blaspheme my King who saved me?'[1]

The last three writings of the Apostolic Fathers are all anonymous. The *Didache*, or *Teachings of the Twelve*, is a collection of writings estimated to date back as far as the middle of the first century. There are indications from several Church Fathers that it was considered to be Scripture for the first few centuries of the church. The *Epistle of Barnabas* was written sometime around the turn of the first century and thus not by the New Testament figure of that name. It deals heavily with Christianity's relationship to Judaism and is a key early document that models the church's developing approach to Old Testament interpretation. The *Shepherd of Hermas* comprises five visions, twelve commandments and ten parables that were given through angelic figures. It was very popular in the early centuries of Christianity as it was simple, clear and practical. Jesus Christ and the Holy Spirit do not figure clearly in the text as the Angel of Repentance is the dominant character. The use of 'spirit' in particular is varied, sometimes referring to a human spirit, sometimes something more akin to the Holy Spirit and often somewhere in between. It is not an easy document to work with for those who seek a systematic theology, but it shows how many in the Early Church were drawn to experiential and practical teachings.

Justin Martyr was a great defender of Christianity – an apologist – in the middle of the second century, having converted from paganism and a devotion to Greek philosophy, primarily Plato. Justin's writings are far more voluminous than those of the Apostolic Fathers and could have been treated separately in this book, but the purpose of this chapter is to set the scene for the more extensive presentations in the following chapters.

In terms of their engagement with ideas of sin, grace and free will, it is certainly the first of these that receives the greatest attention. Grace, with its varied use in Scripture continues to be mentioned briefly in relation to the Christian life without any definitive construct being offered. Free will is strongly upheld in the nature of humanity and Christianity, but only Justin Martyr devotes extended sections of his work to this concept.

1. *Martyrdom of Polycarp*, 9.

1. Early Church Views

Sin

The presentation of sin can be grouped into several themes beginning with the nature of sin and the relationship between this and humans. The next stage is to look at the cause of sin in humanity, in terms of the first humans, and discussing the effects sin has had on society and Christians. Finally, the Apostolic Fathers are noted for their emphasis on righteousness and works. It is important to highlight this value in relation to sin while recognising that this does not imply salvation by works for the writers.

Justin Martyr addresses a question that seems to have become an issue for the earliest church, about what part of the human sins: the soul, the body or the whole? In *Dialogue with Trypho*, Justin presents a discussion on Christianity with a Hebrew who is interested in Greek philosophy. This grants Justin the freedom to examine topics from a variety of perspectives. When dealing with the soul and sin, Justin first distinguishes between animals and humans, claiming that the former are limited in their relationship to God because they do not have souls as humans do:

> 'Do goats or sheep injure any one?'
> 'No one in any respect,' I said.
> 'Therefore these animals will see [God] according to your account,' says he.
> 'No; for their body being of such a nature, is an obstacle to them.'[1]

Following this, Justin Martyr writes that the nature of humanity allows for sin in its differentiation from the nature of God, despite the likeness of nature in the spiritual dimension:

> For those things which exist after God, or shall at any time exist, these have the nature of decay, and are such as may be blotted out and cease to exist; for God alone is unbegotten and incorruptible, and therefore He is God, but all other things after Him are created and corruptible. For this reason souls both die and are punished: since, if they were unbegotten, they would neither sin, nor be filled with folly, nor be cowardly, and again ferocious; nor would they willingly transform into swine, and serpents, and dogs; and it would not indeed be just to compel them, if they be unbegotten.[2]

---

1. Justin Martyr, *Dialogue with Trypho*, 4. Later in this chapter of the work, there is a strange response to Trypho's question about what happens to those who have not seen God: 'They are imprisoned in the bodies of certain wild beasts, and this is their punishment.' There is little surrounding material to help us to understand precisely what Justin Martyr is trying to communicate about sin and punishment in this comment.
2. Ibid., 5.

In *On the Resurrection*, which is widely attributed to Justin, there is clear writing on the union of body and soul in sin as in all things:

> The flesh is a sinner, so much so, that it forces the soul to sin along with it. And thus they vainly accuse it, and lay to its charge alone the sins of both. But in what instance can the flesh possibly sin by itself, if it have not the soul going before it and inciting it? For as in the case of a yoke of oxen, if one or other is loosed from the yoke, neither of them can plough alone; so neither can soul or body alone effect anything, if they be unyoked from their communion. And if it is the flesh that is the sinner, then on its account alone did the Saviour come, as He says, 'I am not come to call the righteous, but sinners to repentance.' Since, then, the flesh has been proved to be valuable in the sight of God, and glorious above all His works, it would very justly be saved by Him.[1]

The nature of sin is therefore seen to involve the corruption of the whole person, body and soul and, as the *Shepherd of Hermas* states, the mind. There are writers later in the history of the church who analyse the role of intention and act in sin, but the basis of the first vision to Hermas is that he sinned in an evil desire towards a young woman who appears to him in his dream:

> And as I prayed, the heavens were opened, and I saw the woman whom I had desired saluting me from the sky, and saying, 'Hail, Hermas!' And looking up to her, I said, 'Lady, what doest thou here?' And she answered me, 'I have been taken up here to accuse you of your sins before the Lord.' 'Lady,' said I, 'are you to be the subject of my accusation?' 'No,' said she; 'but hear the words which I am going to speak to you. God, who dwells in the heavens, and made out of nothing the things that exist, and multiplied and increased them on account of His holy Church, is angry with you for having sinned against me.' I answered her, 'Lady, have I sinned against you? How? Or when spoke I an unseemly word to you? Did I not always think of you as a lady? Did I not always respect you as a sister? Why do you falsely accuse me of this wickedness and impurity?' With a smile she replied to me, 'The desire of wickedness arose within your heart. Is it not your opinion that a righteous man commits sin when an evil desire arises in his heart? There is sin in such a case, and the sin is great,' said she; 'for the thoughts of a righteous man should be righteous. For by thinking righteously his character is established in the heavens, and he has the Lord merciful to him in every business. But those who entertain wicked thoughts in their minds are bringing upon

---

1. Justin Martyr, *On the Resurrection*, 8.

themselves death and captivity; and especially is this the case with those who set their affections on this world, and glory in their riches, and look not forward to the blessings of the life to come. For many will their regrets be; for they have no hope, but have despaired of themselves and their life. But do thou pray to God, and He will heal thy sins, and the sins of thy whole house, and of all the saints.'

After she had spoken these words, the heavens were shut. I was overwhelmed with sorrow and fear, and said to myself, 'If this sin is assigned to me, how can I be saved, or how shall I propitiate God in regard to my sins, which are of the grossest character? With what words shall I ask the Lord to be merciful to me?' While I was thinking over these things, and discussing them in my mind, I saw opposite to me a chair, white, made of white wool, of great size. And there came up an old woman, arrayed in a splendid robe, and with a book in her hand; and she sat down alone, and saluted me, 'Hail, Hermas!' And in sadness and tears I said to her, 'Lady, hail!' And she said to me, 'Why are you downcast, Hermas? For you were wont to be patient and temperate, and always smiling. Why are you so gloomy, and not cheerful?'

I answered her and said, 'O Lady, I have been reproached by a very good woman, who says that I sinned against her.' And she said, 'Far be such a deed from a servant of God. But perhaps a desire after her has arisen within your heart. Such a wish, in the case of the servants of God, produces sin. For it is a wicked and horrible wish in an all-chaste and already well-tried spirit to desire an evil deed; and especially for Hermas so to do, who keeps himself from all wicked desire, and is full of all simplicity, and of great guilelessness.'[1]

2 Clement briefly takes this concept further to conscious and unconscious sin, allowing for the latter in encouraging the readers thus:

And let not us, in our folly, feel displeasure and indignation, whenever anyone admonishes us and turns us from unrighteousness to righteousness. For there are some wicked deeds which we commit, and know it not, because of the double-mindedness and unbelief present in our breasts, and our understanding is darkened by vain desires.[2]

A final theme in the nature of sin extends beyond the individual to the communal. Both 1 Clement and the *Shepherd of Hermas* indicate some kind of corporate element to sin and grace. In the *Shepherd of Hermas*, the elderly woman explains why God is angry at Hermas:

1. *Shepherd of Hermas*, Vision 1.1-2.
2. *2 Clement*, 19.

> But God is not angry with you on account of this, but that you may convert your house, which have committed iniquity against the Lord, and against you, their parents. And although you love your sons, yet did you not warn your house, but permitted them to be terribly corrupted. On this account is the Lord angry with you, but He will heal all the evils which have been done in your house. For, on account of their sins and iniquities, you have been destroyed by the affairs of this world.[1]

Clement writes to the church in Corinth:

> Full of holy designs, and with true earnestness of mind and a godly confidence, you stretched forth your hands to God Almighty, beseeching Him to be merciful to you, if you had been guilty of any involuntary transgression. Day and night you were anxious for the whole brotherhood, that the number of God's elect might be saved with mercy and a good conscience. You were sincere and uncorrupted, and forgetful of injuries between one another. Every kind of faction and schism was abominable in your sight. You mourned over the transgressions of your neighbours: their deficiencies you deemed your own.[2]

We move on now from the nature of sin to the cause of sin. We will start with the first sin of humanity and move on to look at the devil, demons and responsibility for sin. Two texts grant some power to the devil beyond mere temptation in causing the first sin, but it is worth noting that, while they allow dark spirits a role, human responsibility is never forgotten.

In *Hortatory Address to the Greeks*, Justin Martyr speaks of the deception that caused Adam to sin:

> Since, therefore, God knew that the first men remembered the old delusion of their forefathers, whereby the misanthropic demon contrived to deceive them when he said to them, 'If ye obey me in transgressing the commandment of God, ye shall be as gods.' ... Men, therefore, having been duped by the deceiving demon, and having dared to disobey God, were cast out of Paradise, remembering the name of gods, but no longer being taught by God that there are no other gods.[3]

Justin makes a similar point in the *Dialogue with Trypho*:

> For by this, as I previously remarked, He proclaimed the mystery, by which He declared that He would break the power of the serpent which occasioned the transgression of Adam, and [would bring] to

1. *Shepherd*, V.1.3.
2. *1 Clement* 2.
3. Justin Martyr, *Hortatory Address to the Greeks*, 21.

them that believe on Him [who was foreshadowed] by this sign, i.e., Him who was to be crucified, salvation from the fangs of the serpent, which are wicked deeds, idolatries, and other unrighteous acts.

Using this as a base, Justin Martyr goes on to discuss the ongoing role of the devil and demons in the experience of humanity since the Fall. He writes extensively on the nature of demons and fallen angels and their relationship to humanity in his *Second Apology*:

> But the angels transgressed this appointment, and were captivated by love of women, and begat children who are those that are called demons; and besides, they afterwards subdued the human race to themselves, partly by magical writings, and partly by fears and the punishments they occasioned, and partly by teaching them to offer sacrifices, and incense, and libations, of which things they stood in need after they were enslaved by lustful passions; and among men they sowed murders, wars, adulteries, intemperate deeds, and all wickedness. Whence also the poets and mythologists, not knowing that it was the angels and those demons who had been begotten by them that did these things to men, and women, and cities, and nations, which they related, ascribed them to god himself, and to those who were accounted to be his very offspring, and to the offspring of those who were called his brothers, Neptune and Pluto, and to the children again of these their offspring. For whatever name each of the angels had given to himself and his children, by that name they called them.[1]

There is thus some power that results for the demons. Justin writes of, 'the evil demons, who hate us, and who keep such men as these subject to themselves, and serving them in the capacity of judges, incite them, as rulers actuated by evil spirits, to put us to death';[2] while the *Epistle of Barnabas*, talks about the two ways of living:

> There are two ways of doctrine and authority, the one of light, and the other of darkness. But there is a great difference between these two ways. For over one are stationed the light-bringing angels of God, but over the other the angels' of Satan. And He indeed (i.e., God) is Lord for ever and ever, but he (i.e., Satan) is prince of the time of iniquity.[3]

However, the fact that this power exists does not mean that temptation is irresistible. The Angel of Repentance tells Hermas, 'for all luxury is foolish and empty in the servants of God. These, then, are the evil desires

1. Justin Martyr, *Second Apology*, 5.
2. Ibid., 1.
3. *Epistle of Barnabas*, 18.

which slay the servants of God. For this evil desire is the daughter of the devil. You must refrain from evil desires, that by refraining ye may live to God.'[1] This indicates a need to stand against the devil; a line also found in 2 Clement: 'For I myself, though a sinner every whir and not yet fleeing temptation but continuing in the midst of the tools of the devil, study to follow after righteousness, that I may make, be it only some, approach to it, fearing the judgment to come.'[2]

In addition to this role of the human will resisting temptation, there are also promises of divine assistance, such as this from the Angel of Repentance:

> Return, ye who walk in the commandments of the devil, in hard, and bitter, and wild licentiousness, and fear not the devil; for there is no power in him against you, for I will be with you, the angel of repentance, who am lord over him. The devil has fear only, but his fear has no strength. Fear him not, then, and he will flee from you.[3]

Justin Martyr offers a similar message:

> Though we lived in fornication and all kinds of filthy conversation, we have by the grace of our Jesus, according to His Father's will, stripped ourselves of all those filthy wickednesses with which we were imbued. And though the devil is ever at hand to resist us, and anxious to seduce all to himself, yet the Angel of God, i.e., the Power of God sent to us through Jesus Christ, rebukes him, and he departs from us. And we are just as if drawn out from the fire, when purified from our former sins, and [rescued] from the affliction and the fiery trial by which the devil and all his coadjutors try us; out of which Jesus the Son of God has promised again to deliver us, and invest us with prepared garments, if we do His commandments; and has undertaken to provide an eternal kingdom [for us].[4]

Finally, behind these statements about the limited role of the devil and demons is a determination that sin is the responsibility of humans (and angels in their fall) and this should not be avoided by positing external influence: 'Furthermore, I have proved in what has preceded, that those who were foreknown to be unrighteous, whether men or angels, are not made wicked by God's fault, but each man by his own fault is what he will appear to be'.[5] Clement makes this point clearly to the church in Corinth:

1. *Shepherd*, Commandment 12.2.
2. *2 Clement*, 18.
3. *Shepherd*, C.12.4.
4. *Dialogue*, 116.
5. Ibid., 140.

> Hence flowed emulation and envy, strife and sedition, persecution and disorder, war and captivity. So the worthless rose up against the honoured, those of no reputation against such as were renowned, the foolish against the wise, the young against those advanced in years. For this reason righteousness and peace are now far departed from you, inasmuch as every one abandons the fear of God, and is become blind in His faith, neither walks in the ordinances of His appointment, nor acts a part becoming a Christian, but walks after his own wicked lusts, resuming the practice of an unrighteous and ungodly envy, by which death itself entered into the world.[1]

The most complete treatment is found in Justin Martyr's *Second Apology*:

> For so we say that there will be the conflagration, but not as the Stoics, according to their doctrine of all things being changed into one another, which seems most degrading. But neither do we affirm that it is by fate that men do what they do, or suffer what they suffer, but that each man by free choice acts rightly or sins; and that it is by the influence of the wicked demons that earnest men, such as Socrates and the like, suffer persecution and are in bonds, while Sardanapalus, Epicurus, and the like, seem to be blessed in abundance and glory. The Stoics, not observing this, maintained that all things take place according to the necessity of fate. But since God in the beginning made the race of angels and men with free-will, they will justly suffer in eternal fire the punishment of whatever sins they have committed. And this is the nature of all that is made, to be capable of vice and virtue. For neither would any of them be praiseworthy unless there were power to turn to both [virtue and vice]. And this also is shown by those men everywhere who have made laws and philosophised according to right reason, by their prescribing to do some things and refrain from others. Even the Stoic philosophers, in their doctrine of morals, steadily honour the same things, so that it is evident that they are not very felicitous in what they say about principles and incorporeal things. For if they say that human actions come to pass by fate, they will maintain either that God is nothing else than the things which are ever turning, and altering, and dissolving into the same things, and will appear to have had a comprehension only of things that are destructible, and to have looked on God Himself as emerging both in part and in whole in every wickedness; or that neither vice nor virtue is anything; which is contrary to every sound idea, reason, and sense.[2]

The effect of this sin in us is captured well in 2 Clement:

1. *1 Clement*, 3.
2. Martyr, *Second Apology*, 7.

> We were deficient in understanding, worshipping stones and wood, and gold, and silver, and brass, the works of men's hands; and our whole life was nothing else than death. Involved in blindness, and with such darkness before our eyes, we have received sight, and through His will have laid aside that cloud by which we were enveloped.[1]

The *Shepherd of Hermas* speaks of a battle present in the believer between an evil spirit – it is unclear if this is personal (in the sense of a demon) or a distorted human spirit – and a holy spirit (again, the meaning of this is unclear as it does not seem to correspond closely to the Holy Spirit of the New Testament writers). The Angel of Repentance, when speaking to Hermas, is clear that the two spirits cannot coexist well in the same person.

> For if you be patient, the Holy Spirit that dwells in you will be pure. He will not be darkened by any evil spirit, but, dwelling in a broad region, he will rejoice and be glad; and with the vessel in which he dwells he will serve God in gladness, having great peace within himself. But if any outburst of anger take place, forthwith the Holy Spirit, who is tender, is straitened, not having a pure place, and He seeks to depart. For he is choked by the vile spirit, and cannot attend on the Lord as he wishes, for anger pollutes him. For the Lord dwells in long-suffering, but the devil in anger. The two spirits, then, when dwelling in the same habitation, are at discord with each other, and are troublesome to that man in whom they dwell. . . . For when all these spirits dwell in one vessel in which the Holy Spirit also dwells, the vessel cannot contain them, but overflows. The tender Spirit, then, not being accustomed to dwell with the wicked spirit, nor with hardness, withdraws from such a man, and seeks to dwell with meekness and peacefulness. Then, when he withdraws from the man in whom he dwelt, the man is emptied of the righteous Spirit; and being henceforward filled with evil spirits, he is in a state of anarchy in every action, being dragged hither and thither by the evil spirits, and there is a complete darkness in his mind as to everything good. . . . Both these are grievous to the Holy Spirit – doubt and anger. Wherefore remove grief from you, and crush not the Holy Spirit which dwells in you, lest he entreat God against you, and he withdraw from you. For the Spirit of God which has been granted to us to dwell in this body does not endure grief nor straitness.[2]

1. *2 Clement*, 1.
2. *Shepherd*, C.5.1, C.5.2, C.10.2.

1. Early Church Views

Given this emphasis on responsibility, these writers believe that it is incumbent on Christians to pursue righteousness with their whole being. The Apostolic Fathers in particular write massive sections on the need for and nature of Christian righteousness, and have been criticised for this and the comparative absence of grace teaching in their works. Throughout these works, there is a sense that these commandments are the outworking of the reception of the Gospel message. Polycarp states:

> These things, brethren, I write to you concerning righteousness, not because I take anything upon myself, but because ye have invited me to do so. For neither I, nor any other such one, can come up to the wisdom of the blessed and glorified Paul. . . . For if any one be inwardly possessed of these graces, he hath fulfilled the command of righteousness, since he that hath love is far from all sin.[1]

Clement begins his letter to the church at Corinth with a similar exhortation:

> For who ever dwelt even for a short time among you, and did not find your faith to be as fruitful of virtue as it was firmly established? Who did not admire the sobriety and moderation of your godliness in Christ? Who did not proclaim the magnificence of your habitual hospitality? And who did not rejoice over your perfect and well-grounded knowledge? For you did all things without respect of persons, and walked in the commandments of God, being obedient to those who had the rule over you, and giving all fitting honour to the presbyters among you. You enjoined young men to be of a sober and serious mind; you instructed your wives to do all things with a blameless, becoming, and pure conscience, loving their husbands as in duty bound; and you taught them that, living in the rule of obedience, they should manage their household affairs becomingly, and be in every respect marked by discretion.[2]

Likewise, Hermas is told, 'For he who has received remission of his sins ought not to sin any more, but to live in purity . . . if any one is tempted by the devil, and sins after that great and holy calling in which the Lord has called His people to everlasting life, he has opportunity to repent but once. But if he should sin frequently after this, and then repent, to such a man his repentance will be of no avail; for with difficulty will he live'[3] while Justin Martyr writes:

1. Polycarp, *Philippians*, 3.
2. *1 Clement*, 1.
3. *Shepherd*, C.4.3.

> So that it becomes you to eradicate this hope from your souls, and hasten to know in what way forgiveness of sins, and a hope of inheriting the promised good things, shall be yours. But there is no other [way] than this – to become acquainted with this Christ, to be washed in the fountain spoken of by Isaiah for the remission of sins; and for the rest, to live sinless lives.[1]

Clement has the most explicit material on the fact that we are not justified by works, and he then writes about the correct response:

> What shall we do, then, brethren? Shall we become slothful in well-doing, and cease from the practice of love? God forbid that any such course should be followed by us! But rather let us hasten with all energy and readiness of mind to perform every good work. For the Creator and Lord of all Himself rejoices in His works. . . . Having therefore such an example, let us without delay accede to His will, and let us work the work of righteousness with our whole strength.[2]

While this call to righteousness is the result of salvation, there are some passages that indicate merit in relation to sins that have been committed, such as this quote from 2 Clement: 'Good, then, is alms as repentance from sin; better is fasting than prayer, and alms than both; "charity covereth a multitude of sins", and prayer out of a good conscience delivereth from death. Blessed is every one that shall be found complete in these; for alms lightens the burden of sin.'[3] Similarly, the *Didache* teaches:

> Be not a stretcher forth of the hands to receive and a drawer of them back to give. If you have anything, through your hands you shall give ransom for your sins. Do not hesitate to give, nor complain when you give; for you shall know who is the good repayer of the hire.[4]

The topic of sin is thus treated thoroughly in these earliest church writers and from a variety of perspectives. In comparison, the volume of material on grace and free will is much briefer and more isolated.

Grace

The mentions of grace mirror the varied use of the term in Scripture. In the closing of his letter to the church in Smyrna, Ignatius of Antioch sounds distinctly Pauline in two phrases: 'Grace, mercy, peace, and

---

1. Martyr, *Dialogue*, 44.
2. *1 Clement*, 33.
3. *2 Clement*, 16.
4. *Didache*, 4.

1. Early Church Views

patience, be with you in Christ for evermore. . . . Fare ye well in the grace of God.'[1] Perhaps the strangest use of the word appears earlier in the epistle:

> I write to you by Burrhus, whom ye sent with me, together with the Ephesians, your brethren, and who has in all things refreshed me. And I would that all may imitate him, as being a pattern of a minister of God. Grace will reward him in all things.[2]

The application of grace can be roughly grouped together in three areas: salvation, sanctification and charismata – the gifts of the Holy Spirit; literally, the gifts of grace.[3] The *Epistle of Barnabas* brings these three together most clearly in the opening remarks:

> Seeing that the ordinances of God are great and rich unto you, I rejoice with an exceeding great and overflowing joy at your blessed and glorious spirits; so innate is the grace of the spiritual gift that ye have received. Wherefore also I the more congratulate myself hoping to be saved, for that I truly see the Spirit poured out among you from the riches of the fount of the Lord.[4]

The most extensive writer on the grace of salvation is Clement, who repeatedly returns to that which has been won by the Christ event for those who repent. Early in the letter, he writes:

> Let us look steadfastly to the blood of Christ, and see how precious that blood is to God, which, having been shed for our salvation, has set the grace of repentance before the whole world. Let us turn to every age that has passed, and learn that, from generation to generation, the Lord has granted a place of repentance to all who would be converted to Him.[5]

He follows this up in the next chapter by stating:

> The ministers of the grace of God have, by the Holy Spirit, spoken of repentance; and the Lord of all things has himself declared with an oath regarding it, 'As I live, says the Lord, I desire not the death of the sinner, but rather his repentance.'[6]

The next reference is slightly different, speaking of the 'yoke' of grace, implying that the righteousness that Christians are bound to was noted

1. Ignatius of Antioch, *Smyrnaeans*, 12, 13.
2. Ibid., 12.
3. *Charis* being the Greek word for 'grace'.
4. *Barnabas*, 1.
5. *1 Clement*, 7.
6. Ibid., 8.

above in the section on sin: 'You see, beloved, what is the example which has been given us; for if the Lord thus humbled Himself, what shall we do who have through Him come under the yoke of His grace?'[1]

Later in the letter, Clement clarifies that this salvation by grace denies any teaching that we can work towards our own salvation:

> Let us cleave, then, to those to whom grace has been given by God. Let us clothe ourselves with concord and humility, ever exercising self-control, standing far off from all whispering and evil-speaking, being justified by our works, and not our words. For [the Scripture] says, 'He that speaks much, shall also hear much in answer. And does he that is ready in speech deem himself righteous? Blessed is he that is born of woman, who lives but a short time: be not given to much speaking.' Let our praise be in God, and not of ourselves; for God hates those who commend themselves. Let testimony to our good deeds be borne by others, as it was in the case of our righteous forefathers. Boldness, and arrogance, and audacity belong to those that are accursed of God; but moderation, humility, and meekness to such as are blessed by Him.[2]

He follows this with more teaching on the same lines:

> And we, too, being called by His will in Christ Jesus, are not justified by ourselves, nor by our own wisdom, or understanding, or godliness, or works which we have wrought in holiness of heart; but by that faith through which, from the beginning.[3]

Other writers who explicitly mention grace in this context are Polycarp, who begins his letter by writing, '"In whom, though now ye see Him not, ye believe, and believing, rejoice with joy unspeakable and full of glory;" into which joy many desire to enter, knowing that "by grace ye are saved, not of works", but by the will of God through Jesus Christ',[4] and Ignatius of Antioch in his letters to the Ephesians and Smyrnaeans:

> Let us therefore be of a reverent spirit, and fear the long-suffering of God, that it tend not to our condemnation. For let us either stand in awe of the wrath to come, or show regard for the grace which is at present displayed – one of two things. Only [in one way or another] let us be found in Christ Jesus unto the true life.[5]

1. Ibid., 16.
2. Ibid., 30.
3. Ibid., 32.
4. Polycarp, *Philippians*, 1.
5. Ignatius, *Ephesians*, 11.

> Nevertheless, according to the will of God, I have been thought worthy [of this honour], not that I have any sense [of having deserved it], but by the grace of God, which I wish may be perfectly given to me, that through your prayers I may attain to God.[1]

The two writers compare the grace of the new covenant in Christ with that found in the Old Testament. Ignatius argues that the prophets of the Old Testament were teaching salvation by grace through Christ rather than through the law:

> Be not deceived with strange doctrines, nor with old fables, which are unprofitable. For if we still live according to the Jewish law, we acknowledge that we have not received grace. For the divinest prophets lived according to Christ Jesus. On this account also they were persecuted, being inspired by His grace to fully convince the unbelieving that there is one God, who has manifested Himself by Jesus Christ His Son, who is His eternal Word, not proceeding forth from silence, and who in all things pleased Him that sent Him.[2]

Justin Martyr equates grace in the Old Testament, particularly the grace given to Abraham whereby Christians are saved:

> What larger measure of grace, then, did Christ bestow on Abraham? This, namely, that He called him with His voice by the like calling, telling him to quit the land wherein he dwelt. And He has called all of us by that voice, and we have left already the way of living in which we used to spend our days, passing our time in evil after the fashions of the other inhabitants of the earth; and along with Abraham we shall inherit the holy land, when we shall receive the inheritance for an endless eternity, being children of Abraham through the like faith.[3]

There are two areas of grace that result from this salvation: sanctification and gifts. Ignatius writes about sanctification to the church at Smyrna:

> But consider those who are of a different opinion with respect to the grace of Christ which has come unto us, how opposed they are to the will of God. They have no regard for love; no care for the widow, or the orphan, or the oppressed; of the bond, or of the free; of the hungry, or of the thirsty.[4]

Clement, meanwhile, applies this idea to the church:

1. Ignatius, *Smyrnaeans*, 11.
2. Ignatius, *Magnesians*, 8.
3. Martyr, *Dialogue*, 119.
4. Ignatius, *Smyrnaeans*, 6.

> Let us cleave, therefore, to the innocent and righteous, since these are the elect of God. Why are there strifes, and tumults, and divisions, and schisms, and wars among you? Have we not [all] one God and one Christ? Is there not one Spirit of grace poured out upon us?[1]

Justin Martyr makes a similar point in the *Dialogue*:

> But impute it to your own wickedness, that God even can be accused by those who have no understanding, of not having always instructed all in the same righteous statutes. For such institutions seemed to be unreasonable and unworthy of God to many men, who had not received grace to know that your nation were called to conversion and repentance of spirit, while they were in a sinful condition and labouring under spiritual disease; and that the prophecy which was announced subsequent to the death of Moses is everlasting. And this is mentioned in the Psalm, my friends. And that we, who have been made wise by them, confess that the statutes of the Lord are sweeter than honey and the honey-comb, is manifest from the fact that, though threatened with death, we do not deny His name.[2]

In terms of the gifts of grace, the dominant application is to prophecy, which is made by three separate writers. The *Epistle of Barnabas* contains a brief reference: 'The prophets, having obtained grace from Him, prophesied concerning Him';[3] while the *Shepherd of Hermas* confuses spirit and angelic agency in this context, a result of the nature of the book:

> When, then, a man having the divine spirit comes into an assembly of righteous men who have faith in the divine spirit, and this assembly of men offers up prayer to God, then the angel of the prophetic spirit, who is destined for him, fills the man; and the man being filled with the holy spirit, speaks to the multitude as the Lord wishes.[4]

Justin Martyr writes about grace more in terms of the interpretation of the Scriptures:

> Unless, therefore, a man by God's great grace receives the power to understand what has been said and done by the prophets, the appearance of being able to repeat the words or the deeds will not profit him, if he cannot explain the argument of them. . . . Accordingly He revealed to us all that we have perceived by His grace out of the Scriptures, so that we know Him to be the first-begotten

---

1. *1 Clement*, 46.
2. Martyr, *Dialogue*, 30.
3. *Barnabas*, 5.
4. *Shepherd*, C.11.

of God, and to be before all creatures; likewise to be the Son of the patriarchs, since He assumed flesh by the Virgin of their family, and submitted to become a man without comeliness, dishonoured, and subject to suffering.[1]

This brief survey shows that there is little organised teaching about grace at this point in the church's journey, but writers develop some similar themes from the Apostolic Tradition that are in line with teachings in the New Testament.

Free Will

The Apostolic Fathers rarely address free will as a philosophical concept nor link it to the theology that they are teaching. This may be because there was an understood position on the subject, or simply that the nature of their writings, which are more devotional or exhortative, does not naturally lead them into a discussion of this topic. One example of them coming close to discussing free will can be found in Ignatius' letter to the Magnesians, which implies that actions result from being:

> Seeing, then, all things have an end, these two things are simultaneously set before us – death and life; and every one shall go unto his own place. For as there are two kinds of coins, the one of God, the other of the world, and each of these has its special character stamped upon it [so is it also here]. The unbelieving are of this world; but the believing have, in love, the character of God the Father by Jesus Christ, by whom, if we are not in readiness to die into His passion, His life is not in us.[2]

The focus is on the responsibility of believers for their actions, a point reinforced in 2 Clement: 'By what course of conduct, then, shall we attain these things, but by leading a holy and righteous life, and by deeming these worldly things as not belonging to us, and not fixing our desires upon them? For if we desire to possess them, we fall away from the path of righteousness.'[3]

It is only when we reach Justin Martyr's more systematic approach that we find extended sections that deal with free will. These can be divided into two main groups: firstly, there is the belief that free will is an essential part of created human nature, a core part of human identity; secondly, there is teaching on the nature of God's foreknowledge, with some indication of what this means for human will and responsibility.

1. Martyr, *Dialogue*, 92, 100.
2. Ignatius, *Magnesians*, 5.
3. *2 Clement*, 5.

In his *First Apology*, Justin avows free will in light of the work of the devil and the delay to his punishment:

> For He foreknows that some are to be saved by repentance, some even that are perhaps not yet born. In the beginning He made the human race with the power of thought and of choosing the truth and doing right, so that all men are without excuse before God; for they have been born rational and contemplative. And if any one disbelieves that God cares for these things, he will thereby either insinuate that God does not exist, or he will assert that though He exists He delights in vice, or exists like a stone, and that neither virtue nor vice are anything, but only in the opinion of men these things are reckoned good or evil.[1]

In the *Dialogue*, Justin focuses on the honour that God gives humanity in giving them this freedom of choice, recognising that this entails a willingness to punish when that will is not used correctly.

> Now, we know that he [Jesus] did not go to the river because He stood in need of baptism, or of the descent of the Spirit like a dove; even as He submitted to be born and to be crucified, not because He needed such things, but because of the human race, which from Adam had fallen under the power of death and the guile of the serpent, and each one of which had committed personal transgression. For God, wishing both angels and men, who were endowed with free-will, and at their own disposal, to do whatever He had strengthened each to do, made them so, that if they chose the things acceptable to Himself, He would keep them free from death and from punishment; but that if they did evil, He would punish each as He sees fit. . . .[2]
>
> Could He not have at once created a multitude of men? But yet, since He knew that it would be good, He created both angels and men free to do that which is righteous, and He appointed periods of time during which He knew it would be good for them to have the exercise of free-will; and because He likewise knew it would be good, He made general and particular judgments; each one's freedom of will, however, being guarded. Hence Scripture says the following, at the destruction of the tower, and division and alteration of tongues: 'And the Lord said, Behold, the people is one, and they have all one language; and this they have begun to do: and now nothing will be restrained from them of all which they have attempted to do.'[3]

---

1. Martyr, *First Apology*, 28.
2. Martyr, *Dialogue*, 88.
3. Ibid., 102.

The question that this raises, and which Justin addresses, is why does God allow this level of freedom if he foreknows the disastrous consequences that will result? It is interesting that the dominant theme is foreknowledge, rather than predestination, and this allows Justin to maintain a strong line against a Greek idea of fate controlling destiny. A good bridge between created freedom and the theme of God's foreknowledge is found in the *Dialogue*:

> But that you may not have a pretext for saying that Christ must have been crucified, and that those who transgressed must have been among your nation, and that the matter could not have been otherwise, I said briefly by anticipation, that God, wishing men and angels to follow His will, resolved to create them free to do righteousness; possessing reason, that they may know by whom they are created, and through whom they, not existing formerly, do now exist; and with a law that they should be judged by Him, if they do anything contrary to right reason: and of ourselves we, men and angels, shall be convicted of having acted sinfully, unless we repent beforehand. But if the Word of God foretells that some angels and men shall be certainly punished, it did so because it foreknew that they would be unchangeably [wicked], but not because God had created them so.[1]

The fact of God's complete foreknowledge is regularly stated by Justin Martyr: 'For none of you, I suppose, will venture to say that God neither did nor does foresee the events, which are future, nor foreordained his deserts for each one.'[2]

> This has come to pass through the wonderful foreknowledge of God, in order that we, through the calling of the new and eternal covenant, that is, of Christ, might be found more intelligent and God-fearing than yourselves, who are considered to be lovers of God and men of understanding, but are not.[3]

In his *First Apology*, Justin confronts the Greek ideas of fate and seeks to respond from a Christian perspective. The sovereignty of God, with complete foreknowledge, could lead Christians to hold onto a fatalistic determinism that lowers human worth and absolves humanity from the responsibility for sin and its consequences. In successive chapters, Justin deals at length with this issue, upholding God's unique perspective but equally retaining absolute human responsibility:

1. Ibid., 141.
2. Ibid., 16.
3. Ibid., 118.

But lest some suppose, from what has been said by us, that we say that whatever happens, happens by a fatal necessity, because it is foretold as known beforehand, this too we explain. We have learned from the prophets, and we hold it to be true, that punishments, and chastisements, and good rewards, are rendered according to the merit of each man's actions. Since if it be not so, but all things happen by fate, neither is anything at all in our own power. For if it be fated that this man, e.g., be good, and this other evil, neither is the former meritorious nor the latter to be blamed. And again, unless the human race have the power of avoiding evil and choosing good by free choice, they are not accountable for their actions, of whatever kind they be. But that it is by free choice they both walk uprightly and stumble, we thus demonstrate. We see the same man making a transition to opposite things. Now, if it had been fated that he were to be either good or bad, he could never have been capable of both the opposites, nor of so many transitions. But not even would some be good and others bad, since we thus make fate the cause of evil, and exhibit her as acting in opposition to herself; or that which has been already stated would seem to be true, that neither virtue nor vice is anything, but that things are only reckoned good or evil by opinion; which, as the true word shows, is the greatest impiety and wickedness. But this we assert is inevitable fate, that they who choose the good have worthy rewards, and they who choose the opposite have their merited awards. For not like other things, as trees and quadrupeds, which cannot act by choice, did God make man: for neither would he be worthy of reward or praise did he not of himself choose the good, but were created for this end; nor, if he were evil, would he be worthy of punishment, not being evil of himself, but being able to be nothing else than what he was made....[1]

And hence there seem to be seeds of truth among all men; but they are charged with not accurately understanding [the truth] when they assert contradictories. So that what we say about future events being foretold, we do not say it as if they came about by a fatal necessity; but God foreknowing all that shall be done by all men, and it being His decree that the future actions of men shall all be recompensed according to their several value, He foretells by the Spirit of prophecy that He will bestow meet rewards according to the merit of the actions done, always urging the human race to effort and recollection, showing that He cares and provides for men. But by the agency of the devils, death has been decreed against those who read the books of Hystaspes, or of the Sibyl, or of the prophets, that through fear they may prevent men who read them from receiving the knowledge of the good, and may retain them in slavery to themselves; which, however, they could not always effect.[2]

1. Martyr, *First Apology*, 43.
2. Ibid., 44.

There is, therefore, some teaching in these early writings about freedom of will, although it is more implied in the earlier material on sin than explicitly developed in a systematic doctrine of humanity, which only Justin Martyr begins to do. One of the main dangers for this earliest church was the strength of Greek lines of thought. Fatalism was key to this theme and thus Martyr stresses that Christian belief in a sovereign God in no way implies God is involved in the origin or practice of evil. This remains the responsibility of humankind because of their unique created position.

Conclusion

This chapter is important in providing a sense of the progression of Christian thought from the earliest decades of the church, at a time when processing the experience of being a church in a secular society was more important for Christians than the need to develop a systematic theology. In this context, it is the existence and response to sin that provides the major focus in terms of this book. Due to limited space, sections on the need to practice righteousness could not be included. This chapter has highlighted particular teachings on the nature of sin, its causes and the ongoing experience of sin, with the devil and demons playing a major role in the writings but not exerting control over the human psyche.

It is difficult to pick up themes of grace in these works. Instead, sporadic references to the concept can loosely be grouped together under the themes of salvation, sanctification and gifting. Grace seems to be more a reflection on experience rather than something solid underpinning the belief system. Free will is implied rather than stated, although Justin Martyr does sense a need to confront a Greek deterministic worldview head on.

You can find the writings of the Apostolic Fathers and Justin Martyr online at www.earlychristianwritings.com, although a more recent and readable edition is Michael Holmes' *The Apostolic Fathers in English* (Grand Rapids: Baker Books, 2006). The Justin Martyr quotations come from Volume 1 of the *Ante-Nicene Fathers* series, which is available at www.ccel.org, while a more recent version has been published as *The Apologies of Justin Martyr* (London: Aeterna Press, 2015). Michael Holmes' book is useful in providing concise, thorough presentations of the Apostolic Fathers that flesh out the brief introductions given here. Introductions to the thought of these writers are sadly lacking, but fortunately Paul Foster has edited an excellent series of articles entitled

The Writings of the Apostolic Fathers (Edinburgh: T&T Clark, 2007), which allows the reader to gain a solid foundation for approaching the various thinkers and highlights further reading if one wishes to go deeper into any of the texts.

2.
Irenaeus

This chapter looks at Irenaeus of Lyon, a second-century theologian with a clear heritage to the New Testament writings, having listened to the wonderfully-named Polycarp of Smyrna in his youth. Polycarp himself studied under John the Apostle. Although born in Asia, Irenaeus ministered mostly in Gaul – hence his title – where he acted as bishop, evangelist and apologist for the nascent church. Irenaeus' greatest surviving work is his *Against Heresies*, a five-volume treatise combating the plethora of Gnostic teachings that threatened the church in his time – volume one alone deals with fourteen separate major strands of Gnosticism.

Many Christians will have encountered some basic Gnostic beliefs when studying the Gospel and the letters of John, since they were an early influence on this line of thought. Studies will often present a rather simplistic view of Gnosticism – that matter is evil and spirit is good, leading to a denial of any real incarnation in Christ. This would lead someone reading Irenaeus to be rather shocked at the depth of thought he was encountering. For example, the mere title of chapter one, book one of *Against Heresies* is rather daunting: 'Absurd ideas of the disciples of Valentinus as to the origin, name, order, and conjugal productions of their fancied Æons, with the passages of Scripture which they adapt to their opinions.' By the end of the first few sentences, I can well imagine many readers deciding against pursuing this valuable primary source:

> They maintain, then, that in the invisible and ineffable heights above there exists a certain perfect, pre-existent Æon, whom they call Proarche, Propator, and Bythus, and describe as being invisible and incomprehensible. Eternal and unbegotten, he remained throughout innumerable cycles of ages in profound serenity and quiescence. There existed along with him Ennoea, whom they also call Charis and Sige.[1]

---

1. Irenaeus, *Against Heresies*, 1.1.

If this book has one contribution to make, it is perhaps the presentation of views on sin, grace and free will that allows readers access to these ideas without the need to trawl through a mass of material. The Gnosticism that Irenaeus was addressing was diverse in its presentations and incredibly deep in its content. The church owes him a great debt in his refutation of so powerful a doctrine.

Against Heresies must be considered in this context, since the material is consistently focused against the range of Gnostic heresies. The most explicit and elaborate sections written by Irenaeus are undoubtedly those on the freedom of the will, given that one of the strands of Gnostic thought tended towards a strong deterministic position. We will, however, leave this until after the presentation of his ideas on sin, since his understanding of the effects of sin is important as a precursor to the writing on free will and is significant in itself. There is much less of real significance on grace, and this will be examined last. It provides clarification on the free will discussion and is also useful as an indication of Early Church thought.

Sin

Irenaeus wrote one of the most significant passages on the concept of sin in book four of *Against Heresies*. Chapter thirty-eight of that book is entitled 'Why man was not made perfect from the beginning'. This challenges anyone brought up in a purely Augustinian tradition, as well as the Gnostic view that some are good by nature while others are naturally bad. This teaching is questioned in the previous chapter by Irenaeus as he focuses on the nature of free will, which is offered to all and through the exercise of which 'man may finally be brought to maturity at some future time'.[1] The indication already is that humans were created in an immature state in which they wandered into sin through the use of their free will.

Irenaeus starts his discussion on mankind's imperfection by stating that '[I]t was possible for God Himself to have made man perfect from the first, but man could not receive this [perfection], being as yet an infant.'[2] This infantile state is a result of creation, which necessarily makes mankind less perfect than the creator: 'as the latter was only recently created, he could not possibly have received it, or even if he had received it, could he have contained it, or containing it, could he

1. Ibid., 4.37.
2. Ibid., 4.38.

have retained it.'[1] There is therefore a need for humans to be created in an infantile state and to progress gradually towards maturity and perfection:

> By this arrangement, therefore, and these harmonies, and a sequence of this nature, man, a created and organised being, is rendered after the image and likeness of the uncreated God – the Father planning everything well and giving His commands, the Son carrying these into execution and performing the work of creating, and the Spirit nourishing and increasing [what is made], but man making progress day by day, and ascending towards the perfect, that is, approximating to the uncreated One. For the Uncreated is perfect, that is, God. Now it was necessary that man should in the first instance be created; and having been created, should receive growth; and having received growth, should be strengthened; and having been strengthened, should abound; and having abounded, should recover [from the disease of sin]; and having recovered, should be glorified; and being glorified, should see his Lord.[2]

The importance of this teaching is shown by Irenaeus in the next section as he relates this back to a Gnostic teaching that God is responsible for evil (hence the idea that people are naturally good or bad):

> Irrational, therefore, in every respect, are they who await not the time of increase, but ascribe to God the infirmity of their nature. Such persons know neither God nor themselves, being insatiable and ungrateful, unwilling to be at the outset what they have also been created – men subject to passions.[3]

The sin of humankind is thus a necessary part of the self-awareness and maturation process as preparation for perfection, immortality and incorruptibility:

> But since we could not sustain the power of divinity, He adds, 'But ye shall die like men,' setting forth both truths – the kindness of His free gift, and our weakness, and also that we were possessed of power over ourselves. For after His great kindness He graciously conferred good [upon us], and made men like to Himself, [that is] in their own power; while at the same time by His prescience He knew the infirmity of human beings, and the consequences which would flow from it; but through [His] love and [His] power, He shall overcome the substance of created nature. For it

1. Ibid.
2. Ibid.
3. Ibid.

was necessary, at first, that nature should be exhibited; then, after that, that what was mortal should be conquered and swallowed up by immortality, and the corruptible by incorruptibility, and that man should be made after the image and likeness of God, having received the knowledge of good and evil.[1]

Irenaeus does not develop this precise idea too deeply. The next chapter returns to the nature and responsibility of free will, picking up on that which went before. For the rest of *Against Heresies*, there are simply indications of the purposes that Irenaeus would see in God's decision to allow for a sinful humanity. The theme here is that sin points humanity towards the need for a saviour. This is worked out both in the biblical accounts of sin, which are included:

> not for the sake of those who did then transgress, but as a means of instruction unto us, and that we should understand that it is one and the same God against whom these men sinned, and against whom certain persons do now transgress from among those who profess to have believed in Him[2]

and in terms of the individual:

> He, the same against whom we had sinned in the beginning, grants forgiveness of sins in the end. But if indeed we had disobeyed the command of any other, while it was a different being who said, 'Thy sins are forgiven thee;' such an one is neither good, nor true, nor just. For how can he be good, who does not give from what belongs to himself? Or how can he be just, who snatches away the goods of another? And in what way can sins be truly remitted, unless that He against whom we have sinned has Himself granted remission 'through the bowels of mercy of our God' . . . . Therefore, by remitting sins, He did indeed heal man, while He also manifested Himself who He was.[3]

This is linked into the role of the law in revealing sin:

> But the law coming, which was given by Moses, and testifying of sin that it is a sinner, did truly take away his (death's) kingdom, showing that he was no king, but a robber; and it revealed him as a murderer. It laid, however, a weighty burden upon man, who had sin in himself, showing that he was liable to death. For as the law was spiritual, it merely made sin to stand out in relief, but did not destroy it.[4]

1. Ibid.
2. Ibid., 4.27.
3. Ibid., 5.17.
4. Ibid., 3.18.

This is the foundational thought by Irenaeus on the concept of sin. He believed people wandered into sin from a position of immaturity and, through sin, death and redemption, achieved a maturity for which they were not initially fitted. This leaves two areas of thought on sin in *Against Heresies* that need to be discussed. The first concerns the question of who was responsible for sin and the second addresses the results of sin in the changed nature of humanity. The latter naturally leads into a discussion of the extent to which people retain free will in a sinful condition.

The Origin of Sin

The first point that Irenaeus makes is that God can in no way be held accountable for the existence of sin. For a book like this that seeks to help someone read through the various authors, it would have been ideal if Irenaeus had stated this matter-of-factly. Instead, because of the context into which he was writing, Irenaeus makes the point as part of a refutation of the elaborate Gnostic creation mythologies. There are pages of description about Aeons, Ogdads and the Pleroma showing how the various Gnostic teachers ascribe evil to the material world created by the Demiurge rather than the true God who is pure spirit and pure goodness, shown in this passage regarding the formation of the Demiurge:

> They further teach that the spirits of wickedness derived their origin from grief. Hence the devil, whom they also call Cosmocrator (the ruler of the world), and the demons, and the angels, and every wicked spiritual being that exists, found the source of their existence. They represent the Demiurge as being the son of that mother of theirs (Achamoth), and Cosmocrator as the creature of the Demiurge. Cosmocrator has knowledge of what is above himself, because he is a *spirit* of wickedness; but the Demiurge is ignorant of such things, inasmuch as he is merely *animal*. Their mother dwells in that place which is above the heavens, that is, in the intermediate abode; the Demiurge in the heavenly place, that is, in the hebdomad; but the Cosmocrator in this our world. The corporeal elements of the world, again, sprang, as we before remarked, from bewilderment and perplexity, as from a more ignoble source. Thus the earth arose from her state of stupor; water from the agitation caused by her fear; air from the consolidation of her grief; while fire, producing death and corruption, was inherent in all these elements, even as they teach that ignorance also lay concealed in these three passions.[1]

1. Ibid., 1.5.

This passage contains a lot of confusing terminology for the modern day, but the basic point is that they create an alternative source of existence to explain evil. He later states:

> Impious indeed, beyond all impiety, are these men, who assert that the Maker of heaven and earth, the only God Almighty, besides whom there is no God, was produced by means of a defect, which itself sprang from another defect, so that, according to them, He was the product of the third defect.[1]

Against this, Irenaeus repeatedly argues that it is one God who has made all things, which is the foundation statement of his Rule of Truth:

> The rule of truth which we hold, is, that there is one God Almighty, who made all things by His Word, and fashioned and formed, out of that which had no existence, all things which exist. Thus saith the Scripture, to that effect 'By the Word of the Lord were the heavens established, and all the might of them, by the spirit of His mouth.' And again, 'All things were made by Him, and without Him was nothing made.' There is no exception or deduction stated; but the Father made all things by Him, whether visible or invisible, objects of sense or of intelligence, temporal, on account of a certain character given them, or eternal; and these eternal things He did not make by angels, or by any powers separated from His Ennoea. For God needs none of all these things, but is He who, by His Word and Spirit, makes, and disposes, and governs all things, and commands all things into existence – He who formed the world (for the world is of all) – He who fashioned man – He [who] is the God of Abraham, and the God of Isaac, and the God of Jacob, above whom there is no other God, nor initial principle, nor power, nor Pleroma.[2]

Because it is this Almighty God who created all things, it is an unworthy accusation for the various Gnostic groups to attribute faults to this creation:

> Let them cease, therefore, to affirm that the world was made by any other; for as soon as God formed a conception in His mind, that was also done which He had thus mentally conceived. . . . Since, then, it is just such as the Father had [ideally] formed in counsel with Himself, it must be worthy of the Father. But to affirm that what was mentally conceived and pre-created by the Father of all, just as it has been actually formed, is the fruit of defect, and the production of ignorance, is to be guilty of great blasphemy. For,

1. Ibid., 1.16.
2. Ibid., 1.22.

> according to them, the Father of all will thus be [regarded as] generating in His breast, according to His own mental conception, the emanations of defect and the fruits of ignorance, since the things which He had conceived in His mind have actually been produced.[1]

This leaves Irenaeus with the task of explaining how a world created by this Being could result in this broken and sinful place. There is an important context that he introduces at the end of book two, in a chapter entitled, 'Perfect knowledge cannot be attained in the present life: many questions must be submissively left in the hands of God.'[2] This deals with various questions, including a fascinating short section on the origins and pervasiveness of sin:

> In like manner, also, we must leave the cause why, while all things were made by God, certain of His creatures sinned and revolted from a state of submission to God, and others, indeed the great majority, persevered, and do still persevere, in [willing] subjection to Him who formed them, and also of what nature those are who sinned, and of what nature those who persevere – [we must, I say, leave the cause of these things] to God and His Word.[3]

With this basic position in mind, Irenaeus investigates the process of the Fall of humankind, primarily using the account in Genesis 3. For this, we must remember Irenaeus' teaching about humans being created in an infantile state because this affects the nature of the origin of sin. Rather than purely emphasising the responsibility of Adam, the devil or tempter is held partly responsible, while Eve also assumes some of the blame for her role between the serpent and Adam.

The dominant section on the serpent is found in book three, where Irenaeus argues that Adam should be the first to partake of the salvation offered in Christ. The reason for this is that Satan 'had led man captive', and that Adam was 'injured by the serpent that had corrupted him'.[4] When looking at the curses that were the results of disobedience, Irenaeus states that God 'put no question to the serpent; for He knew that he had been the prime mover in the guilty deed.'[5] Therefore, 'the curse in all its fullness fell upon the serpent, which had beguiled them.'[6]

1. Ibid., 2.3.
2. Ibid., 2.28.
3. Ibid.
4. Ibid., 3.23.
5. Ibid.
6. Ibid.

The power of the serpent comes to bear on Eve, who was first deceived by the devil. This is noted in the section on the manner in which Satan was able to tempt, but the implications of this are seen more strongly in Irenaeus' famous parallel between Eve and Mary. Here Mary's obedience is contrasted with Eve's disobedience, which make her 'the cause of death, both to herself and the whole human race'.[1] On this basis, Irenaeus states that, 'it was that the knot of Eve's disobedience was loosed by the obedience of Mary. For what the virgin Eve had bound fast through unbelief, this did the virgin Mary set free through faith.'[2]

There are three caveats in place in Irenaeus' thought when discussing Adam as the originator of sin in humankind. These must be borne in mind when considering this earliest phase of thought: the infant state of humanity at their creation, the role of the devil as tempter and 'prime mover', and Eve's causal role. That said, it is Adam's disobedience that remains the crucial factor in the Fall into sin, and this is emphasised in passages that look at the results of sin.

There are two major results of sin in *Against Heresies*: slavery to the devil and death. Irenaeus states that, 'the first Adam becomes a vessel in his (Satan's) possession, whom he did also hold under his power, that is, by bringing sin on him iniquitously'.[3] He develops this later by writing that the devil 'obtained' man as 'the first-fruits of his own apostasy', 'got him into his power' and 'obtained dominion over man by apostasy'.[4] This dominion seems to be the crucial element for Irenaeus, since much of the material on death is put within this framework. For example: '[man] who had been drawn by sin into bondage, but was held by death'; or, 'man, who had been created by God that he might live, after losing life, through being injured by the serpent that had corrupted him, should not any more return to life'.[5]

One of the reasons for this is a repeated parallel drawn between Adam and Christ, which is the basis of that between Eve and Mary mentioned above. There are few mentions of sin that are not accompanied by material on Christ's redemptive act freeing humankind from bondage and death. So the passage above on man being 'drawn into sin by bondage' continues, 'so that sin should be destroyed by man and man should go forth from death. . . . God recapitulated Himself the ancient formation of man, that He might kill sin, deprive death of its power, and vivify man.'[6]

1. Ibid., 3.22.
2. Ibid.
3. Ibid., 3.23.
4. Ibid., 3.23, 5.21, 5.24.
5. Ibid., 3.18, 3.23.
6. Ibid., 3.18.

The most powerful section brings this analysis of sin full circle because it comes in the section on why man was not made perfect from the beginning, the major cause of the fall or wandering into sin. The whole question of why sin exists in a creation made by a perfect being is answered thus:

> For it was necessary, at first, that nature should be exhibited; then, after that, that what was mortal should be conquered and swallowed up by immortality, and the corruptible by incorruptibility, and that man should be made after the image and likeness of God, having received the knowledge of good and evil.[1]

Free Will

One of the biggest questions raised by Irenaeus' focus on bondage as a result of sin is the effects of this on human free will. Before looking at this, however, it is important to note the foundational concept behind this whole section: God has free will and the existence of this in humankind is part of the *imago Dei* in which they were created: '. . . man is possessed of free will from the beginning, and God is possessed of free will, in whose likeness man was created.'[2]

The importance of God's free will for Irenaeus is the power in response to a Gnostic view of creation, which absolves God from responsibility for evil by positing the Demiurge as the creator of matter. Against this, Irenaeus states that it is the one God of the whole Bible who created everything and that humankind, influenced by the devil, wandered into sin. Therefore, in beginning his response in chapter one of book two to the Gnostic claims outlined in book one, Irenaeus states:

> It is proper, then, that I should begin with the first and most important head, that is, God the Creator, who made the heaven and the earth, and all things that are therein (whom these men blasphemously style the fruit of a defect), and to demonstrate that there is nothing either above Him or after Him; nor that, influenced by any one, but of His own free will, He created all things, since He is the only God, the only Lord, the only Creator, the only Father, alone containing all things, and Himself commanding all things into existence.[3]

Later in the same chapter, Irenaeus makes the same point again: 'For it must be either that there is one Being who contains all things, and formed in His own territory all those things which have been created,

1. Ibid., 4.38.
2. Ibid., 4.37.
3. Ibid., 2.1.

according to His own will.'[1] This will continue free and unimpeded even by the advent of sin, since it is impossible that, 'the serpent would have prevailed over the will of God' in light of the fact that God is 'invincible'.[2] This freedom of God leads to a privileged position of God in relating to his creation, briefly worked out in terms of his foreknowledge and predestination of events.

Irenaeus does not devote a great deal of material to the sovereignty of God as it is worked out in themes such as predestination, but underlying the whole work is a sense of God's continuing control over the affairs of the world that naturally results from his strong creation theology. For example, in responding to some of the Gnostic claims of Marcion, Irenaeus quotes Plato's perceived truth about God, that he is 'also the ancient Word, possessing the beginning, the end, and the mean of all existing things, does everything rightly, moving round about them according to their nature.'[3]

Earlier in this section is one of two major passages in *Against Heresies* that talk about God's providence in a chapter that seeks to demonstrate God's justice in punishing the wicked and his goodness in blessing the pious:

> God does, however, exercise a providence over all things, and therefore He also gives counsel; and when giving counsel, He is present with those who attend to moral discipline. It follows then of course, that the things which are watched over and governed should be acquainted with their ruler; which things are not irrational or vain, but they have understanding derived from the providence of God. And, for this reason certain of the Gentiles, who were less addicted to [sensual] allurements and voluptuousness, and were not led away to such a degree of superstition with regard to idols, being moved, though but slightly, by His providence, were nevertheless convinced that they should call the Maker of this universe the Father, who exercises a providence over all things, and arranges the affairs of our world.

The other section on predestination comes earlier in the work and focuses on the establishment of things in their proper place as part of the pre-eminence of God:

> But He Himself in Himself, after a fashion which we can neither describe nor conceive, predestinating all things, formed them as He pleased, bestowing harmony on all things, and assigning them their own place, and the beginning of their creation.[4]

1. Ibid.
2. Ibid., 3.23.
3. Ibid., 3.25, quoting from Plato, *De Legibus*, 4.
4. Ibid., 2.2.

In neither of these cases does Irenaeus deal with potential effects on the nature of human free will if God has predestined sovereignty over all things, but the implication is that human free will is retained to a very high degree.

The final passage that needs to be highlighted in this section concerns his foreknowledge, which has been used to stand in between concepts of predestination and free will:

> For all these things were foreknown by the Father; but the Son works them out at the proper time in perfect order and sequence. This was the reason why, when Mary was urging [Him] on to [perform] the wonderful miracle of the wine, and was desirous before the time to partake of the cup of emblematic significance, the Lord, checking her untimely haste, said, 'Woman, what have I to do with thee? mine hour is not yet come' – waiting for that hour which was foreknown by the Father. . . . Paul also says: 'But when the fulness of time came, God sent forth His Son.' By which is made manifest, that all things which had been foreknown of the Father, our Lord did accomplish in their order, season, and hour, foreknown and fitting, being indeed one and the same, but rich and great.[1]

Again, there is no direct connection made about the effect on human free will, however, it is important to note the nature of God as having free will in order to understand the application of this to humankind made in the image of God. It is also essential to bear in mind the transcendent nature of God, overseeing all things, as we consider the high anthropology that is taught.

Before looking at the continued existence of free will in humankind, it is right to look first at the effects of sin on this aspect of the *imago Dei*. Irenaeus provides a number of stages to the constraints that result from sin. Firstly, there are the effects of the Adamic sin that result in a servitude from which humankind needs to be liberated. This is declared in a passage dealing with redemption, which states that the children of Adam are 'bound', 'captive' and 'in servitude'.[2] This bondage is confirmed in the 'laws of bondage' that were promulgated by Moses that served as a sign of the need for the 'new covenant of liberty'.[3] At this stage, there is still no precise application of these concepts of slavery to sin on the will of people with exception of this being part of their whole being entering into this condition.

1. Ibid., 3.16.
2. Ibid., 3.23.
3. Ibid., 4.16.

There are two specific examples given of people's wills being overcome: the first is important as it is worked out in relation to God's foreknowledge and the salvation of humankind. The second is a bridge to our continuing free will in discussing whether we are held responsible for sins that we commit without a direct act of will.

The first example is that of Pharaoh, whose heart was hardened by God according to the account in Exodus (9:35). Marcion had used this passage to state that God was therefore the author of sin, an accusation that Irenaeus seeks to refute. In this task, Irenaeus makes note of several New Testament passages that teach how God blinds those who do not believe: 2 Corinthians 4:4, Romans 1:28 and 2 Thessalonians 2:11.[1] The apparent implication is that human free will is denied by a direct act of God. Irenaeus does not directly deny this as he instead argues that this action of God is a result of his foreknowledge of their unbelief:

> If, therefore, in the present time also, God, knowing the number of those who will not believe, since He foreknows all things, has given them over to unbelief, and turned away His face from men of this stamp, leaving them in the darkness which they have themselves chosen for themselves, what is there wonderful if He did also at that time give over to their unbelief, Pharaoh, who never would have believed, along with those who were with him? As the Word spake to Moses from the bush: 'And I am sure that the king of Egypt will not let you go, unless by a mighty hand.' And for the reason that the Lord spake in parables, and brought blindness upon Israel, that seeing they might not see, since He knew the [spirit of] unbelief in them, for the same reason did He harden Pharaoh's heart.[2]

The implication is that while God is held to act, this is in response to the will of people rather than in subjection of that will.

The second specific example is a very strange passage concerning Lot and his daughters, in which it appears that God works through a sinful situation for which Lot is not held responsible. The question at stake here, which will be revisited by other writers, is whether we can be held accountable for sins that we commit unknowingly. Irenaeus is questioning whether we are in a position to judge characters in Scripture who commit sinful actions but are not condemned for these in the text:

> An example is found in the case of Lot, who led forth his daughters from Sodom, and these then conceived by their own father; and who left behind him within the confines [of the land] his wife, [who remains] a pillar of salt unto this day. For Lot, not acting

1. Ibid.
2. Ibid.

> under the impulse of his own will, nor at the prompting of carnal concupiscence, nor having any knowledge or thought of anything of the kind, did [in fact] work out a type [of future events]. As says the Scripture: 'And that night the elder went in and lay with her father; and Lot knew not when she lay down, nor when she arose.' And the same thing took place in the case of the younger: 'And he knew not,' it is said, 'when she slept with him, nor when she arose.' Since, therefore, Lot knew not [what he did], nor was a slave to lust [in his actions], the arrangement [designed by God] was carried out, by which the two daughters (that is, the two churches), who gave birth to children begotten of one and the same father, were pointed out, apart from [the influence of] the lust of the flesh.[1]

Irenaeus' position is that Lot is not judged for his unconscious part in these deeds and that therefore we should not pass judgement. There is thus a question about what this means more generally for sins that are committed unknowingly.

The issue of responsibility in the stories of Pharaoh, and particularly Lot, is important as it is an essential element of Irenaeus' wider discourse about the continuing free will that exists in humankind after the Fall. There is an indication of this, albeit for those redeemed by God, in the continuation of thought on the role of the Mosaic Law, which was stated above as being a sign of the need for the covenant of liberty. Under this new covenant, God has

> increased and widened those laws which are natural, and noble, and common to all, granting to men largely and without grudging, by means of adoption, to know God the Father, and to love Him with the whole heart, and to follow His word unswervingly, while they abstain not only from evil deeds, but even from the desire after them. . . . [All this is declared,] that we may know that we shall give account to God not of deeds only, as slaves, but even of words and thoughts, as those who have truly received the power of liberty, in which [condition] a man is more severely tested, whether he will reverence, and fear, and love the Lord. And for this reason Peter says 'that we have not liberty as a cloak of maliciousness,' but as the means of testing and evidencing faith.[2]

The clearest material comes towards the end of book four of *Against Heresies*, in chapters that analyse Irenaean thought on the creation of humankind as imperfect. The chapter preceding that particular teaching is entitled 'Men are possessed of free will, and endowed with the faculty of

1. Ibid., 4.31.
2. Ibid., 4.16.

making a choice. It is not true, therefore, that some are by nature good, and others bad'.[1] The opening statements not only explicate this fundamental nature of humankind in possessing free will, they also immediately engage with the resulting responsibility that we are given for our actions:

> This expression [of our Lord], 'How often would I have gathered thy children together, and thou wouldest not,' set forth the ancient law of human liberty, because God made man a free [agent] from the beginning, possessing his own power, even as he does his own soul, to obey the behests of God voluntarily, and not by compulsion of God. For there is no coercion with God, but a good will [towards us] is present with Him continually. And therefore does He give good counsel to all. And in man, as well as in angels, He has placed the power of choice (for angels are rational beings), so that those who had yielded obedience might justly possess what is good, given indeed by God, but preserved by themselves.[2]

There is a relational aspect to Irenaeus' anthropology, in that while God does give counsel, the fundamental nature of man is to be in control of his own will. There are passages quoted by Irenaeus in order to

> demonstrate the independent will of man, and at the same time the counsel which God conveys to him, by which He exhorts us to submit ourselves to Him, and seeks to turn us away from [the sin of] unbelief against Him, without, however, in any way coercing us . . .[3]

including a reference to Jesus weeping over Jerusalem:

> In the same manner therefore the Lord, both showing His own goodness, and indicating that man is in his own free will and his own power, said to Jerusalem, 'How often have I wished to gather thy children together, as a hen [gathereth] her chickens under her wings, and ye would not! Wherefore your house shall be left unto you desolate.'[4]

Within this created nature, there is also the capacity to distinguish between good and evil, so that there is no excuse for an incorrect use of the will. This is made clear two chapters after that, where Irenaeus discusses how man was created imperfect:

> Man has received the knowledge of good and evil. It is good to obey God, and to believe in Him, and to keep His commandment, and this is the life of man; as not to obey God is evil, and this is his

1. Ibid., 4.37.
2. Ibid.
3. Ibid.
4. Ibid.

> death. Since God, therefore, gave [to man] such mental power man knew both the good of obedience and the evil of disobedience, that the eye of the mind, receiving experience of both, may with judgement make choice of the better things; and that he may never become indolent or neglectful of God's command; and learning by experience that it is an evil thing which deprives him of life, that is, disobedience to God, may never attempt it at all, but that, knowing that what preserves his life, namely, obedience to God, is good, he may diligently keep it with all earnestness. Wherefore he has also had a twofold experience, possessing knowledge of both kinds, that with discipline he may make choice of the better things.[1]

In Irenaean thought, freedom of will by nature and the knowledge of good and evil combine to make humankind fully responsible for their actions. There is no excuse allowed that some may have been created better than others, since:

> If some had been made by nature bad, and others good, these latter would not be deserving of praise for being good, for such were they created; nor would the former be reprehensible, for thus they were made [originally]. But since all men are of the same nature, able both to hold fast and to do what is good; and, on the other hand, having also the power to cast it from them and not to do it – some do justly receive praise even among men who are under the control of good laws (and much more from God), and obtain deserved testimony of their choice of good in general, and of persevering therein; but the others are blamed, and receive a just condemnation, because of their rejection of what is fair and good.[2]

People are therefore rightly held accountable for their actions and are judged on this basis.

> The prophets used to exhort men to what was good, to act justly and to work righteousness, as I have so largely demonstrated, because it is in our power so to do, and because by excessive negligence we might become forgetful, and thus stand in need of that good counsel which the good God has given us to know by means of the prophets.[3]

There is a further step in the debate on free will, which goes beyond mere human action to the issue of salvation and the extent to which people are engaged with the grace that is offered to them. Irenaeus is adamant that even in this regard, humans retain their free will:

1. Ibid., 4.39.
2. Ibid., 4.37.
3. Ibid.

And not merely in works, but also in faith, has God preserved the will of man free and under his own control, saying, 'According to thy faith be it unto thee;' thus showing that there is a faith specially belonging to man, since he has an opinion specially his own. And again, 'All things are possible to him that believeth;' and, 'Go thy way; and as thou hast believed, so be it done unto thee.' Now all such expressions demonstrate that man is in his own power with respect to faith. And for this reason, 'he that believeth in Him has eternal life while he who believeth not the Son hath not eternal life, but the wrath of God shall remain upon him.'[1]

Shortly before this section, Irenaeus argues a similar point:

No doubt, if any one is unwilling to follow the Gospel itself, it is in his power [to reject it], but it is not expedient. For it is in man's power to disobey God, and to forfeit what is good; but [such conduct] brings no small amount of injury and mischief. And on this account Paul says, 'All things are lawful to me, but all things are not expedient;' referring both to the liberty of man, in which respect 'all things are lawful,' God exercising no compulsion in regard to him; and [by the expression] 'not expedient' pointing out that we 'should not use our liberty as a cloak of maliciousness,' for this is not expedient.[2]

It is therefore clear that Irenaeus would hold to a continuing, absolute freedom of human will despite the effects of sin and the Fall. This extends beyond our mere actions to the faith journey and response to the Gospel. Irenaeus is aware of a question that results from all this: why did God create humans as this kind of free moral agent when sin, rejection and judgement were the consequences? His answer is that God sought a precious relationship with humankind that is only possible through a choice that results from the free will that is a fundamental part of human nature:

'But He should not,' say they, 'have created angels of such a nature that they were capable of transgression, nor men who immediately proved ungrateful towards Him; for they were made rational beings, endowed with the power of examining and judging, and were not [formed] as things irrational or of a [merely] animal nature, which can do nothing of their own will, but are drawn by necessity and compulsion to what is good, in which things there is one mind and one usage, working mechanically in one groove, who are incapable of being anything else except just what they had been created.' But upon this supposition, neither would what is good be grateful to them, nor communion with God be precious, nor would the good be very much to be sought after, which would present itself without

1. Ibid.
2. Ibid.

2. Irenaeus

their own proper endeavour, care, or study, but would be implanted of its own accord and without their concern. Thus it would come to pass, that their being good would be of no consequence, because they were so by nature rather than by will, and are possessors of good spontaneously, not by choice.[1]

Grace

Irenaeus does not devote extensive sections of his work to the concept of grace, including it more in sporadic references that give some indication of its nature, while he concentrates on other areas of faith. Given the variety of uses of grace in the New Testament, it is perhaps unsurprising that there is little evidence of a doctrine of grace towards the end of the second century. This short section will highlight the range of areas in which grace is applied to build up a picture of Irenaeus' thought. One contrasting section will be highlighted as he confronts what he views as a heretical position taught on the relationship between grace and works.

For understanding the nature of grace, Irenaeus makes it clear that we must start with the Christ event both as an example of grace and as the source of our experience of grace. So book five, chapter two has as the beginning of its title: 'When Christ visited us in His grace, He did not come to what did not belong to Him.'[2] From this event, while God remains just in judging those who rebel against him:

> [he] may, in the exercise of His grace, confer immortality on the righteous, and holy, and those who have kept His commandments, and have persevered in His love, some from the beginning [of their Christian course], and others from [the date of] their repentance, and may surround them with everlasting glory.[3]

Irenaeus later quotes the promise of grace in redemption from Romans 7:24, concluding that, 'Here we see, that not by ourselves, but by the help of God, we must be saved.'[4]

One aspect that Irenaeus comes back to three times in the course of his work is the measure of grace that is received, which he argues has increased after the arrival of Christ but still not complete in this world.

> As, therefore, He has promised to give very much to those who do now bring forth fruit, according to the gift of His grace, but not according to the changeableness of 'knowledge;' for the Lord

1. Ibid.
2. Ibid., 5.2.
3. Ibid., 1.10.
4. Ibid., 3.20.

remains the same, and the same Father is revealed; thus, therefore, has the one and the same Lord granted, by means of His advent, a greater gift of grace to those of a later period, than what He had granted to those under the Old Testament dispensation. For they indeed used to hear, by means of [His] servants, that the King would come, and they rejoiced to a certain extent, inasmuch as they hoped for His coming; but those who have beheld Him actually present, and have obtained liberty, and been made partakers of His gifts, do possess a greater amount of grace, and a higher degree of exultation, rejoicing because of the King's arrival.[1]

Later in the same passage he writes:

If, therefore, the self-same person is present who was announced by the prophets, our Lord Jesus Christ, and if His advent has brought in a fuller [measure of] grace and greater gifts to those who have received Him, it is plain that the Father also is Himself the same who was proclaimed by the prophets.[2]

There are earlier indications that, despite this growth in grace after the incarnation, it remains a measure rather than the fullness:

Since, therefore, we know but in part, we ought to leave all sorts of [difficult] questions in the hands of Him who in some measure, [and that only,] bestows grace on us. . . . It becomes us, therefore, to leave the knowledge of this matter to God, even as the Lord does of the day and hour [of judgement], and not to rush to such an extreme of danger, that we will leave nothing in the hands of God, even though we have received only a measure of grace [from Him in this world].[3]

From this it is clear that grace is related to the Spirit: 'For where the Church is, there is the Spirit of God; and where the Spirit of God is, there is the Church, and every kind of grace; but the Spirit is truth.'[4] Some of the results of this relationship are the interpretation of Scripture ('in regard to those things which we investigate in the Scriptures (which are throughout spiritual), we are able by the grace of God to explain some of them, while we must leave others in the hands of God'),[5] the gift of prophecy ('only those to whom God sends His grace from above possess the divinely-bestowed power

1. Ibid., 4.11.
2. Ibid.
3. Ibid., 2.28.
4. Ibid., 3.24.
5. Ibid., 2.28.

2. Irenaeus

of prophesying')[1] and the gift of miracles ('those who are in truth His disciples, receiving grace from Him, do in His name perform [miracles], so as to promote the welfare of other men').[2]

Irenaeus addresses grace in one other context: its perceived abuse by certain Gnostic teachers who claim that their measure of grace means that they do not need to do good works, whereas lesser Christians are required to work out their salvation. A division is seemingly drawn between 'animal' men (most Christians) and 'spiritual' men (the Gnostics).

> Animal men, again, are instructed in animal things; such men, namely, as are established by their works, and by a mere faith, while they have not perfect knowledge. We of the Church, they say, are these persons. Wherefore also they maintain that good works are necessary to us, for that otherwise it is impossible we should be saved. But as to themselves, they hold that they shall be entirely and undoubtedly saved, not by means of conduct, but because they are spiritual by nature.[3]

This allows them to 'addict themselves without fear to all those kinds of forbidden deeds of which the Scriptures assure us that "they who do such things shall not inherit the kingdom of God"'.[4] Part of this Gnostic teaching is that other Christians only have grace temporarily:

> They run us down (who from the fear of God guard against sinning even in thought or word) as utterly contemptible and ignorant persons, while they highly exalt themselves, and claim to be perfect, and the elect seed. For they declare that we simply receive grace for use, wherefore also it will again be taken away from us; but that they themselves have grace as their own special possession, which has descended from above by means of an unspeakable and indescribable conjunction; and on this account more will be given them.[5]

Irenaeus rebuts their teaching, arguing that all are in the same condition and are saved by grace – 'for men are saved through his grace, and not on account of their own righteous actions'[6] – but are also held accountable for their actions, hence his condemnation of the Gnostics' 'forbidden deeds'.

1. Ibid., 1.13.
2. Ibid., 2.32.
3. Ibid., 1.6.
4. Ibid.
5. Ibid.
6. Ibid., 1.23.

Conclusion

In the context of this work, Irenaeus is most loquacious on the topic of human free will, arguing for a radical continuation of this as part of the ongoing *imago Dei* after the Fall. As one of the first major systematic writers on Christianity, however, his understanding of sin and grace gives us indications of how the Early Church was beginning to process their understanding in these areas.

If you wish to read *Against Heresies*, you can find a copy online at www.ccel.org or look at the recent published translation (London: Aeterna Press, 2016). For more background on Irenaeus, read either Eric Osborn's *Irenaeus of Lyon* (Cambridge: CUP, 2001) or Denis Minns' *Irenaeus: An Introduction* (London: T&T Clark, 2010).

3.
Tertullian

Tertullian of Carthage (c.155-c.240) stands out among Early Church Christian writers because he wrote in Latin, rather than in Greek. A powerful rhetorician and often a witty writer (by historical theological standards – all things are relative), Tertullian wrote a number of works defending Christianity against attack from suspect teachings and advocating the strengths of the growing religion. Like Irenaeus, Gnosticism – particularly the form taught by Marcion – was a major focus and Tertullian's longest surviving work is entitled *Against Marcion*. He wrote another significant apologetic against Praxeas, a teacher who held to one God to the exclusion of any notion of Trinity. In this task, Tertullian notably coined both the term '*Trinitas*' to refer to the godhead and '*Persona*' for the individuated substances within the divinity.

Tertullian also wrote a number of more philosophical works and is famous for his dictum, 'What has Athens to do with Jerusalem?'[1] In this, he takes an opposite line to Justin Martyr, who sought truth in any thought system and took ownership of it for Christians, in refuting any wisdom found outside the revelation of God in the Bible. In engaging with philosophy, Tertullian wrote *A Treatise on the Soul*, which is particularly important for this work as will be shown below.

Tertullian writes with an aggressive (some would say overly aggressive) tone, which demonstrates the passion that he held for the Christian faith. The precise nature of his legacy is affected by his move later in life towards Montanism, a hyper-spiritual movement that began in the Near East and questioned the authority of Scripture and the Church in light of the internal presence of the Holy Spirit in a person's life. Despite this blot on his copybook, the main reason that Tertullian was never made a saint, his writings are a valuable source for gauging the beliefs of the church at this early stage on the topics of sin, grace and free will.

1. Tertullian, *On the Prescription of Heretics*, 7.

Sin

Tertullian covers some of the same ground as Irenaeus, and this examination will again begin with his views on the origins of sin and the respective roles of God, the devil and humankind. As with Irenaeus, Tertullian writes about the nature of sin generically, embodied in Adam. One major new element that he addresses is the transmission of sin, linked to the transmission of the soul from one generation to the next. What is now known as original sin, a doctrine that owes its most complete early elucidation to Augustine of Hippo, is hinted at in a number of passages here. Finally, there are the consequences of sin for humankind in their nature and in the judgement of God and this presents an interesting case study today in a minor work on entertainment. As with Irenaeus, these effects of sin on humankind naturally lead to a discussion of Tertullian's views on continuing free will as part of the *imago Dei* after the advent of sin.

Tertullian's view of God in relation to sin comes as a response to Marcion's teaching that evil exists as a result of a second, evil God rather than the first, perfect God, a fairly standard Gnostic line of thought. Tertullian notes that this is partly a result of Marcion's correct understanding that evil cannot proceed from a perfect God. Therefore, by engaging with Isaiah 45:7, where God declares himself the root of evil ('disaster' in the NIV), Marcion is forced to attribute this to a second God:

> When he found the Creator declaring, 'I am He that createth evil,' inasmuch as he had already concluded from other arguments, which are satisfactory to every perverted mind, that God is the author of evil, so he now applied to the Creator the figure of the corrupt tree bringing forth evil fruit, that is, moral evil, and then presumed that there ought to be another god, after the analogy of the good tree producing its good fruit.[1]

Tertullian gradually deconstructs Marcion's theory, ultimately showing that the two 'gods' posited, which Marcion wants to be equal but different, can have no equality: '[W]e know full well that Marcion makes his gods unequal: one judicial, harsh, mighty in war; the other mild, placid, and simply good and excellent.'[2] This is part of his defence of the existence of one supreme God who made all things, yet who is not the origin of evil. Rather God's goodness must be 'perpetual and

---

1. Tertullian, *Against Marcion*, 1.2.
2. Ibid., 1.6.

3. Tertullian

unbroken', cannot 'fail in power' and 'knows nothing of inactivity'.[1] One of these must have happened to Marcion's god, which shows him to be false; none can affect Tertullian's God, and we must therefore look elsewhere for the origin of sin.

Tertullian makes the same point in a work against another Gnostic writer, Hermogenes. He argues that any argument that seeks to make evil a fundamental part of nature will always result in laying the blame for its origin with the perfect God:

> For observe how God is found to be, if not the Author of, yet at any rate the conniver at, evil, inasmuch as He, with all His extreme goodness, endured evil in Matter before He created the world, although, as being good, and the enemy of evil, He ought to have corrected it. For He either was able to correct it, but was unwilling; or else was willing, but being a weak God, was not able. If He was able and yet unwilling, He was Himself evil, as having favoured evil; and thus He now opens Himself to the charge of evil, because even if He did not create it yet still, since it would not be existing if He had been against its existence, He must Himself have then caused it to exist, when He refused to will its non-existence.[2]

Tertullian's solution to Hermogenes is that all that comes from God is good, including the creation of matter, but, because of the nature of creation, this matter then becomes the source of evil: '[L]et the good be God's, and the evil belong to Matter – then, on the one hand, evil must not be ascribed to God, nor, on the other hand, good to Matter.'[3]

In heading towards humankind as the origin of sin (is there a need for a spoiler alert?), there is one more step to take when dealing with the role of the devil. The devil and demons do play a role but Tertullian hastens to clarify that this is not a function derived from their creation, nor is it overwhelming in force to deny human responsibility.

Tertullian deals with the origin of the devil in his work against Marcion, answering 'whence originated this malice of lying and deceit towards man, and slandering of God?' with 'Most certainly not from God, who made the angel good after the fashion of His good works.'[4] After the devil chose corruption, he became the 'very author of sin', a phrase that needs addressing as it may seem to absolve humanity.[5]

1. Ibid., 1.22.
2. Tertullian, *Against Hermogenes*, 10.
3. Ibid., 16.
4. Tertullian, *Marcion*, 2.10.
5. Ibid.

Tertullian does not agree with this, and devotes a number of passages in various works to discussing the relationship of the devil and demons to humanity and sin.

In his *Apology*, which seeks to defend Christianity from false accusations about its teaching, Tertullian addresses the concept of demons at length. Having noted that both Socrates and Plato discuss spiritual beings in their works, he writes:

> Their great business is the ruin of mankind. So, from the very first, spiritual wickedness sought our destruction. They inflict, accordingly, upon our bodies diseases and other grievous calamities, while by violent assaults they hurry the soul into sudden and extraordinary excesses. Their marvellous subtleness and tenuity give them access to both parts of our nature. As spiritual, they can do no harm; for, invisible and intangible, we are not cognisant of their action save by its effects, as when some inexplicable, unseen poison in the breeze blights the apples and the grain while in the flower, or kills them in the bud, or destroys them when they have reached maturity; as though by the tainted atmosphere in some unknown way spreading abroad its pestilential exhalations. So, too, by an influence equally obscure, demons and angels breathe into the soul, and rouse up its corruptions with furious passions and vile excesses; or with cruel lusts accompanied by various errors, of which the worst is that by which these deities are commended to the favour of deceived and deluded human beings, that they may get their proper food of flesh-fumes and blood when that is offered up to idol-images. What is daintier food to the spirit of evil, than turning men's minds away from the true God by the illusions of a false divination?[1]

In the short work on *The Soul's Testimony*, Tertullian seems to attribute a greater role to the demon in sin:

> In expressing vexation, contempt, or abhorrence, thou hast Satan constantly upon thy lips; the very same we hold to be the angel of evil, the source of error, the corrupter of the whole world, by whom in the beginning man was entrapped into breaking the commandment of God....[2]

In contrast to this, he also wrote passages such as this one from *On Exhortation to Chastity*: '[Y]ou think yourself to have been subverted by the devil; who, albeit he does *will* that you should will something which

1. Tertullian, *Apology*, 22.
2. Tertullian, *The Soul's Testimony*, 3.

3. Tertullian

God nills still does not *make* you will it.'[1] The devil and demons thus play their part as an 'incentive to sin', or the 'instigator', but there needs to be an act of will in response to this that originates in the human being.[2]

Tertullian is clear that evil is not natural for humankind:

> If, again, the evil of sin was developed in him, this must not be accounted as a *natural* disposition: it was rather produced by the instigation of the (old) serpent as far from being incidental to his nature as it was from being *material* in him.[3]

In his opinion, it is the result of Adam's free choice: 'Or who will hesitate to declare the great sin of Adam to have been heresy, when he committed it by the choice of his own will rather than of God's?'[4] Tertullian makes the same point again later in *Against Marcion*, contrasting the choice of humankind with the nature of God:

> To conclude: the goodness of God, then fully considered from the beginning of His works, will be enough to convince us that nothing evil could possibly have come forth from God; and the liberty of man will, after a second thought, show us that it alone is chargeable with the fault which itself committed.'[5]

Perhaps the clearest, most complete statement comes in his work on chastity:

> And accordingly we ought not to lay to the account of the Lord's will that which lies subject to our own choice; (on the hypothesis) that He does not will, or else (positively) nills what is good, who does nill what is evil. Thus, it is a volition of our own when we will what is evil, in antagonism to God's will, who wills what is good. Further, if you inquire whence comes that volition whereby we will anything in antagonism to the will of God, I shall say, it has its source in ourselves. And I shall not make the assertion rashly – for you must needs correspond to the seed whence you spring – if indeed it be true, (as it is), that the originator of our race and our sin, Adam, willed the sin which he committed. For the devil did not impose upon him the volition to sin, but subministered material to the volition.[6]

1. Tertullian, *On Exhortation to Chastity*, 2.
2. Tertullian, *Treatise on the Soul*, 16; *Marcion*, 5.17.
3. Tertullian, *Treatise on the Soul*, 21.
4. Tertullian, *Marcion*, 2.2.
5. Ibid., 2.6.
6. Tertullian, *Chastity*, 2.

From this basis, Tertullian briefly argues that sin results from a being who is created by good to do good yet who chooses to reject this path and succumb to the temptation to sin. There are two words that Tertullian uses as the basis of all sin: idolatry and irrationality. In his work *On Idolatry*, he states at the outset:

> The principal crime of the human race, the highest guilt charged upon the world, the whole procuring cause of judgement, is idolatry. For, although each single fault retains its own proper feature, although it is destined to judgement under its own proper name also, yet it is marked off under the *general* account of idolatry.[1]

The important aspect here is that sin is an 'offence done to God', and thus always has God as its object.[2] The second term, irrational, is more an offence to the created nature of humanity: 'All sin, however, is irrational: therefore the irrational proceeds from the devil, from whom sin proceeds; and it is extraneous to God, to whom also the irrational is an alien principle.'[3] Both of these words affirm the root of sin in people's independent actions.

The next area of Tertullian's beliefs to explore is the transmission of sin. This is an ongoing theme as writers consider how later generations relate to Adam's sin. In *The Soul's Testimony*, Tertullian writes, 'And (the man) being given over to death on account of his [Adam's] sin, the entire human race, tainted in their descent from him, were made a channel for transmitting his condemnation.'[4]

These next references come with a warning about sexual content, as Tertullian discusses the origin of the soul, which potentially carries with it the taint of sin. Tertullian states:

> Well, now, in this usual function of the sexes which brings together the male and the female in their common intercourse, we know that both the soul and the flesh discharge a duty together: the soul supplies desire, the flesh contributes the gratification of it; the soul furnishes the instigation, the flesh affords the realisation. The entire man being excited by the one effort of both natures, his seminal substance is discharged, deriving its fluidity from the body, and its warmth from the soul.[5]

1. Tertullian, *On Idolatry*, 1.
2. Ibid.
3. Tertullian, *Treatise on the Soul*, 16.
4. Tertullian, *Soul's Testimony*, 3.
5. Tertullian, *Treatise on the Soul*, 27. There is more detail contained in this chapter, but I do not want this section overburdened with this material, however much that may increase the popularity of Tertullian.

The importance of this for the nature of the soul in people when born is clarified later: 'Every soul, then, by reason of its birth, has its nature in Adam until it is born again in Christ; moreover, it is unclean all the while that it remains without this regeneration.'[1]

The results of sin can thus be found in a new identity that people are born into, in a sinful state and a tendency to sin. Tertullian believes that there is a progression in a person's life in relation to this, with the soul advancing as the body does 'by a gradual growth through the stages of life' so that, 'the *puberty* of the soul coincides with that of the body, and that they attain both together to this full growth at about the fourteenth year of life'.[2] Tertullian is firm is stating that the sins that result are both physical and spiritual and that each carry equal weight in their seriousness before God:

> Still it will not be irksome briefly to touch upon the fact that, of sins, some are carnal, that is, corporeal; some spiritual. For since man is composed of this combination of a two-fold substance, the sources of his sins are no other than the sources of his composition. But it is not the fact that body and spirit are two things that constitute the sins mutually different – otherwise they are on this account rather *equal*, because the *two* make up *one* – lest any make the distinction between their *sins* proportionate to the difference between their *substances*, so as to esteem the one lighter, or else heavier, than the other: if it be true, (as it is,) that both flesh and spirit are creatures of God; one wrought by His hand, one consummated by His *afflatus*. Since, then, they equally pertain to the Lord, whichever of them *sins* equally *offends* the Lord.[3]

One result of sin is the judgement of God. In two separate works, Tertullian makes some interesting statements that seem to suggest that while God is just intrinsically (in his being), he is a judge only after sin exists. This seems to tie God into a linear relationship to time: 'Up to the fall of man, therefore, from the beginning God was simply good; after that He became a judge both severe and, as the Marcionites will have it, cruel.'[4] In arguing against this charge of cruelty, Tertullian argues that this is a righteous and just severity in response to sin:

> Thus God's prior goodness was from nature, His subsequent severity from a cause. The one was innate, the other accidental; the one His own, the other adapted; the one issuing from Him, the other

1. Ibid., 40.
2. Ibid., 38.
3. Tertullian, *On Repentance*, 3.
4. Tertullian, *Marion*, 2.11.

admitted by Him. But then *nature* could not have rightly permitted His goodness to have gone on inoperative, nor the *cause* have allowed His severity to have escaped in disguise or concealment. God provided the one for Himself, the other for the occasion.... It follows, then, that as injustice is an evil, so in the same degree is justice a good. Nor should it be regarded as simply a species of goodness, but as the practical observance of it, because goodness (unless justice be so controlled as to be just) will not be goodness, if it be unjust.[1]

The second occasion when Tertullian argues this point reads even more strangely, as he parallels God becoming a judge after the advent of sin with His becoming Father after the incarnation of the Son:

Because God is in like manner a Father, and He is also a Judge; but He has not always been Father and Judge, merely on the ground of His having always been God. For He could not have been the Father previous to the Son, nor a Judge previous to sin. There was, however, a time when neither sin existed with Him, nor the Son; the former of which was to constitute the Lord a Judge, and the latter a Father.[2]

Tertullian is not intentionally claiming that there was a time when God existed without Word and Spirit, as Arius later argued, but it is a strange choice of example to demonstrate the right reaction in God's decision to judge sin that could be interpreted as having Trinitarian implications.

One work of Tertullian's which merits a mention in this context, but sadly cannot be explored more fully, is *The Shows*. This is a fascinating discussion of the correct attitude that the church should take to the entertainment on offer in the early third-century Roman Empire. There seem to be many aspects drawn out that mirror elements of twenty-first century culture, and Tertullian encourages his readers to be wary of their engagement because of the dangers of falling into various forms of sin. The work begins as follows:

Ye Servants of God, about to draw near to God, that you may make solemn consecration of yourselves to Him, seek well to understand the condition of faith, the reasons of the Truth, the laws of Christian Discipline, which forbid among other sins of the world, the pleasures of the public shows. Ye who have testified and confessed that you have done so already, review the subject, that there may be no sinning whether through real or wilful ignorance.

1. Ibid.
2. Tertullian, *Hermogenes*, 3.

> For such is the power of earthly pleasures, that, to retain the opportunity of still partaking of them, it contrives to prolong a willing ignorance, and bribes knowledge into playing a dishonest part.[1]

Tertullian thus has much to say on the subject of sin in a wide variety of areas from its roots to the results and in application for Christian life. There is some impact from Adam's sin on the human individual and therefore the next question to be addressed is the extent to which the *imago Dei,* and particularly the element of free will, is affected by the ubiquity of sin. As will become increasingly clear (hopefully), Tertullian maintains a high view of humankind in this area even after the Fall:

> There is, then, besides the evil which supervenes on the soul from the intervention of the evil spirit, an antecedent, and in a certain sense natural, evil which arises from its corrupt origin. For, as we have said before, the corruption of our nature is another nature having a god and father of its own, namely the author of (that) corruption. Still there is a portion of good in the soul, of that original, divine, and genuine good, which is its proper nature. For that which is derived from God is rather obscured than extinguished. It can be obscured, indeed, because it is not God; extinguished, however, it cannot be, because it comes from God.[2]

Free Will

Tertullian's construction of human free will is found in a discussion of the nature of humanity, rather than a result of a clear doctrine of God, as was the case with Irenaeus. This idea does at times inform his thought, but it is not separately stated. Angelic free will is stated in the *Apology* as part of their created nature:

> We are instructed, moreover, by our sacred books how from certain angels, who fell of their own free-will, there sprang a more wicked demon-brood, condemned of God along with the authors of their race, and that chief we have referred to.[3]

This is relatively unimportant in itself and will be returned to later as Tertullian compares the nature of human free will with that of the angels.

1. Tertullian, *The Shows,* 1.
2. Tertullian, *Treatise on the Soul,* 41.
3. Tertullian, *Apology,* 22.

As with Irenaeus, it is good to set the presentation of human free will within the context of Tertullian's understanding of the sovereignty of God. This is in order to do justice to the nuances that are present in his theology. If this were not done, there would be some danger of misreading Tertullian as a pure libertarian whose God was impotent in the face of human free will. In a number of works, Tertullian teaches that God is sovereign and ordains elements within creation. For example, in writing to the philosophers of his age, he states:

> Bear thy testimony, if thou knowest this to be the truth; for openly and with a perfect liberty, such as we do not possess, we hear thee both in private and in public exclaim, 'Which may God grant,' and, 'If God so will.' By expressions such as these thou declarest that there is one who is distinctively God, and thou confessest that all power belongs to him to whose will, as Sovereign, thou dost look.[1]

In the *Apology*, Tertullian replies to critics who contended that the suffering of Christians indicates a lack of power in the God they trust in. Tertullian replies:

> But admit first of all His providential arrangings, and you will not make this retort. For He who once for all appointed an eternal judgement at the world's close, does not precipitate the separation, which is essential to judgement, before the end. Meanwhile He deals with all sorts of men alike, so that all together share His favours and reproofs. His will is, that outcasts and elect should have adversities and prosperities in common, that we should have all the same experience of His goodness and severity. . . . Nay, though we are likewise involved in troubles because of our close connection with you, we are rather glad of it, because we recognise in it divine foretellings, which, in fact, go to confirm the confidence and faith of our hope.[2]

This teaching is backed up elsewhere by a firm belief in the ordination of God exemplified in the prophecies contained in Scripture, some of which have been fulfilled while other await their fulfilment:

> For what is written, must needs come to pass. Besides, what is written will then come to pass, if something different does not. But, lo! we are both regarded as persons to be hated by all men for the sake of the name, as it is written; and are delivered up by our nearest of kin. . . . So the Lord ordained. If He ordained these events otherwise, why do they not come to pass otherwise

1. Tertullian, *Testimony*, 2.
2. Tertullian, *Apology*, 41.

than He ordained them, that is, as He ordained them? And yet they do not come to pass otherwise than He ordained. Therefore, as they come to pass, so He ordained; and as He ordained, so they come to pass. For neither would they have been permitted to occur otherwise than He ordained, nor for His part would He have ordained otherwise than He would wish them to occur.[1]

The concept of human free will is explored in great depth in two of Tertullian's works: *Treatise on the Soul* and *Against Marcion*. In the latter, this is in light of a reassertion of God's sovereignty:

> By such a conclusion all is reserved unimpaired to God; both His natural goodness, and the purposes of His governance and foreknowledge, and the abundance of His power. You ought, however, to deduct from God's attributes both His supreme earnestness of purpose and most excellent truth in His whole creation, if you would cease to inquire whether anything could have happened against the will of God.[2]

We will now look through the two presentations of human free will, beginning with this instance in Tertullian's writings against Marcion. It starts with the created nature of man through the inspiration of a soul from the great Goodness that is God: 'Who indeed was so worthy of dwelling amongst the works of God, as he who was His own image and likeness? . . . Goodness breathed into him a soul, not dead but living.'[3] The question this raises, looked at in the section above on sin, is how God could have allowed this good created to fall from obedience into evil in light of his omnipotent nature. The answer begins with the creation of humanity:

> I find, then, that man was by God constituted free, master of his own will and power; indicating the presence of God's image and likeness in him by nothing so well as by this constitution of his nature. For it was not by his face, and by the lineaments of his body, though they were so varied in his human nature, that he expressed his likeness to the form of God; but he showed his stamp in that essence which he derived from God Himself (that is, the spiritual, which answered to the form of God), and in the freedom and power of his will.[4]

Tertullian questions whether God was right to create humanity in this state and initially responds by once again looking at the being of God in whose likeness they were created:

1. Tertullian, *Antidote for the Scorpion's Sting*, 11.
2. Tertullian, *Marcion*, 2.7.
3. Ibid., 2.4.
4. Ibid., 2.5.

Proper also was it that there should be something worthy of knowing God. What could be found so worthy as the image and likeness of God? This also was undoubtedly good and reasonable. Therefore it was proper that (he who is) the image and likeness of God should be formed with a free will and a mastery of himself; so that this very thing – namely, freedom of will and self-command – might be reckoned as the image and likeness of God in him. For this purpose such an essence was adapted to man as suited this character, even the afflatus of the Deity, Himself free and uncontrolled.[1]

In the following passage, a distinction is drawn between the created goodness that exists in humankind and the goodness that is found in the innate nature of God. It is key for understanding Tertullian's anthropology in this area:

> Now, God alone is good by nature. For He, who has that which is without beginning, has it not by creation, but by nature. Man, however, who exists entirely by creation, having a beginning, along with that beginning obtained the form in which he exists; and thus he is not by nature disposed to good, but by creation, not having it as his own attribute to be good, because, (as we have said,) it is not by nature, but by creation, that he is disposed to good, according to the appointment of his good Creator, even the Author of all good. In order, therefore, that man might have a goodness of his own, bestowed on him by God, and there might be henceforth in man a property, and in a certain sense a natural attribute of goodness, there was assigned to him in the constitution of his nature, as a formal witness of the goodness which God bestowed upon him, freedom and power of the will, such as should cause good to be performed spontaneously by man, as a property of his own, on the ground that no less than this would be required in the matter of a goodness which was to be voluntarily exercised by him, that is to say, by the liberty of his will, without either favour or servility to the constitution of his nature, so that man should be good just up to this point, if he should display his goodness in accordance with his natural constitution indeed, but still as the result of his will, as a property of his nature; and, by a similar exercise of volition, should show himself to be too strong in defence against evil also (for even this God, of course, foresaw), being free, and master of himself; because, if he were wanting in this prerogative *of self-mastery*, so as to perform even good by necessity and not will, he would, in the helplessness of his servitude, become subject to the usurpation of evil, a slave as much to evil as to good. Entire freedom of will, therefore, was conferred upon him in both tendencies; so that,

---

1. Ibid., 2.6.

as master of himself, he might constantly encounter good by spontaneous observance of it, and evil by its spontaneous avoidance; because, were man even otherwise circumstanced, it was yet his bounden duty, in the judgement of God, to do justice according to the motions of his will regarded, of course, as free. But the reward neither of good nor of evil could be paid to the man who should be found to have been either good or evil through necessity and not choice. In this really lay the law which did not exclude, but rather prove, *human* liberty by a spontaneous rendering of obedience, or a spontaneous commission of iniquity; so patent was the liberty of man's will for either issue.[1]

The conclusion that is drawn is clear:

> [T]he goodness of God, then fully considered from the beginning of His works, will be enough to convince us that nothing evil could possibly have come forth from God; and the liberty of man will, after a second thought, show us that it alone is chargeable with the fault which itself committed.[2]

In the next chapter, Tertullian seeks to resolve the difficulty of why a perfectly good God would allow his created humanity to sin when he could foresee this eventuality and had it in his power to prevent a wrong use of human liberty. The answer given is that God chose to rein in his power in order to be faithful to who he is.

> For, since He had once for all allowed (and, as we have shown, worthily allowed) to man freedom of will and mastery of himself, surely He from His very authority in creation permitted *these gifts* to be enjoyed: to be enjoyed, too, so far as lay in Himself, according to His own character as God, that is, for good (for who would permit anything hostile to himself?); and, so far as lay in man, according to the impulses of his liberty (for who does not, when giving anything to any one to enjoy, accompany the gift with a permission to enjoy it with all his heart and will?). The necessary consequence, therefore, was, that God must separate from the liberty which He had once for all bestowed upon man (in other words, keep within Himself), both His foreknowledge and power, through which He might have prevented man's falling into danger when attempting wrongly to enjoy his liberty. Now, if He had interposed, He would have rescinded the liberty of man's will, which He had permitted with set purpose, and in goodness. But, suppose God had interposed; suppose Him to have abrogated man's liberty, by warning him from the tree, and

1. Ibid.
2. Ibid.

> keeping off the subtle serpent from his interview with the woman; would not Marcion then exclaim, What a frivolous, unstable, and faithless Lord, cancelling the gifts He had bestowed! Why did He allow any liberty of will, if He afterwards withdrew it? Why withdraw it after allowing it? Let Him choose where to brand Himself with error, either in His original constitution of man, or in His subsequent abrogation thereof! If He had checked (man's freedom), would He not then seem to have been rather deceived, through want of foresight into the future? But in giving it full scope, who would not say that He did so in ignorance of the issue of things? God, however, did foreknow that man would make a bad use of his created constitution; and yet what can be so worthy of God as His earnestness of purpose, and the truth of His created works, be they what they may?[1]

The next stage in Tertullian's argument, which logically follows on from this quotation, concerns the responsibility for sinning founded in this free will. This means that God is not to blame for evil and that the devil's role is limited to that of tempter:

> No doubt it was an angel who was the seducer; but then the victim of that seduction was free, and master of himself; and as being the image and likeness of God, was stronger than any angel; and as being, too, the *afflatus* of the Divine Being, was nobler than that material spirit of which angels were made.[2]

This is then clarified and developed as follows:

> The *possibility* lay in its slenderness of nature, as being the breath and not the spirit; the *impropriety*, however, arose from its power of will, as being free, and not a slave. It was furthermore assisted by the warning against committing sin under the threat of incurring death, which was meant to be a support for its slender nature, and a direction for its liberty of choice. So that the soul can no longer appear to have sinned, because it has an affinity with God, that is to say, through the *afflatus*, but rather through that which was an addition to its nature, that is, through its free-will, which was indeed given to it by God in accordance with His purpose and reason, but recklessly employed by man according as he chose. This, then, being the case, the entire course of God's action is purged from all imputation to evil. For the liberty of the will will not retort its own wrong on Him by whom it was bestowed, but on him by whom it was improperly used.[3]

1. Ibid., 2.7.
2. Ibid., 2.8.
3. Ibid., 2.9.

3. Tertullian

It is thus apparent that Tertullian holds a high view of free will in the nature of humankind against a strong determinism, and thus an absolute responsibility for sin. There remains the question of the extent to which the Fall affected this and impacted the ability for humanity to choose right or wrong. Tertullian's response again is emphatic: the introduction of the law demonstrates that absolute free will is retained so that people continue to be held rightly responsible for their actions. This teaching is repeated twice in this section of *Against Marcion*:

> This his state was confirmed even by the very law which God then imposed upon him. For a law would not be imposed upon one who had it not in his power to render that obedience which is due to law; nor again, would the penalty of death be threatened against sin, if a contempt of the law were impossible to man in the liberty of his will. So in the Creator's subsequent laws also you will find, when He sets before man good and evil, life and death, that the entire course of discipline is arranged in precepts by God's calling men from sin, and threatening and exhorting them; and this on no other ground than that man is free, with a will either for obedience or resistance. . . .[1]
>
> Nor would He have put the burden of law upon him, if he had been incapable of sustaining so great a weight; nor, again, would He have threatened with the penalty of death a creature whom He knew to be guiltless on the score of his helplessness: in short, if He had made him infirm, it would not have been by liberty and independence of will, but rather by the withholding from him these endowments. And thus it comes to pass, that even now also, the same human being, the same substance of his soul, the same condition as Adam's, is made conqueror over the same devil by the self-same liberty and power of his will, when it moves in obedience to the laws of God.[2]

This theological teaching in response to Marcion is backed up by more philosophical material in Tertullian's *Treatise on the Soul*, which examines the nature of the human soul. This again affirms a core element in 'the freedom of our will, which is described as αὐτεξούσιος (of independent authority); and inasmuch as this faculty is itself also natural and mutable, in whatsoever direction it turns, it inclines of its own nature'.[3] This is further developed in the next chapter:

1. Ibid., 2.5.
2. Ibid., 2.8.
3. Tertullian, *Treatise*, 21 (in a chapter entitled, 'As Free-Will Actuates an Individual, so May his Character Change').

> We have assigned, then, to the soul both that freedom of the will which we just now mentioned, and its dominion over the works of nature. . . . The soul, then, we define to be sprung from the breath of God, immortal, possessing body, having form, simple in its substance, intelligent in its own nature, developing its power in various ways, free in its determinations, subject to be changes of accident, in its faculties mutable, rational, supreme, endued with an instinct of presentiment, evolved out of one (archetypal soul).[1]

Tertullian thus defines the 'proper condition' of the soul as being 'immortality, rationality, sensibility, intelligence, and freedom of the will'.[2] As in the work against Marcion, Tertullian again affirms that the initial state of the soul is retained after the Fall, although here he does allow for some corruption:

> For, as we have said before, the corruption of our nature is another nature having a god and father of its own, namely the author of (that) corruption. Still there is a portion of good in the soul, of that original, divine, and genuine good, which is its proper nature. For that which is derived from God is rather obscured than extinguished. It can be obscured, indeed, because it is not God; extinguished, however, it cannot be, because it comes from God.[3]

In this section, Tertullian goes so far as to declare that when people exclaim 'Good God!' or 'God knows!' they are bearing witness to a consciousness of the origin of the soul.[4]

The final significant writing on free will in the works of Tertullian is found in *On Exhortation to Chastity*, which contains important passages in chapters two and three on the power of human volition. The focus here is on the sin that we now commit and repeats Tertullian's teaching that it is our responsibility. It cannot be excused by imputing effective influence to either God or the devil:

> Thus, it is a volition of our own when we will what is evil, in antagonism to God's will, who wills what is good. Further, if you inquire whence comes that volition whereby we will anything in antagonism to the will of God, I shall say, It has its source in ourselves. . . . In like manner you, too, if you fail to obey God, who has trained you by setting before you the precept of free action, will, through the liberty of your will, willingly turn into the downward

---

1. Ibid., 22.
2. Ibid., 38.
3. Ibid., 41.
4. Ibid.

> course of doing what God nills: and thus you think yourself to have been subverted by the devil; who, albeit he does *will* that you should will something which God nills still does not *make* you will it, inasmuch as he did not *reduce* those our protoplasts to the volition of sin; nay, nor (did *reduce* them at all) against their will, or in ignorance as to what God nilled. For, of course, He nilled (a thing) to be done when He made death the destined consequence of its commission. Thus the work of the devil is one: to make trial whether you do will that which it rests with you to will. But when you *have* willed, it follows that he subjects you to himself; not by having *wrought* volition in you, but by having found a favourable opportunity in your volition.[1]

God's engagement with us in this is one of permission, rather than our actions resulting from his absolute and irrevocable will:

> For, albeit some things seem to savour of 'the will of God,' seeing that they are *allowed* by Him, it does not forthwith follow that everything which is *permitted* proceeds out of the mere and absolute will of him who permits. *Indulgence* is the source of all *permission*.[2]

It is God's revealed desire in creating humanity with free will and holding them responsible for their use of that will that evil is permitted or 'indulged'.

Given the strength of this teaching on human free will as part of the created and ongoing nature, there are naturally questions as to the role of grace in a person's life and whether God is able within his faithfulness to his creation, to intervene in encouraging people towards all that is good if their will is set against it.

Grace

Tertullian follows the general pattern of the earliest church writings in not having a developed doctrine of grace. However, there are some passages that deal with key issues related to grace, such as the relationship between faith and works and the possibility of losing grace. One area where Tertullian has significant input is baptism, where clear beginnings of the sacramental understanding can be found.

The first aspect of grace to be mentioned briefly is common grace; the ongoing experience of God after the Fall. Tertullian does not explicitly use the word grace in this context, but the teaching appears in a number of his works. For example:

1. Tertullian, *Chastity*, 2.
2. Ibid., 3.

> Even fallen as it is, the victim of the great adversary's machinations, it does not forget its Creator, His goodness and law, and the final end both of itself and of its foe. Is it singular then, if, divine in its origin, its revelations agree with the knowledge God has given to His own people?[1]

A similar point is made against Marcion, showing that, even in their sin, humans still receive that which is necessary from the creator:

> You are an enemy to the sky, and yet you are glad to catch its freshness in your houses. You disparage the earth, although the elemental parent of your own flesh, as if it were your undoubted enemy, and yet you extract from it all its fatness for your food. The sea, too, you reprobate, but are continually using its produce, which you account the more sacred diet. If I should offer you a rose, you will not disdain its Maker.[2]

There are effects from the Fall, however, which mean that not everyone experiences grace in the same way. Those who are considered worthy receive God's goodness more fully than those who are unworthy: 'And this is the result: the divine goodness, being interrupted in that free course whereby God was spontaneously good, is now dispensed according to the deserts of every man.'[3]

Moving onto the salvific role of grace, there is a question in light of the strong teaching on free will about the effects of grace and the extent of human agency in salvation. Tertullian makes the point that the initiative in saving people comes from God in the offer of mercy and grace:

> For God – after so many and so great sins of human temerity, begun by the first of the race, Adam, after the condemnation of man, together with the dowry of the world after his ejection from paradise and subjection to death – when He had hasted back to His own mercy, did from that time onward inaugurate repentance in His own self, by rescinding the sentence of His first wrath, engaging to grant pardon to His own work and image. And so He gathered together a people for Himself, and fostered them with many liberal distributions of His bounty, and, after so often finding them most ungrateful, ever exhorted them to repentance and sent out the voices of the universal company of the prophets to prophesy. By and by, promising freely the grace which in the last times He was intending to pour as a flood of light on the universal world through His Spirit, He bade the baptism

---

1. Tertullian, *Testimony*, 5.
2. Tertullian, *Marcion*, 1.14.
3. Ibid., 2.13.

of repentance lead the way, with the view of first preparing, by means of the sign and seal of repentance, them whom He was calling, through grace, to (inherit) the promise surely made to Abraham.[1]

There is also a note in relation to the letter to the Galatians about a move away from salvation by works in obeying the law to a Gospel of grace: 'Therefore the entire purport of this epistle is simply to show us that the supersession of the law comes from the appointment of the Creator.'[2]

Tertullian does not devote any great material to the specific relationship between divine grace and human free will, but this one explicit engagement shows an emphasis on the strength of the latter:

> Stones also will become children of Abraham, if educated in Abraham's faith; and a generation of vipers will bring forth the fruits of penitence, if they reject the poison of their malignant nature. This will be the power of the grace of God, more potent indeed than nature, exercising its sway over the faculty that underlies itself within us – even the freedom of our will, which is described as αὐτεξούσιος (of independent authority); and inasmuch as this faculty is itself also natural and mutable, in whatsoever direction it turns, it inclines of its own nature.[3]

There is thus a role that grace plays, but it is not a controlling one. Rather, humans are free to reject grace and lose its effects if they so choose. This is a point that Tertullian reiterates in a number of different works and contexts. In *The Prescription Against Heretics*, Tertullian highlights a number of different characters who fell away from faith, indicating the importance of the human response to grace:

> This again is, I suppose, an extraordinary thing, that one who has been approved should afterwards fall back? Saul, who was good beyond all others, is afterwards subverted by envy. David, a good man 'after the Lord's own heart,' is guilty afterwards of murder and adultery. Solomon, endowed by the Lord with all grace and wisdom, is led into idolatry, by women. For to the Son of God alone was it reserved to persevere to the last without sin. But what if a bishop, if a deacon, if a widow, if a virgin, if a doctor, if even a martyr, have fallen from the rule (of faith), will heresies on that account appear to possess the truth? Do we prove the faith by the persons, or the persons by the faith? No one is wise, no one is faithful, no one excels in dignity, but the Christian; and no one is a Christian but he who perseveres even to the end.[4]

1. Tertullian, *On Repentance*, 2.
2. Tertullian, *Marcion*, 5.2.
3. Tertullian, *Treatise*, 21.
4. Tertullian, *The Prescription Against Heretics*, 3.

Against Marcion, he makes the same point whilst shifting the focus onto God and his response to people's actions:

> Now, although you will have it that He is inconstant in respect of persons, sometimes disapproving where approbation is deserved; or else wanting in foresight, bestowing approbation on men who ought rather to be reprobated, as if He either censured His own past judgements, or could not forecast His future ones; yet nothing is so consistent for even a good judge as both to reject and to choose on the merits of the present moment. . . . Now, who is so faultless among men, that God could always have him in His choice, and never be able to reject him? Or who, on the other hand, is so void of any good work, that God could reject him for ever, and never be able to choose him? Show me, then, the man who is always good, and he will not be rejected; show me, too, him who is always evil, and he will never be chosen. Should, however, the same man, being found on different occasions in the pursuit of both (good and evil) be recompensed in both directions by God, who is both a good and judicial Being, He does not change His judgements through inconstancy or want of foresight, but dispenses reward according to the deserts of each case with a most unwavering and provident decision.[1]

This possibility of losing the effects of grace is dealt with again in *On Repentance*, in which, having encouraged readers to persevere in the benefits and fruit of receiving grace, Tertullian states:

> For what I say is this, that the repentance which, being shown us and commanded us through God's grace, recalls us to grace with the Lord, when once learned and undertaken by us ought never afterward to be cancelled by repetition of sin. No pretext of ignorance now remains to plead on your behalf; in that, after acknowledging the Lord, and accepting His precepts – in short, after engaging in repentance of (past) sins – you again betake yourself to sins. Thus, in as far as you are removed from ignorance, in so far are you cemented to contumacy. . . . Now, that man does despise Him, who, after attaining by His help to an understanding of things good and evil, often an affront to his own understanding – that is, to God's gift – by resuming what he understands ought to be shunned, and what he has already shunned: he rejects the Giver in abandoning the gift; he denies the Benefactor in not honouring the benefit.[2]

1. Tertullian, *Marcion*, 2.23.
2. Tertullian, *On Repentance*, 5.

Later in the same work, Tertullian argues further on these lines against those who indicate by their actions that they believe God is constrained to save by the gift of grace:

> But some think as if God were under a *necessity* of bestowing even on the unworthy, what He has engaged (to give); and they turn His liberality into slavery. But if it is of necessity that God grants us the symbol of death, then He does so *unwillingly*. But who permits a gift to be permanently retained which he has granted unwillingly? For do not many afterward fall out of (grace)? Is not this gift taken away from many? These, no doubt, are they who do steal a march upon (the treasure), who, after approaching to the faith of repentance, set up on the sands a house doomed to ruin. Let no one, then, flatter himself on the ground of being assigned to the 'recruit-classes' of learners, as if on that account he have a licence even now to sin.[1]

It is thus clear that Tertullian would not have held to an absolute assurance of salvation from the moment of repentance. One element that is important in all this for Tertullian, and where Tertullian is influential in the history of the church, is the area of baptism. The previous quotation warning Christians about their conduct after coming to faith is from a chapter in *On Repentance* entitled 'Baptism Not to Be Presumptuously Received. It Requires Preceding Repentance, Manifested by Amendment of Life.'[2] Baptism thus has a very high status, linked to the reception of grace and the Holy Spirit, rather than being merely symbolic.

Tertullian is not one of the Church Fathers who advocated infant baptism, rather encouraging an understanding of faith before one is baptised:

> And so, according to the circumstances and disposition, and even age, of each individual, the delay of baptism is preferable; principally, however, in the case of little children. For why is it necessary – if (baptism itself) is not so necessary – that the sponsors likewise should be thrust into danger? Who both themselves, by reason of mortality, may fail to fulfil their promises, and may be disappointed by the development of an evil disposition, *in those for whom they stood?* The Lord does indeed say, 'Forbid them not to come unto me.' Let them 'come,' then, while they are growing up; let them 'come' while they are learning, while they are learning whither to come; let them become Christians when they have become able to know Christ.[3]

1. Ibid., 6.
2. Ibid.
3. Tertullian, *On Baptism*, 18.

Earlier in *On Baptism*, Tertullian delineates the relationship between the outward sign and the inward grace:

> All waters, therefore, in virtue of the pristine privilege of their origin, do, after invocation of God, attain the sacramental power of sanctification; for the Spirit immediately supervenes from the heavens, and rests over the waters, sanctifying them from Himself; and being thus sanctified, they imbibe at the same time the power of sanctifying.[1]

The following chapter clarifies what this sanctification involves: 'And thus, when the grace of God advanced to higher degrees among men, an accession *of efficacy* was granted to the waters and to the angel.'[2]

Tertullian uses this high doctrine of baptism to argue against Marcion's evil, creator-of-matter god, who removes from the good God the powers of generation, judgement and vivification (giving of life):

> For what end does baptism serve, according to him? If the remission of sins, how will he make it evident that he remits sins, when he affords no evidence that he retains them? Because he would retain them, if he performed the functions of a judge. If deliverance from death, how could he deliver *from* death, who has not delivered *to* death? For he must have delivered the sinner to death, if he had from the beginning condemned sin. If the regeneration of man, how can he regenerate, who has never generated? For the repetition of an act is impossible to him, by whom nothing any time has been ever done. If the bestowal of the Holy Ghost, how will he bestow the Spirit, who did not at first impart the life?[3]

This teaching comes in a chapter entitled 'This Perverse Doctrine Deprives Baptism of All Its Grace'. There is thus a close relationship in Tertullian's thought between the act of baptism and the experience of grace.

The last brief mention from Tertullian on the topic of grace is a short, beautiful phrase concerning the effect of grace in a believer, in the context of the temptation to lust. Tertullian declares, 'But a Christian with grace-healed eyes is sightless in this matter; he is mentally blind against the assaults of passion.'[4]

1. Ibid., 4.
2. Ibid., 5.
3. Tertullian, *Marcion*, 1.28.
4. Tertullian, *Apology*, 46.

Conclusion

As with Irenaeus, Tertullian's greatest contribution is in the area of free will, on which he writes extensively in support of human control of, and therefore responsibility for, one's actions. There is also a quantity of material on sin in terms of its origin and transmission, while grace does not have the same core role in his theology.

Tertullian's works are contained in Philip Schaff's *Ante-Nicene Fathers*, volumes three and four, which can be accessed at www.ccel.org. The various works of Tertullian have been published separately, but there are no single volume collections that encompass the major works that have been presented in this chapter. For more background material on Tertullian and for a wider look at his thought, look at Eric Osborn's *Tertullian: First Theologian of the West* (Cambridge: CUP, 1997) or Geoffrey Dunn's *Tertullian* (London: Routledge, 2004).

4.
Origen

Origen of Alexandria (c.185-c.255) is one of the most fascinating and controversial thinkers in the Early Church. His devotion to the Christian faith is unquestioned, seeking martyrdom with his father as a young man and going on to achieve martyrdom when he died from injuries sustained through torture during the Decian persecution. Origen was heavily influenced by Platonic philosophy, and this has always raised questions about his relationship with orthodox Christianity. He certainly favoured a strong allegorical approach to certain Scriptures, particularly Old Testament passages that can make for awkward reading.

Origen's Trinitarian thought has been criticised as overly hierarchical and the root of many early heresies, such as Arianism, but he also laid the foundations for many key defenders of orthodoxy and contributors to early Christian theology, including Athanasius and the Cappadocian Fathers. He remains a cornerstone of the theology of the Orthodox churches today.

Origen amassed an enormous body of work over the course of his life and the wealth of material that could be engaged with here, particularly in the area of free will, means that this presentation will necessarily be more selective than was the case with Irenaeus and Tertullian.

Sin

The first area to look at in Origen's views on sin is the nature of God and the created nature of humankind, including the nature of the human soul. This is one of the areas in which he has received criticism for his views. Writing at a similar time to Irenaeus and Tertullian, it is unsurprising that one of the first tasks that faced Origen was to show that God was not responsible for sin against any Gnostic charge that one God through the whole of Scripture would be the root of evil. With this in mind, we will then look at Origen's views on the human soul before moving onto the causes of sin in creation and the effects of this in humankind.

4. Origen

Origen's main passages on the perfection of God and against his involvement in sin and evil are found in *Against Celsus*. Celsus was a Platonist philosopher and stern critic of the Christian religion, belittling those who would follow the faith for their lack of education and reason. Whilst the second-century church seemed to lack some intellectual rigour, Origen's work in the third century was a thorough response to Celsus.

Celsus had raised scriptural passages that seemed to indicate a role for God in evil, such as Job 2:10, Isaiah 45:7 and Micah 1:12-13. The Isaiah verse in the Septuagint reads, 'I make peace, and create evil'. On this basis, Celsus asked how it could be that God created evil, to which Origen replied:

> We, on the other hand, maintain that 'evil,' or 'wickedness,' and the actions which proceed from it, were *not* created by God. For if God created that which is *really* evil, how was it possible that the proclamation regarding (the last) judgement should be confidently announced, which informs us that the wicked are to be punished for their evil deeds in proportion to the amount of their wickedness, while those who have lived a virtuous life, or performed virtuous actions, will be in the enjoyment of blessedness, and will receive rewards from God?[1]

Rather than originating in God, evil results from that which God has made:

> Evils, then, if those be meant which are *properly* so called, were *not* created by God; but some, although *few* in comparison with the order of the *whole* world, *have* resulted from His principal works, as there follow from the chief works of the carpenter such things as spiral shavings and sawdust, or as architects might appear to be the cause of the rubbish which lies around their buildings in the form of the filth which drops from the stones and the plaster.[2]

This is the defence against the Gnostic writings of Celsus, who argued that the God who created this world is responsible for the evil that happens within it, necessitating the need for another creative force that is different to the supreme God. Origen's contention is that, were this the case, the supreme God would retain the same position because evil would still result from his works, whether directly or indirectly:

> He hastily concludes, as if it were a consequence of our maintaining that this world also is a work of the universal God, that in *our* judgement *God* is the author of evil. Let it be, however, regarding

---

1. Origen, *Against Celsus*, 6.55.
2. Ibid.

evil as it may – whether created by God or not – it nevertheless follows only as a *result* when you compare the principal design. And I am greatly surprised if the inference regarding God's authorship of evil, which he thinks follows from our maintaining that this world also is the work of the universal God, does not follow too from his *own* statements.[1]

Origen emphatically states that it is impossible for God to do anything which is evil because he is constrained by his character, so that it is not within his rightly-understood omnipotence to commit wickedness:

> Now in our judgement God can do everything which it is possible for Him to do without ceasing to be God, and good, and wise. But Celsus asserts – not comprehending the meaning of the expression 'God can do all things' – 'that He will not desire to do anything wicked,' admitting that He has the *power*, but not the *will*, to commit evil. We, on the contrary, maintain that as that which by nature possesses the property of sweetening other things through its own inherent sweetness cannot produce bitterness contrary to its own peculiar nature, nor that whose nature it is to produce light through its being light can cause darkness; so neither is God able to commit wickedness, for the power of doing evil is contrary to His deity and its omnipotence.[2]

Origen does not make the link that Irenaeus and Tertullian make between this nature of God and the created nature of humanity in the image of God, leading to an initial purity. There is a clear distinction between the uncreated and all created things. One interesting passage that shows this, and links to the nature of the human soul, is found in Origen's *De Principiis*. Here he examines whether the sun, moon and stars can be considered sinful, based on Job 25:5: 'The stars also are not clean in Thy sight.' The conclusion reached is that stars can be considered sinful because they count as living beings for two reasons: 'they are said to receive commandments from God, which is ordinarily the case only with rational beings'; and from their movement, as Origen states:

> Neither can the movement of that body take place without a soul, nor can living things be at any time without motion. And seeing that the stars move with such order and regularity, that their movements never appear to be at any time subject to derangement, would it not be the height of folly to say that so orderly an observance of method and plan could be carried out or accomplished by irrational beings?[3]

1. Ibid., 6.53.
2. Ibid., 3.70.
3. Origen, *De Principiis*, 1.7.

4. Origen

This may seem to be a rather frivolous argument, but its importance comes from the context in discussing the nature and transmission of the human soul, which has implications for the nature of fallen humanity. The question that Origen asks in this context is whether the heavenly bodies received their souls when they received their bodies and seeks an answer in a parallel study of humanity – which is far more applicable here. Origen's reply is from two examples, Jacob and John the Baptist, connected to a teaching that God knows people before their birth, which results in his thinking in a pre-existent soul that is implanted into a living person from without:

> For, as regards man, how could the soul of him, viz., Jacob, who supplanted his brother in the womb, appear to be formed along with his body? Or how could his soul, or its images, be formed along with his body, who, while lying in his mother's womb, was filled with the Holy Ghost? I refer to John leaping in his mother's womb, and exulting because the voice of the salutation of Mary had come to the ears of his mother Elisabeth. How could his soul and its images be formed along with his body, who, before he was created in the womb, is said to be known to God, and was sanctified by Him before his birth?[1]

Origen holds that the soul is given to the individual from God, rather than being inherited from the parents: 'the soul, when implanted in the body, moves all things in it, and exerts its force over everything on which it operates.'[2] The soul that a person receives is thus pure but not a defining quality of the soul in the same sense that it is a core part of divinity. Rather, it is deemed 'accidental', i.e. something that can be lost, as Origen shows in a passage looking at the opposing powers of the devil and God:

> If then they are called opposing powers, and are said to have been once without stain, while spotless purity exists in the essential being of none save the Father, Son, and Holy Spirit, but is an accidental quality in every created thing; and since that which is accidental may also fall away, and since those opposite powers once were spotless, and were once among those which still remain unstained, it is evident from all this that no one is pure either by essence or nature, and that no one was by nature polluted.[3]

One result of these beliefs on the soul is a suspicion of the material in Origen's thought and some linking of matter to sinfulness or, at least, the vanity spoken of in Ecclesiastes: 'Let us see then, in the first place,

1. Ibid.
2. Ibid., 2.8.
3. Ibid., 1.5.

what is the vanity to which the creature is subject. I apprehend that it is nothing else than the body.'[1] Origen therefore interprets Paul's writing in Philippians 1 on abiding in the body rather than returning to Christ as implying a continuing connection with his sinful self from which he will be released at death.

In terms of the origin of evil, as indicated above, the first step is to exonerate God from any part:

> If, then, it is written, that 'carnal wisdom is enmity against God,' and if this be declared to be a result of creation, God Himself will appear to have formed a nature hostile to Himself, which cannot be subject to Him nor to His law.[2]

In writing against Celsus, Origen finds some common ground in that, 'it is sufficient for the multitude to say that they [evils] do not proceed from God'.[3] In this passage, Origen holds to a certain mystery in the origin of evil, stating:

> Now, to this we say, that the origin of evils is a subject which is not easy even for a philosopher to master, and that perhaps it is impossible even for such to attain a clear understanding of it, unless it be revealed to them by divine inspiration, both what evils are, and how they originated, and how they shall be made to disappear.[4]

This is particularly the case when considering the devils and his angels, Origen writes.

In seeking to provide what answer he can to this mystery, Origen focuses on the responsibility of humankind, while allowing some influence to evil spirits. One of the most interesting factors in Origen's presentation deals with the Genesis narrative, since he takes the story of Adam to be typological rather than historical, meaning that Adam becomes a 'type' of human as opposed to a definite founding father from whom all humankind receive their sinfulness:

> The subjects of Adam and his son will be philosophically dealt with by those who are aware that in the Hebrew language Adam signifies man: and that in those parts of the narrative which appear to refer to Adam as an individual, Moses is discoursing upon the nature of man in general. For 'in Adam' (as the Scripture says) 'all die,' and were condemned in the likeness of Adam's

1. Ibid., 1.7.
2. Ibid., 3.4.
3. Origen, *Celsus*, 4.65.
4. Ibid.

transgression, the Word of God asserting this not so much of *one particular individual* as of the *whole human race*. For in the connected series of statements which appears to apply as to one particular individual, the curse pronounced upon Adam is regarded as common to all (the members of the race), and what was spoken with reference to the woman is spoken of *every* woman without exception.[1]

As a result, there is no necessary created sinfulness present in humankind from birth, but rather each individual sins, corrupting their nature, and is responsible for that sin:

> Let the learned Greeks say that the human soul at its birth is placed under the charge of demons: Jesus has taught us not to despise even the little ones in His Church, saying, 'Their angels do always behold the face of My Father which is in heaven.'[2]

This sin is inevitable in humanity and can become naturalised in a person:

> We, however, who know of only one nature in every rational soul, and who maintain that none has been created evil by the Author of all things, but that many have *become* wicked through education, and perverse example, and surrounding influences, so that wickedness has been naturalised in some individuals, are persuaded that for the Word of God to change a nature in which evil has been naturalised is not only not impossible, but is even a work of no very great difficulty.[3]

In the same passage, Origen argues against Celsus' teaching that it is possible for a person to live a perfect life from the beginning, although he seems to hold out a hope for complete transformation for a view after they are saved:

> He alleges, in the next place, that 'they who are without sin are partakers of a better life;' not making it clear what he means by 'those who are without sin,' whether those who are so from the beginning (of their lives), or those who become so by a transformation. Of those who were so from the beginning of their lives, there cannot possibly be any; while those who are so after a transformation (of heart) are found to be few in number, being those who have become so after giving in their allegiance to the saving word.[4]

1. Ibid., 4.40.
2. Ibid., 8.34.
3. Ibid., 3.69.
4. Ibid.

On the same topic, Origen teaches that it is 'impossible for a man thus to be without sin . . . it is impossible for a man to look up to God (adorned) with virtue from the beginning. For wickedness must necessarily first exist in men.'[1]

In addition to this teaching on the human role in sin, there is the possibility of external, evil agency present in a person from this earliest time of life:

> It is shown beyond a doubt, that some have been possessed by hostile spirits from the very beginning of their lives: i.e., some were born with an evil spirit; and others, according to credible histories, have practised divination from childhood. Others have been under the influence of the demon called Python, i.e., the ventriloquial spirit, from the commencement of their existence. To all which instances, those who maintain that everything in the world is under the administration of Divine Providence (as is also our own belief), can, as it appears to me, give no other answer, so as to show that no shadow of injustice rests upon the divine government, than by holding that there were certain causes of prior existence, in consequence of which the souls, before their birth in the body, contracted a certain amount of guilt in their sensitive nature, or in their movements, on account of which they have been judged worthy by Divine Providence of being placed in this condition.[2]

This writing on divine providence, which we will return to as it affects human free will, is picked up in one other place in relation to sin as Origen seeks to evince one reason why a good God who has complete power would allow his created people to sin:

> And let the Jews assert what they will when we charge them with guilt, and say, 'Is not the providence and goodness of God most wonderfully displayed in your punishment, and in your being deprived of Jerusalem, and of the sanctuary, and of your splendid worship?' For whatever they may say in reply with respect to the providence of God, we shall be able more effectually to answer it by remarking, that the providence of God was wonderfully manifested in using the transgression of that people for the purpose of calling into the kingdom of God, through Jesus Christ, those from among the Gentiles who were strangers to the covenant and aliens to the promises.[3]

1. Ibid., 3.62.
2. Origen, *De Principiis*, 3.3.
3. Origen, *Celsus*, 2.78.

Origen thus has a high view of the human soul, like Irenaeus and Tertullian, but holds to the idea of a universal corruption of human nature more clearly than either of the earlier writers. The next stage is to look at the effects of this on human free will, a topic to which Origen devotes extended passages in his works.

Free Will

While Origen has many sections that pertain to free will, there is an important extended passage at the beginning of book three of *De Principiis*. In subsequent chapters he writes 'On the Freedom of the Will' and 'On the Opposing Powers', the latter discussing the effects of temptations to evil and lures to good on the human person and thus relating to the effectiveness of the human will. These chapters will be dealt with first in this presentation, because they are the most developed, cohesive and coherent expression of Origen's thought, and the themes that are raised will then be clarified and expanded in looking at the rest of his work.

The basis from which Origen approaches the concept of free will is the justice of God, and the chapter therefore starts:

> Since in the preaching of the Church there is included the doctrine respecting a just judgement of God, which, when believed to be true, incites those who hear it to live virtuously, and to shun sin by all means, inasmuch as they manifestly acknowledge that things worthy of praise and blame are within our own power, come and let us discuss by themselves a few points regarding the freedom of the will – a question of all others most necessary.[1]

Origen begins with a slightly strange assessment of the cause of movement of inanimate objects and the nature of animals before engaging with rational animals, who

> are in the nature of reason aids towards the contemplation of virtue and vice, by following which, after beholding good and evil, we select the one and avoid the other, we are deserving of praise when we give ourselves to the practice of virtue, and censurable when we do the reverse.[2]

He allows for external factors to impact people and to affect decisions that are made while asserting that this is never a controlling factor and calling on his readers to attest this from their own experiences:

1. Origen, *De Principiis*, 3.1.
2. Ibid.

> if any one maintain that this very external cause is of such a nature that it is impossible to resist it when it comes in such a way, let him turn his attention to his own feelings and movements, (and see) whether there is not an approval, and assent, and inclination of the controlling principle towards some object on account of some specious arguments.[1]

He provides an example in the case of a man tempted to engage in sex, with one allowing his will to succumb to temptation, while another who has developed further discipline is able to refrain:

> To take an instance, a woman who has appeared before a man that has determined to be chaste, and to refrain from carnal intercourse, and who has incited him to act contrary to his purpose, is not a perfect cause of annulling his determination. For, being altogether pleased with the luxury and allurement of the pleasure, and not wishing to resist it, or to keep his purpose, he commits an act of licentiousness. Another man, again (when the same things have happened to him who has received more instruction, and has disciplined himself), encounters, indeed, allurements and enticements; but his reason, as being strengthened to a higher point, and carefully trained, and confirmed in its views towards a virtuous course, or being near to confirmation, repels the incitement, and extinguishes the desire.[2]

Origen therefore states that we cannot avoid the responsibility for our actions, and anyone who seeks to blame an external force destroys the freedom of the human will by reducing it to circumstances when there is no force acting on a person but their own will – a rare occurrence.

> To say that we are moved from without, and to put away the blame from ourselves, by declaring that we are like to pieces of wood and stones, which are dragged about by those causes that act upon them from without, is neither true nor in conformity with reason, but is the statement of him who wishes to destroy the conception of free-will. For if we were to ask such an one what was free-will, he would say that it consisted in this, that when purposing to do some thing, no external cause came inciting to the reverse.[3]

Citing the examples of people who have changed in their tempers through their lives, Origen argues that people have the power of reason to engage with external forces and use these to their advantage, rather than being subject to their control:

1. Ibid.
2. Ibid.
3. Ibid.

> Reason, therefore, demonstrates that external events do not depend on us, but that it is our own business to use them in this way or the opposite, having received reason as a judge and an investigator of the manner in which we ought to meet those events that come from without.[1]

This is the reflective foundational thought on free will, covering two and a half pages. The remaining seventeen pages of the chapter engage with a variety of biblical texts for and against the concept of free will as Origen seeks to engage with the paradoxes that seem to be thrown up. He first deals with passages that support his initial notion of a just God who deals with people on the basis of their free choices:

> Now, that it is our business to live virtuously, and that God asks this of us, as not being dependent on Him nor on any other, nor, as some think, upon fate, but as being our own doing, the prophet Micah will prove when he says: 'If it has been announced to thee, O man, what is good, or what does the Lord require of thee, except to do justice and to love mercy?'[2]

This is supported by a range of Scriptures from Deuteronomy, Isaiah, Psalms and Matthew, all showing choices that are set before people with results dependent on their decisions. He cites a lengthy passage from Romans 2 to show 'how Paul also converses with us as having freedom of will, and as being ourselves the cause of ruin or salvation'.[3] The conclusion: 'There are, indeed, innumerable passages in the Scriptures which establish with exceeding clearness the existence of freedom of will.'[4]

Against this, Origen allows that there are certain sections in both the Old and New Testaments that could 'lead to the opposite conclusion – namely, that it does not depend on ourselves to keep the commandments and to be saved, or to transgress them and to be lost'.[5] He chooses to tackle these individually and devotes himself to demonstrating a correct reading in light of the teachings he has mentioned that advocate free will. Noting the passages, he states that they 'are 'sufficient of themselves to trouble the multitude, as if man were not possessed of free-will, but as if it were God who saves and destroys whom He will'.[6] Origen is concerned that 'certain of those

1. Ibid.
2. Ibid.
3. Ibid.
4. Ibid.
5. Ibid.
6. Ibid.

who hold different opinions misuse these passages, themselves also almost destroying free-will by introducing ruined natures incapable of salvation, and others saved which it is impossible can be lost'.[1]

The first story that Origen highlights is that of Pharaoh, whose heart was hardened by God against the entreaties of Moses, seemingly to his own and Egypt's loss. If God did harden Pharaoh's heart, to what extent can he be considered responsible for refusing Moses' demand to let the Israelites leave? It would seem that Pharaoh had what Origen called a 'ruined nature', with the question of whether he was destined for ruin as a result of God's hardening his heart or whether this was something that happened to a nature that was already wicked.

For illustration of this latter view, Origen engages with Hebrews 6:

> God has mercy upon one man while He hardens another, although not intending to harden; but, (although) having a good purpose, hardening follows as a result of the inherent principle of wickedness in such persons, and so He is said to harden him who is hardened.[2]

He gives an example in the rain, which can fall evenly on different ground, producing fruit in cultivated ground and thorns in barren and neglected ground. 'In the same way, therefore, the wonderful works also done by God are, as it were, the rain; while the differing purposes are, as it were, the cultivated and neglected land, being (yet), like earth, of one nature.'[3] Origen thus seeks to soften the impact of the phrase being discussed, highlighting that Pharaoh himself ultimately gave the Israelites leave to depart for a time and choosing to see the hardening as revealing the true nature of Pharaoh rather than changing that nature: '[T]he announcements made to him will be understood to have been made with peculiar fitness, as to one who, according to his hardness and unrepentant heart, was treasuring up to himself wrath.'[4]

The next section deals with prophetical declarations of those who have experienced God's favour and then struggled with sin. This is less clear in its application to free will, concentrating rather on God's timing in judgement. He returns to his main theme in addressing a passage similar to that on Pharaoh, this time from Ezekiel 36:26-7: 'I shall take away their stony hearts, and will put in them hearts of flesh, that they may walk in My statutes and keep My precepts.' Origen outlines an interpretation of this passage that would seem to negate human free will:

1. Ibid.
2. Ibid.
3. Ibid.
4. Ibid.

> For if God, when He wills, takes away the stony hearts, and implants hearts of flesh, so that His precepts are obeyed and His commandments are observed, it is not in our power to put away wickedness. For the taking away of the stony hearts is nothing else than the taking away of the wickedness, according to which one is hardened, from him from whom God wills to take it; and the implanting of a heart of flesh, so that a man may walk in the precepts of God and keep His commandments, what else is it than to become somewhat yielding and unresistant to the truth, and to be capable of practising virtues? And if God promises to do this, and if, before He takes away the stony hearts, we do not lay them aside, it is manifest that it does not depend upon ourselves to put away wickedness; and if it is not we who do anything towards the production within us of the heart of flesh, but if it is God's doing, it will not be our own act to live agreeably to virtue, but altogether (the result of) divine grace. Such will be the statements of him who, from the mere words (of Scripture), annihilates free-will.[1]

Origen's approach to the passage assumes that God's action is in response to a first move by the believer: '[T]he Word of God promises to take away wickedness, which it calls a stony heart, from those who come to it, not if they are unwilling, but (only) if they submit themselves to the Physician of the sick.'[2]

He now moves to a statement of Jesus in Mark 4:12 that seems to contradict starkly with Origen's main thesis: 'seeing they may not see, and hearing they may not understand; lest they should be converted, and their sins be forgiven them', indicating that such people do not have the ability to be saved. At the heart of Origen's response is the following passage, indicating that those who would hear and repent quickly may fall back into former sins, and thus a more gradual path to faith would lead to a more solid result:

> It is probable, then, that those 'without,' of whom we are speaking, having been foreseen by the Saviour, according to our supposition, as not (likely) to prove steady in their conversion, if they should hear more clearly the words that were spoken, were (so) treated by the Saviour as not to hear distinctly the deeper (things of His teaching), lest, after a rapid conversion, and after being healed by obtaining remission of sins, they should despise the wounds of their wickedness, as being slight and easy of healing, and should again speedily relapse into them.[3]

1. Ibid.
2. Ibid.
3. Ibid.

The next passage from Romans 9:16 is on similar lines: 'So, then, it is not of him that willeth, nor of him that runneth, but of God that showeth mercy.' Origen offers a number of analogies to explain how he reads this, all along the lines of God being given thanks for a work that he does not directly achieve, but is rightly praised as the source of all: a building, the defence of a city, athletes in a game and crops that are planted. In each of these cases, it is 'understood that something also had been done by human means, but the benefit being gratefully referred to God who brought it to pass'.[1] In the last of these examples, Origen shows the parallel that he is making:

> Now we could not piously assert that the production of full crops was the work of the husbandman, or of him that watered, but the work of God. So also our own perfection is brought about, not as if we ourselves did nothing; for it is not completed by us, but God produces the greater part of it.[2]

Origen links this passage to another that is thrown against him from Philippians 2:13: 'Both to will and to do are of God.' If this is taken simply and literally, then it would seem that humans have no free will, rather:

> seeing that willing and doing are from God, it is not we who have done the more excellent things, but we only appeared (to perform them), while it was God that bestowed them; so that even in this respect we do not possess free-will.[3]

Given that this interpretation would lead to even an evil will coming from God, Origen argues that it is the faculty of willing and doing that is received from God, as opposed to specific decisions and actions:

> to will in a general way, and to run in a general way, (are from Him). For as we have from God (the property) of being living things and human beings, so also have we that of willing generally, and, so to speak, of motion in general.[4]

If this point is allowed, Origen's opponents' next step is to question free will in salvation on the basis of Romans 9 and the indication that God forms some for honour and others for dishonour, in which case 'salvation or ruin does not depend upon ourselves, nor are we possessed of free-will'.[5] In response, Origen asks whether the Apostle Paul can contradict

1. Ibid.
2. Ibid.
3. Ibid.
4. Ibid.
5. Ibid.

4. Origen

himself as much as this suggests, given that he censures people for sinning and praises them for good actions:

> It is not consistent for the same apostle to blame the sinner as worthy of censure, and to praise him who had done well as deserving of approval; and again, on the other hand, to say, as if nothing depended on ourselves.[1]

This statement indicates a judgement based on the actions of people. The result is that the formation of vessels that Paul teaches must result from people's actions and decisions and take place after this, rather than being a pre-existent condition based on his foreknowledge:

> For the Creator makes vessels of honour and vessels of dishonour, not from the beginning according to His foreknowledge, since He does not condemn or justify beforehand according to it; but (He makes) those into vessels of honour who purged themselves, and those into vessels of dishonour who allowed themselves to remain unpurged: so that it results from older causes (which operated) in the formation of the vessels unto honour and dishonour, that one was created for the former condition, and another for the latter.[2]

The chapter ends with a final reflection on this point, indicating a symbiosis between human action and God's knowledge and will:

> Neither does our own power, apart from the knowledge of God, compel us to make progress; nor does the knowledge of God (do so), unless we ourselves also contribute something to the good result; nor does our own power, apart from the knowledge of God, and the use of the power that worthily belongs to us, make a man become (a vessel) unto honour or dishonour; nor does the will of God alone form a man to honour or to dishonour, unless He hold our will to be a kind of matter that admits of variation, and that inclines to a better or worse course of conduct. And these observations are sufficient to have been made by us on the subject of freewill.

The next chapter is titled 'On the Opposing Powers' and engages with how human free will is affected by the influence of the spiritual powers, primarily the devil. Origin shows the importance of this by citing various Scriptures and apocryphal texts that indicate a controlling role for these in people's actions. One passage that is mentioned is 2 Kings 22:19-23. Here, the Lord requests a spirit to deceive King Achab so that he would be led to his death, from which Origen states:

1. Ibid.
2. Ibid.

it is clearly shown that a certain spirit, from his own (free) will and choice, elected to deceive (Achab), and to work a lie, in order that the Lord might mislead the king to his death, for he deserved to suffer.[1]

The result of these passages for some Christians is summarised thus:

> Whence, also, the more simple among the believers in the Lord Christ are of opinion, that all the sins which men have committed are caused by the persistent efforts of these opposing powers exerted upon the minds of sinners, because in that invisible struggle these powers are found to be superior (to man). For if, for example, there were no devil, no single human being would go astray.[2]

Origen's first stage in denying this view is to look at the natural appetites of people such as hunger and thirst and, following maturity, sexual desire. Any such human appetite has the capacity for abuse without specific temptation and such indulgence is possible in any area of a person's will. God does allow for temptation, and this will not be beyond our power to resist, although there is no guarantee that we will resist:

> each one is tempted in proportion to the amount of his strength or power of resistance. Now, although we have said that it is by the just judgement of God that every one is tempted according to the amount of his strength, we are not therefore to suppose that he who is tempted ought by all means to prove victorious in the struggle.[3]

The important factor for Origen is that this power that we are given to use in response to temptation is the decisive element, whether or not there is a clear external agency involved in the temptation:

> But this power which is given us to enable us to conquer may be used, according to our faculty of free-will, either in a diligent manner, and then we prove victorious, or in a slothful manner, and then we are defeated. For if such a power were wholly given us as that we must by all means prove victorious, and never be defeated, what further reason for a struggle could remain to him who cannot be overcome? Or what merit is there in a victory, where the power of successful resistance is taken away? . . . Now from these points which we have discussed to the best of our power, it is, I think, clearly evident that there are certain transgressions which we by no means commit under the pressure of malignant powers; while there are others, again, to which we are incited by instigation on their part to excessive and immoderate indulgence.[4]

1. Ibid., 3.2.
2. Ibid.
3. Ibid.
4. Ibid.

4. Origen

Origen clarifies that we retain this power whether the influence on us is evil or good:

> We are not, however, to imagine that any other result follows from what is suggested to our heart, whether good or bad, save a (mental) commotion only, and an incitement instigating us either to good or evil. For it is quite within our reach, when a malignant power has begun to incite us to evil, to cast away from us the wicked suggestions, and to resist the vile inducements, and to do nothing that is at all deserving of blame. And, on the other hand, it is possible, when a divine power calls us to better things, not to obey the call; our freedom of will being preserved to us in either case.[1]

There is one aspect of engaging with temptation that Origen highlights against any idea that it is purely people against demonic forces. This is the support of God for the limitations that are present in humanity:

> For it is impossible for any man, although he were a saint, to carry on a contest against all of them [adversaries] at the same time. If that indeed were by any means to be the case, as it is certainly impossible it should be so, human nature could not possibly bear it without undergoing entire destruction . . . the struggle having, indeed, to be maintained against all, but by single individuals either with individual powers, or at least in such manner as shall be determined by God, who is the just president of the struggle. For I am of opinion that there is a certain limit to the powers of human nature, although there may be a Paul, of whom it is said, 'He is a chosen vessel unto Me;' or a Peter, against whom the gates of hell do not prevail; or a Moses, the friend of God: yet not one of them could sustain, without destruction to himself, the whole simultaneous assault of these opposing powers, unless indeed the might of Him alone were to work in him. . . . On account, then, of this power, which certainly is not of human origin operating and speaking in him, Paul could say, 'For I am persuaded that neither death, nor life, nor angels, nor principalities, nor powers, nor things present, nor things to come, nor height, nor depth, nor power, nor any other creature, shall be able to separate us from the love of God, which is in Christ Jesus our Lord.' For I do not think that human nature can alone of itself maintain a contest with angels, and with the powers of the height and of the abyss, and with any other creature; but when it feels the presence of the Lord dwelling within it, confidence in the divine help will lead it.[2]

1. Ibid.
2. Ibid.

This concludes the summary of the most concentrated material in Origen on free will. There are many other references to look at, starting with angelic free will. The divine element is less present in Origen than it was in Irenaeus or Tertullian, and in fact there is some contrast suggested in a phrase such as this:

> that will be called its better part which was made in the image and likeness of God; whereas the other part, that which afterwards, through its fall by the exercise of free-will, was assumed contrary to the nature of its original condition of purity – this part, as being the friend and beloved of matter, is punished with the fate of unbelievers.[1]

The concentration is instead on created beings having free will, beginning with the angelic beings. Are the holy angels such by their created nature? If so, reasons Origen, then the evil angels would likewise be so created, which would be unreasonable given the nature of their creator. As a result, Origen argues:

> But if to entertain this view regarding malignant and opposing powers seem to be absurd, as it is certainly absurd that the cause of their wickedness should be removed from the purpose of their own will, and ascribed of necessity to their Creator, why should we not also be obliged to make a similar confession regarding the good and holy powers, that, viz., the good which is in them is not theirs by essential being, which we have manifestly shown to be the case with Christ and the Holy Spirit alone, as undoubtedly with the Father also? For it was proved that there was nothing compound in the nature of the Trinity, so that these qualities might seem to belong to it as accidental consequences. From which it follows, that in the case of every creature it is a result of his own works and movements, that those powers which appear either to hold sway over others or to exercise power or dominion, have been preferred to and placed over those whom they are said to govern or exercise power over, and not in consequence of a peculiar privilege inherent in their constitutions, but on account of merit.[2]

It is this that is the basis for holding that all rational creatures have this power of will to choose right or wrong:

> As he [the devil], then, possessed the power either of receiving good or evil, but fell away from a virtuous course, and turned to evil with all the powers of his mind, so also other creatures, as having a capacity for either condition, in the exercise of the freedom of their will, flee from evil, and cleave to good.[3]

1. Ibid., 2.10.
2. Ibid., 1.5.
3. Ibid., 1.8.

When looking at the incarnate Christ, there is therefore this move from creation to Christology in that, in taking on human nature, Christ must have had the freedom of will to choose between right and wrong:

> That the nature, indeed, of His soul was the same as that of all others cannot be doubted, otherwise it could not be called a soul were it not truly one. But since the power of choosing good and evil is within the reach of all, this soul which belonged to Christ elected to love righteousness, so that in proportion to the immensity of its love it clung to it unchangeably and inseparably, so that firmness of purpose, and immensity of affection, and an inextinguishable warmth of love, destroyed all susceptibility (*sensum*) for alteration and change; and that which formerly depended upon the will was changed by the power of long custom into nature; and so we must believe that there existed in Christ a human and rational soul, without supposing that it had any feeling or possibility of sin.

The importance of human free will is shown in the extensive section found in the preface to the *De Principiis*, which makes a strong case for this being at the core of both humanity and the Gospel:

> This also is clearly defined in the teaching of the Church, that every rational soul is possessed of freewill and volition; that it has a struggle to maintain with the devil and his angels, and opposing influences, because they strive to burden it with sins; but if we live rightly and wisely, we should endeavour to shake ourselves free of a burden of that kind. From which it follows, also, that we understand ourselves not to be subject to necessity, so as to be compelled by all means, even against our will, to do either good or evil. For if we are our own masters, some influences perhaps may impel us to sin, and others help us to salvation; we are not forced, however, by any necessity either to act rightly or wrongly, which those persons think is the case who say that the courses and movements of the stars are the cause of human actions, not only of those which take place beyond the influence of the freedom of the will, but also of those which are placed within our own power. But with respect to the soul, whether it is derived from the seed by a process of traducianism, so that the reason or substance of it may be considered as placed in the seminal particles of the body themselves, or whether it has any other beginning; and this beginning, itself, whether it be by birth or not, or whether bestowed upon the body from without or no, is not distinguished with sufficient clearness in the teaching of the Church.[1]

---

1. Ibid., Preface.

It is through using this free will that humans are to do the good they are intended for, and through misuse that they fall into sin:

> For the Creator gave, as an indulgence to the understandings created by Him, the power of free and voluntary action, by which the good that was in them might become their own, being preserved by the exertion of their own will; but slothfulness, and a dislike of labour in preserving what is good, and an aversion to and a neglect of better things, furnished the beginning of a departure from goodness.[1]

On the same lines, Origen later writes, 'For a soul is always in possession of free-will, as well when it is in the body as when it is without it; and freedom of will is always directed either to good or evil.'[2] Even when we talk of God as Lord and as having dominion, Origen would not have this understood as something that overrides the freedom of the human will:

> We certainly do say that He [Christ] has dominion over all things which have been subjected to Him in this capacity, but not that His dominion extends over the God and Father who is Ruler over all. Besides, as the Word rules over none against their will, there are still wicked beings – not only men, but also angels, and all demons – over whom we say that in a sense He does not rule, since they do not yield Him a willing obedience; but, in another sense of the word, He rules even over them, in the same way as we say that man rules over the irrational animals – not by persuasion, but as one who tames and subdues lions and beasts of burden. Nevertheless, he leaves no means untried to persuade even those who are still disobedient to submit to His authority.[3]

One application of the principle of free will in Origen's thought is against the determinate teachings of Celsus, which indicate a cyclical course of events that humanity cannot break out of. To this, Origen replies, 'Now, if this be true, our free-will is annihilated.'[4] Instead, Origen shows that diversity exists in creation because of the use of free will, which allows for contingent events:

> As He Himself, then, was the cause of the existence of those things which were to be created, in whom there was neither any variation nor change, nor want of power, He created all whom He made equal and alike, because there was in Himself no reason for producing variety and diversity. But since those rational creatures themselves, as we have frequently shown, and will yet show in the proper place,

1. Ibid., 2.9.
2. Ibid., 3.3.
3. Origen, *Celsus*, 8.15.
4. Ibid., 4.70.

4. Origen

> were endowed with the power of free-will, this freedom of will incited each one either to progress by imitation of God, or reduced him to failure through negligence. And this, as we have already stated, is the cause of the diversity among rational creatures, deriving its origin not from the will or judgement of the Creator, but from the freedom of the individual will.[1]

He even seems to engage with some kind of multiverse theory in which 'worlds sometimes come into existence which are not dissimilar to each other, but in all respects equal'.[2] Origen states that it is impossible to know if this is the case ('But what may be the number or measure of this I confess myself ignorant, although, if any one can tell it, I would gladly learn'), but if there *were* other worlds then there would be no necessity for the same events to have unfolded as free will could have led situations in any direction:

> For if there is said to be a world similar in all respects (to the present), then it will come to pass that Adam and Eve will do the same things which they did before . . . and everything which has been done in this life will be said to be repeated – a state of things which I think cannot be established by any reasoning, if souls are actuated by freedom of will, and maintain either their advance or retrogression according to the power of their will. For souls are not driven on in a cycle which returns after many ages to the same round, so as either to do or desire this or that; but at whatever point the freedom of their own will aims, thither do they direct the course of their actions. For what these persons say is much the same as if one were to assert that if a medimnus of grain were to be poured out on the ground, the fall of the grain would be on the second occasion identically the same as on the first, so that every individual grain would lie for the second time close beside that grain where it had been thrown before. . . . So therefore it seems to me impossible for a world to be restored for the second time, with the same order and with the same amount of births, and deaths, and actions; but that a diversity of worlds may exist with changes of no unimportant kind, so that the state of another world may be for some unmistakeable reasons better (than this), and for others worse, and for others again intermediate.[3]

Origen holds so strongly to free will that, even as he agrees with Celsus on the matter of God's foreknowledge, he holds that this does not mean that events are foreordained. Things are foreknown because they will happen; they do not happen because they are foreknown:

1. Origen, *De Principiis*, 2.9.
2. Ibid., 2.3.
3. Ibid.

Celsus imagines that an event, predicted through foreknowledge, comes to pass because it was predicted; but we do not grant this, maintaining that he who foretold it was not the cause of its happening, because he foretold it would happen; but the future event itself, which would have taken place though not predicted, afforded the occasion to him, who was endowed with foreknowledge, of foretelling its occurrence. Now, certainly this result is present to the foreknowledge of him who predicts an event, when it is possible that it may or may not happen, viz., that one or other of these things will take place. For we do not assert that he who foreknows an event, by secretly taking away the possibility of its happening or not, makes any such declaration as this: 'This shall infallibly happen, and it is impossible that it can be otherwise.' And this remark applies to all the foreknowledge of events dependent upon ourselves, whether contained in the sacred Scriptures or in the histories of the Greeks.[1]

Origen thus follows Irenaeus and Tertullian in holding to a high view of human free will in a fallen creation. This is maintained despite the agency of external forces, spiritual and material and we therefore now need to examine what Origen writes about grace and its effects on humanity.

Grace

Origen does not develop any theology of grace, and the sporadic mentions do not greatly help the reader to understand precisely what Origen understands by the concept of grace. Even in the chapter 'On the Holy Spirit' in *De Principiis*, where one might expect to find something more substantial, there are only sporadic references. These do at least cover the main areas of application elsewhere and thus serve as a useful introduction to this section.

The first reference to the grace of the Spirit concerns salvation and the new life that the Christian receives:

> the Holy Spirit, who, after sinners and unworthy persons have been taken away and destroyed, creates for Himself a new people, and renews the face of the earth, when, laying aside, through the grace of the Spirit, the old man with his deeds, they begin to walk in newness of life.[2]

---

1. Origen, *Celsus*, 2.20.
2. Origen, *Principiis*, 1.3.

4. Origen

This grace seems to equate to the experience of salvation in the presence of the Spirit: 'that men should walk in newness of life ... i.e., the newness of grace of the Holy Spirit'.[1] After this first grace, there is then highlighted 'another grace of the Holy Spirit, which is bestowed upon the deserving', the gifts of the Holy Spirit referenced in 1 Corinthians 7.

This survey of Origen's writings on grace will follow this simple pattern, looking first at grace in terms of salvation and briefly querying in this the extent to which the grace that is presented impacts human free will and whether it is possible to lose this grace; and then examining how Origen treats the gifts of grace, the charismata.

Origen's main focus on the theme of grace is in the work of the Holy Spirit in the Christian life but there are a few references to grace in the context of salvation. He writes of the 'grace and revelation of the Holy Spirit bestowed by the imposition of the Apostles' hands after baptism', with the effects that

> men should walk in newness of life, that they might receive the new wine, i.e., the newness of grace of the Holy Spirit. In this manner, then, is the working of the power of God the Father and of the Son extended without distinction to every creature; but a share in the Holy Spirit we find possessed only by the saints.[2]

There are two occasions when Origen highlights that salvation is not due to the merit of the individual, but is a gift of grace. In *De Principiis*, he states:

> From which it appears to me that the divine mysteries were concealed from the wise and prudent, according to the statement of Scripture, that 'no flesh should glory before God', and revealed to children – to those, namely, who, after they have become infants and little children, i.e., have returned to the humility and simplicity of children, then make progress; and on arriving at perfection, remember that they have obtained their state of happiness, not by their own merits, but by the grace and compassion of God.[3]

Against any sense of pride, he writes:

> It seems a possible thing that rational natures, from whom the faculty of free-will is never taken away, may be again subjected to movements of some kind, through the special act of the Lord

1. Ibid.
2. Ibid.
3. Ibid., 3.1.

> Himself, lest perhaps, if they were always to occupy a condition that was unchangeable, they should be ignorant that it is by the grace of God and not by their own merit that they have been placed in that final state of happiness.[1]

Earlier in this same chapter, Origen highlights the effects that this grace has on the believer:

> But as they will not be able immediately to escape all bodily clothing, they are just to be considered as inhabiting more refined and purer bodies, which possess the property of being no longer overcome by death, or of being wounded by its sting; so that at last, by the gradual disappearance of the material nature, death is both swallowed up, and even at the end exterminated, and all its sting completely blunted by the divine grace which the soul has been rendered capable of receiving, and has thus deserved to obtain incorruptibility and immortality.[2]

Origen twice uses the metaphor of medicine to illustrate the work of grace. Firstly, in the section on the Holy Spirit, he states: 'He is manifestly a sanctifying power, in which all are said to have a share who have deserved to be sanctified by His grace.'[3] Recognising the dissimilarity of the analogy that he is providing, he nevertheless seeks to compare this aspect of the Holy Spirit's incorporeal ministry with the physical effects of medicine:

> There are many persons who take a part in the science or art of medicine: are we therefore to suppose that those who do so take to themselves the particles of some body called medicine, which is placed before them, and in this way participate in the same? Or must we not rather understand that all who with quick and trained minds come to understand the art and discipline itself, may be said to be partakers of the art of healing? But these are not to be deemed altogether parallel instances in a comparison of medicine to the Holy Spirit, as they have been adduced only to establish that that is not necessarily to be considered a body, a share in which is possessed by many individuals. For the Holy Spirit differs widely from the method or science of medicine, in respect that the Holy Spirit is an intellectual existence and subsists and exists in a peculiar manner, whereas medicine is not at all of that nature.

Rather more briefly he writes on the same lines of the grace of Christ's compassion:

1. Ibid., 2.3.
2. Ibid.
3. Ibid., 1.1.

4. Origen

> For all things were created by the Word of God, and by His Wisdom, and were set in order by His Justice. And by the grace of His compassion He provides for all men, and encourages all to the use of whatever remedies may lead to their cure, and incites them to salvation.[1]

Origen briefly discusses the affect that salvation by grace has on human free will in response to Celsus, who seeks a more controlling God than Origen is willing to admit, replying that there is a need for human agency in responding to the offer of salvation:

> Now all this on his part is silly talk; for God, by means of His word, which is continually passing from generation to generation into holy souls, and constituting them friends of God and prophets, does improve those who listen to His words; and by the coming of Christ He improves, through the doctrine of Christianity, not those who are unwilling, but those who have chosen the better life, and that which is pleasing to God. I do not know, moreover, what kind of improvement Celsus wished to take place when he raised the objection, asking, 'Is it then not possible for him, by means of his divine power, to make (men) better, unless he send some one for that special purpose?' Would he then have the improvement to take place by God's filling the minds of men with new ideas, removing at once the (inherent) wickedness, and implanting virtue (in its stead)? Another person now would inquire whether this was not inconsistent or impossible in the very nature of things; we, however, would say, 'Grant it to be so, and let it be possible.' Where, then, is our free will? and what credit is there in assenting to the truth? or how is the rejection of what is false praiseworthy? But even if it were once granted that such a course was not only possible, but could be accomplished with propriety (by God), why would not one rather inquire (asking a question like that of Celsus) why it was not possible for God, by means of His divine power, to create men who needed no improvement, but who were of themselves virtuous and perfect, evil being altogether non-existent? These questions may perplex ignorant and foolish individuals, but not him who sees into the nature of things; for if you take away the spontaneity of virtue, you destroy its essence.[2]

Given this symbiotic nature of salvation in Origen, it is perhaps unsurprising that he is willing to accept that the grace that has been received is also capable of being lost:

1. Ibid., 2.9.
2. Origen, Celsus, 4.3.

> In like manner, also, the nature of the Holy Spirit, being holy, does not admit of pollution; for it is holy by nature, or essential being. If there is any other nature which is holy, it possesses this property of being made holy by the reception or inspiration of the Holy Spirit, not having it by nature, but as an accidental quality, for which reason it may be lost, in consequence of being accidental. So also a man may possess an accidental righteousness, from which it is possible for him to fall away.[1]

While recognising this first grace of the Holy Spirit in salvation, Origen moves on and gives a greater volume of material on a second grace in the gifts of the Spirit:

> There is also another grace of the Holy Spirit, which is bestowed upon the deserving, through the ministry of Christ and the working of the Father, in proportion to the merits of those who are rendered capable of receiving it. This is most clearly pointed out by the Apostle Paul, when demonstrating that the power of the Trinity is one and the same, in the words, 'There are diversities of gifts, but the same Spirit; there are diversities of administrations, but the same Lord; and there are diversities of operations, but it is the same God who worketh all in all. But the manifestation of the Spirit is given to every man to profit withal.' From which it most clearly follows that there is no difference in the Trinity, but that which is called the gift of the Spirit is made known through the Son, and operated by God the Father.[2]

In both *De Principiis* and *Against Celsus*, Origen deals with the gifts of the Spirit in the context of the Spirit's ongoing work of sanctification in the life of the believer. In the first work, in the context of participation in Christ, he writes of:

> the grace of the Holy Ghost present, that those beings which are not holy in their essence may be rendered holy by participating in it. Seeing, then, that firstly, they derive their existence from God the Father; secondly, their rational nature from the Word; thirdly, their holiness from the Holy Spirit – those who have been previously sanctified by the Holy Spirit are again made capable of receiving Christ, in respect that He is the righteousness of God; and those who have earned advancement to this grade by the sanctification of the Holy Spirit, will nevertheless obtain the gift of wisdom according to the power and working of the Spirit of God.[3]

1. Origen, *Principiis*, 1.8.
2. Ibid., 1.3.
3. Ibid.

4. Origen

On this occasion, the spiritual gifts that are mentioned are those of wisdom and knowledge, which help in the process of sanctification:

> Whence also the working of the Father, which confers existence upon all things, is found to be more glorious and magnificent, while each one, by participation in Christ, as being wisdom, and knowledge, and sanctification, makes progress, and advances to higher degrees of perfection; and seeing it is by partaking of the Holy Spirit that any one is made purer and holier, he obtains, when he is made worthy, the grace of wisdom and knowledge, in order that, after all stains of pollution and ignorance are cleansed and taken away, he may make so great an advance in holiness and purity, that the nature which he received from God may become such as is worthy of Him who gave it to be pure and perfect, so that the being which exists may be as worthy as He who called it into existence.[1]

In *Against Celsus*, Origen divides human wisdom from divine wisdom, which 'comes, through the grace of God who bestows it, to those who have evinced their capacity for receiving it'.[2] He goes on to develop this grace of divine wisdom:

> Divine wisdom, accordingly, being different from faith, is the 'first' of the so-called 'charismata' of God; and the 'second' after it – in the estimation of those who know how to distinguish such things accurately – is what is called 'knowledge;' and the 'third' – seeing that even the more simple class of men who adhere to the service of God, so far as they can, must be saved – is faith.[3]

Origen writes of the gifts of grace, particularly prophecy, that were present in the Old Testament:

> There might also be found in the writings of Moses and of the prophets, who are older not only than Plato, but even than Homer and the invention of letters among the Greeks, passages worthy of the grace of God bestowed upon them, and filled with great thoughts, to which they gave utterance.[4]

He also makes it clear that the grace received through the Holy Spirit after Christ results in each believer receiving gifts, whereas in the Old Testament it was only given to a few:

1. Ibid.
2. Origen, *Celsus*, 6.13.
3. Ibid.
4. Ibid., 6.7.

> By the grace, then, of the Holy Spirit, along with numerous other results, this most glorious consequence is clearly demonstrated, that with regard to those things which were written in the prophets or in the law of Moses, it was only a few persons at that time, viz., the prophets themselves, and scarcely another individual out of the whole nation, who were able to look beyond the mere corporeal meaning and discover something greater, i.e., something spiritual, in the law or in the prophets.[1]

Now, however, 'this method of apprehension is undoubtedly suggested to the minds of all by the power of the Holy Spirit'.[2] Origen develops this wider access to the gifts of the Holy Spirit, writing,

> as there are many ways of apprehending Christ . . . so also I think is it with the Holy Spirit, in whom is contained every kind of gifts. For on some is bestowed by the Spirit the word of wisdom, on others the word of knowledge, on others faith; and so to each individual of those who are capable of receiving Him, is the Spirit Himself made to be that quality, or understood to be that which is needed by the individual who has deserved to participate.[3]

Beyond this more systematic teaching on the charismata, there are references to spiritual gifts that are experiences of grace in the life of the believer. In the preface to *De Principiis*, he writes: '[T]he spiritual meaning which the law conveys is not known to all, but to those only on whom the grace of the Holy Spirit is bestowed in the word of wisdom and knowledge.'[4] Origen writes about this same gift in relation to the wisdom of the world: '[W]e hold that he who is adorned by the Holy Spirit with that gift which is called "the word of wisdom," far excels all those who have not received the same grace.'[5] In relation to this gift, Origen holds that it is in need of exercise or it will be taken away:

> For if this Spirit is of divine nature, i.e., is understood to be a Holy Spirit, we shall understand this to be said of the gift of the Holy Spirit: that when, whether by baptism, or by the grace of the Spirit, the word of wisdom, or the word of knowledge, or of any other gift, has been bestowed upon a man, and not rightly administered, i.e., either buried in the earth or tied up in a napkin, the gift of the Spirit will certainly be withdrawn from his soul.[6]

1. Origen, *Principiis*, 1.3.
2. Ibid.
3. Ibid.
4. Ibid., Preface.
5. Origen, *Celsus*, 7.23.
6. Origen, *Principiis*, 2.10.

Reinforcing this point, Origen indicates an element of merit in the reception and use of the spiritual gifts:

> As holy and immaculate souls, after devoting themselves to God with all affection and purity, and after preserving themselves free from all contagion of evil spirits, and after being purified by lengthened abstinence, and imbued with holy and religious training, assume by this means a portion of divinity, and earn the grace of prophecy, and other divine gifts.[1]

Conclusion

While Origen was heavily influenced by Platonic cosmology and thought, with accompanying results in some areas of his theology, to a large extent we see the same approaches to the doctrines of sin, grace and free will present in the work of both Irenaeus and Tertullian. Responsibility for sin is placed firmly on humankind, yet there is a largely optimistic view of continuing human free will. Grace remains a background area of thought at this stage, firmly related to the particular work of the Holy Spirit.

Origen's theological works are contained in Philip Schaff's *Ante-Nicene Fathers*, volume four, which can be accessed at www.ccel.org. As with Tertullian, there are various more recent translations of parts of Origen's works, but no handy single volume compilations that can be recommended. For more background material on Origen and for a wider look at his thought, look at Joseph Trigg's *Origen* (London: Routledge, 1998), while Mark Scott has written an in-depth look at Origen's view of sin in *Journey Back to God: Origen on the Problem of Evil* (Oxford: OUP, 2012).

---

1. Ibid., 3.3.

5.
The Greek Fathers on Sin

We turn now to a second group of writers who can be considered to be similar in their views on sin, grace and free will. The Early Church writings were collected because of their date, while these writers are grouped together because of a common theological climate, although most were working around the same time in the second half of the fourth century. Eight writers in all are presented here, with only one – John of Damascus (676-749 CE) – living substantially later than the others; John is included as one of the last major formative thinkers in Greek Christianity and he also shares something of the theological climate with the earlier writers, albeit without the stimulus in perceived heretical thought that was so important in the fourth century. John is most famous for his work on icons, but his *Exposition of the Christian Faith* is a wide-ranging work that is useful to consider here, particularly for what it says about human free will.

Many of these writers were key in forming an orthodox understanding of the Trinity in response to teachings that denied the status of Christ or the Holy Spirit in ways that undermined the developing Christian theology. Of those who would be labelled heretics, Arius was the most influential, and his main opponent, Athanasius (who is often given the title, 'Defender of Orthodoxy'), is the earliest of those looked at in this chapter (296-373 CE). As is the case with many of these writers, large swathes of his work are devoted to the Trinity and an understanding of the nature and relation of the persons (or hypostases, as the Greeks term this), leaving little space devoted to our themes of sin, grace and free will. When discussing the nature of God and the resultant nature of humankind, however, there are shorter passages that can be grouped, as in former chapters, to help us build a picture of their thought in these areas.

Three of the writers, Basil of Caesarea (330-379 CE), Gregory of Nazianzus (329-390 CE) and Gregory of Nyssa (335-394 CE) are often grouped together under the collective name 'The Cappadocian Fathers'. Basil and Gregory of Nyssa were brothers, Gregory of Nazianzus was Basil's close friend, and together they worked in the middle of the fourth century against Arianism, being particularly influential in establishing the divinity of the Holy Spirit alongside the Father and the Son. Whereas Athanasius was often in a direct battle with Arius, these thinkers were fighting more against a theological system. Of the three, Gregory of Nyssa is the most philosophical, providing more writing on free will, while the others were more pastoral and theological.[1] A lesser-known direct contemporary of these three, Cyril of Jerusalem, was not an automatic inclusion, but his *Catechetical Lectures* are an excellent engagement with a range of theological themes and thus contribute well to an understanding of views on sin, grace and free will at that time.

The last two writers examined are John Chrysostom (347-407 CE) and Cyril of Alexandria (378-444 CE). Chrysostom is most famous for his preaching (Chrysostom means 'golden-mouthed') and his writings reflect something of the devotional style for which he received his name. Two of his books are particularly important here: his work *On the Priesthood*, which has sections on grace and sin in that ministry, and his *Homilies Concerning the Power of Demons*, which is influential on sin and free will. Cyril of Alexandria is a slightly later defender of orthodox Trinitarian belief, and his main focus was to refute the teachings of Nestorius, who was the sometime Patriarch of Constantinople. As with those who wrote against Arianism, the concentration of Cyril on a given heresy means that there are not extended sections devoted to sin, grace and free will, although there are some passages that are relevant in his work against Nestorius.

In presenting the views of the Greek Fathers on the topic of sin, we will begin by looking at their views on the nature of God, the nature of humanity and the nature of sin. This provides a foundation for their engagement with human sin and its root in the will, both for Adam and, subsequently, humanity. These writers devote a large amount of material to the devil and demons in light of this, asserting human responsibility and clarifying the role of the devils in relation to humans. Finally, there are passages on the effects of sin and the purpose of sin that will conclude this chapter.

---

1. This is not to say that Basil and Gregory of Nazianzus did not engage with philosophy, or that Gregory of Nyssa was not pastoral and theological, but merely that the balance of their work shifted more towards one or the other.

The Natures of God, Humanity and Sin

The basis for all teaching on sin in these writers is that sin and evil are in no way derived from God, any weakness in his being or his creative act. So Athanasius writes:

> But the godly teaching and the faith according to Christ brands their foolish language as godlessness. For it knows that it was not spontaneously, because forethought is not absent; nor of existing matter, because God is not weak; but that out of nothing, and without its having any previous existence, God made the universe to exist through His word. . . . For God is good, or rather is essentially the source of goodness: nor could one that is good be niggardly of anything: whence, grudging existence to none, He has made all things out of nothing by His own Word, Jesus Christ our Lord.[1]

Basil of Caesarea and Gregory of Nyssa both teach against a Manichean idea that would seek to absolve God from any responsibility for evil by positing a second deity. Gregory shows that this ultimately fails in its intent, since such a being would have to derive from the one good God:

> Manes thought he was pleading on the side of the Origin of Good, when he represented that Evil could derive thence none of its causes; so he linked the chain of things which are on the list of the bad to a separate Principle, in his character of the Almighty's champion, and in his pious aversion to put the blame of any unjustifiable aberrations upon that Source of Good . . . they say that a Good Deity is the Cause of another Deity who in nature diverges from His; and they all but openly exclaim in their teaching, that there is in existence something opposite to the nature of the good, deriving its personality from the good itself.[2]

Basil raises two issues with any idea of a second source of being from which evil is derived. Firstly, he describes the struggle between good and bad that does not explain continued evil if good is stronger:

> In reality two rival principles of equal power, if engaged without ceasing in a war of mutual attacks, will end in self destruction. But if one should gain the mastery it would completely annihilate the conquered. Thus, to maintain the balance in the struggle between good and evil is to represent them as engaged in a war without end and in perpetual destruction, where the opponents are at the same time conquerors and conquered. If good is the stronger, what is there to prevent evil being completely annihilated?[3]

1. Athanasius, *On the Incarnation of the Word*, 3.
2. Gregory of Nyssa, *Against Eunomius*, 1.35.
3. Basil of Caesarea, *Hexaemeron*, 2.

Secondly, he shows that evil cannot be traced either to God or to some intermediary between God and man, but is in Basil's view a negation, or 'falling away from', the virtue of humanity:

> It is equally impious to say that evil has its origin from God; because the contrary cannot proceed from its contrary. Life does not engender death; darkness is not the origin of light; sickness is not the maker of health. In the changes of conditions there are transitions from one condition to the contrary; but in genesis each being proceeds from its like, and not from its contrary. If then evil is neither uncreated nor created by God, from whence comes its nature? Certainly that evil exists, no one living in the world will deny. What shall we say then? Evil is not a living animated essence; it is the condition of the soul opposed to virtue, developed in the careless on account of their falling away from good.[1]

In a later homily, Basil attacks an astrological approach to the origin of evil with undisguised scorn:

> Now, at the hour of birth, it is very important whether one is looked upon by a beneficent star or by an evil one, to speak their language. Often then the astrologers do not seize the moment when a good star shows itself, and, on account of having let this fugitive moment escape, they enrol the newborn under the influence of a bad genius. I am compelled to use their own words. What madness! But, above all, what impiety! For the evil stars throw the blame of their wickedness upon Him Who made them. If evil is inherent in their nature, the Creator is the author of evil. If they make it themselves, they are animals endowed with the power of choice, whose acts will be free and voluntary. Is it not the height of folly to tell these lies about beings without souls? Again, what a want of sense does it show to distribute good and evil without regard to personal merit; to say that a star is beneficent because it occupies a certain place; that it becomes evil, because it is viewed by another star; and that if it moves ever so little from this figure it loses its malign influence.[2]

In terms of humanity, the Greek Fathers recognise a purity of the created nature, but they believe sin enters in an impact on the soul that affects the whole person. There is a focus on the soul because this was the locus of reason and will but as we will see this does not imply a fundamental separation in humans between body and soul. Athanasius writes that:

1. Ibid.
2. Ibid., 8.

> In the beginning wickedness did not exist. Nor indeed does it exist even now in those who are holy, nor does it in any way belong to their nature. But men later on began to contrive it and to elaborate it to their own hurt.[1]

Cyril of Jerusalem expands on this, including another reference to astrology as not responsible for sin:

> Next to the knowledge of this venerable and glorious and all-holy Faith, learn further what thou thyself art: that as man thou art of a two-fold nature, consisting of soul and body; and that, as was said a short time ago, the same God is the Creator both of soul and body. Know also that thou hast a soul self-governed, the noblest work of God, made after the image of its Creator: immortal because of God that gives it immortality; a living being, rational, imperishable, because of Him that bestowed these gifts: having free power to do what it willeth. For it is not according to thy nativity that thou sinnest, nor is it by the power of chance that thou committest fornication, nor, as some idly talk, do the conjunctions of the stars compel thee to give thyself to wantonness. Why dost thou shrink from confessing thine own evil deeds, and ascribe the blame to the innocent stars?[2]

There does seem to be some agreement that it is the virtue of the soul which is affected by sin. Gregory of Nyssa states:

> Now the soul is not sin though it is capable of admitting sin into it as the result of being ill-advised: and this He sanctifies by union with Himself for this end, that so the lump may be holy along with the first-fruits.[3]

Cyril of Jerusalem agrees with this, writing:

> The soul is immortal, and all souls are alike both of men and women; for only the members of the body are distinguished. There is not a class of souls sinning by nature, and a class of souls practising righteousness by nature: but both act from choice, the substance of their souls being of one kind only, and alike in all.[4]

Basil of Caesarea contrasts virtue and vice:

> Virtues exist in us also by nature, and the soul has affinity with them not by education, but by nature herself. We do not need lessons to

1. Athanasius, *Against the Heathen*, 2.
2. Cyril of Jerusalem, *Catechetical Lectures*, 4.18.
3. Gregory of Nyssa, *Against Eunomius*, 2.13.
4. Cyril of Jerusalem, *Catechetical Lectures*, 4.20.

hate illness, but by ourselves we repel what afflicts us, the soul has no need of a master to teach us to avoid vice. Now all vice is a sickness of the soul as virtue is its health.[1]

However, while virtues and vices are primarily attributable to the soul, this does not divorce sin from the body. Cyril of Jerusalem writes:

> Tell me not that the body is a cause of sin. For if the body is a cause of sin, why does not a dead body sin? Put a sword in the right hand of one just dead, and no murder takes place. Let beauties of every kind pass before a youth just dead, and no impure desire arises. Why? Because the body sins not of itself, but the soul through the body. The body is an instrument, and, as it were, a garment and robe of the soul: and if by this latter it be given over to fornication, it becomes defiled: but if it dwell with a holy soul, it becomes a temple of the Holy Ghost.[2]

On the same lines, Gregory of Nyssa teaches about the effects of sin:

> Now it was not the body merely, but the whole man, compacted of soul and body, that was lost: indeed, if we are to speak more exactly, the soul was lost sooner than the body. For disobedience is a sin, not of the body, but of the will: and the will properly belongs to the soul, from which the whole disaster of our nature had its beginning, as the threat of God, that admits of no falsehood, testifies in the declaration that, in the day that they should eat of the forbidden fruit, death without respite would attach to the act. Now since the condemnation of man was twofold, death correspondingly effects in each part of our nature the deprivation of the twofold life that operates in him who is thus mortally stricken. For the death of the body consists in the extinction of the means of sensible perception, and in the dissolution of the body into its kindred elements: but 'the soul that sinneth,' he saith, 'it shall die.' Now sin is nothing else than alienation from God, Who is the true and only life.[3]

In terms of the nature of sin, Athanasius follows on from the teaching we looked at earlier, denying its root in God, by also denying that it is substantial in any way:

> Now certain of the Greeks, having erred from the right way, and not having known Christ, have ascribed to evil a substantive and independent existence. In this they make a double mistake: either in denying the Creator to be maker of all things, if evil had an independent subsistence and being of its own; or again, if they mean

1. Basil, *Hexaemeron*, 9.
2. Cyril of Jerusalem, *Catechetical Lectures*, 4.23.
3. Gregory of Nyssa, *Against Eunomius*, 2.13.

that He is maker of all things, they will of necessity admit Him to be maker of evil also. For evil, according to them, is included among existing things. But this must appear paradoxical and impossible. For evil does not come from good, nor is it in, or the result of, good, since in that case it would not be good, being mixed in its nature or a cause of evil. But the sectaries, who have fallen away from the teaching of the Church, and made shipwreck concerning the Faith, they also wrongly think that evil has a substantive existence. But they arbitrarily imagine another god besides the true One, the Father of our Lord Jesus Christ, and that he is the unmade producer of evil and the head of wickedness, who is also artificer of Creation.[1]

Gregory of Nyssa develops the idea of sin along these lines, indicating that it is a lack of existence:

> Now all wickedness has its form and character in the deprivation of the good; it exists not by itself, and cannot be contemplated as a subsistence. For no evil of any kind lies outside and independent of the will; but it is the non-existence of the good that is so denominated. Now that which is not has no substantial existence, and the Maker of that which has no substantial existence is not the Maker of things that have substantial existence. Therefore the God of things that are is external to the causation of things that are evil, since He is not the Maker of things that are non-existent. He Who formed the sight did not make blindness. He Who manifested virtue manifested not the deprivation thereof.[2]

John Chrysostom draws a distinction between evil that is sinful as direct human action and evil that is the product of the punishment for sin, such as natural disasters:

> There is then evil, which is really evil; fornication, adultery, covetousness, and the countless dreadful things, which are worthy of the utmost reproach and punishment. Again there is evil, which rather is not evil, but is called so, famine, pestilence, death, disease, and others of a like kind. For these would not be evils. On this account I said they are called so only. Why then? Because, were they evils, they would not have become the sources of good to us, chastening our pride, goading our sloth, and leading us on to zeal, making us more attentive. . . . He *calls* this evil therefore which chastens them, which makes them purer, which renders them more zealous, which leads them on to love of wisdom; not that which comes under suspicion and is worthy of reproach; for that is not a work of God, but an invention of our own will, but this is for the destruction of the other. He calls then by the

1. Athanasius, *Against the Heathen*, 6.
2. Gregory of Nyssa, *On the Catechism*, 7.

name of evil the affliction, which arises from our punishment; thus naming it not in regard to its own nature, but according to that view which men take of it. For since we are accustomed to call by the name of evil, not only thefts and adulteries, but also calamities; so he has called the matter, according to the estimate of mankind.[1]

Cyril of Jerusalem distinguishes between sin and the devil:

> But some one will say, What can sin be? Is it a living thing? Is it an angel? Is it a demon? What is this which works within us? It is not an enemy, O man, that assails thee from without, but an evil shoot growing up out of thyself.[2]

Finally, the Cappadocian Fathers have a couple of interesting comments on the nature of sin. Gregory of Nazianzus describes all sin as adultery: 'For it is not only bodily sin which is called fornication and adultery, but any sin you have committed, and especially transgression against that which is divine.'[3] Cyril of Jerusalem, meanwhile, seems to indicate that sin as the product of ignorance is different from wilful sin: 'Sin committed in the state of ignorance is pardoned, but persistent wickedness is condemned.'[4]

Sin and the Will

One aspect of the approach to sin that we have noted in previous chapters is the emphasis on human responsibility. This continues in the Greek Fathers, firstly by affirming the role of the human will in sin, and secondly by extended discussion of the nature and role of the devil and demons, since there seems to have been a trend to seek to absolve humans by appealing to demonic influence. Most of the writers that we are looking at in this chapter taught on these lines from different angles, so we will deal with each in turn.

The importance of the humans as agents of their own sin begins by looking at Adam, who was created with free will and who had a commandment placed before him that he could have obeyed, as Gregory of Nazianzus states:

> This being He placed in Paradise, whatever the Paradise may have been, having honoured him with the gift of Free Will (in order that God might belong to him as the result of his choice, no less than to

---

1. Chrysostom, *Power of Demons*, 1.5.
2. Cyril of Jerusalem, *Catechetical Lectures*, 2.2.
3. Gregory of Nazianzus, *Oration 37*.
4. Cyril of Jerusalem, *Catechetical Lectures*, 3.8.

Him who had implanted the seeds of it), to till the immortal plants, by which is meant perhaps the Divine Conceptions, both the simpler and the more perfect; naked in his simplicity and inartificial life, and without any covering or screen; for it was fitting that he who was from the beginning should be such. Also He gave him a Law, as a material for his Free Will to act upon. This Law was a Commandment as to what plants he might partake of, and which one he might not touch. This latter was the Tree of Knowledge; not, however, because it was evil from the beginning when planted; nor was it forbidden because God grudged it to us. . . . Let not the enemies of God wag their tongues in that direction, or imitate the Serpent.[1]

Cyril of Jerusalem writes along similar lines, drawing out this responsibility for sin from the created nature of humanity noted above:

But these things perhaps thou knowest not: thou wouldest have nothing in common with the creatures which are without thee. Enter now into thyself, and from thine own nature consider its Artificer. What is there to find fault with in the framing of thy body? Be Master of thyself, and nothing evil shall proceed from any of thy members. Adam was at first without clothing in Paradise with Eve, but it was not because of his members that he deserved to be cast out. The members then are not the cause of sin, but they who use their members amiss; and the Maker thereof is wise.[2]

This theme repeatedly appears in Cyril's *Catechetical Lectures* as he moves from the creation of humanity onto our current experience, in which the will remains key: 'And learn this also, that the soul, before it came into this world, had committed no sin, but having come in sinless, we now sin of our free-will.'[3] Cyril moves on to support this idea by appealing to the punishment of God, which is just because it is carried out on wilful agents:

The soul is self-governed: and though the devil can suggest, he has not the power to compel against the will. He pictures to thee the thought of fornication: if thou wilt, thou acceptest it; if thou wilt not, thou rejectest. For if thou wert a fornicator by necessity, then for what cause did God prepare hell? If thou were a doer of righteousness by nature and not by will, wherefore did God prepare crowns of ineffable glory? The sheep is gentle, but never was it crowned for its gentleness: since its gentle quality belongs to it not from choice but by nature.[4]

1. Gregory of Nazianzus, *Oration 38*.
2. Cyril of Jerusalem, *Catechetical Lectures*, 9.15.
3. Ibid., 4.19.
4. Ibid., 4.21.

There is certainly an effect on human nature that results (more of which later in this chapter) but this does not mean that a person is bound by sin so that one cannot be free from it:

> A fearful thing is sin, and the sorest disease of the soul is transgression, secretly cutting its sinews, and becoming also the cause of eternal fire; an evil of a man's own choosing, an offspring of the will. For that we sin of our own free will the Prophet says plainly in a certain place: *Yet I planted thee a fruitful vine, wholly true: how art thou turned to bitterness, (and become) the strange vine?* The planting was good, the fruit coming from the will is evil; and therefore the planter is blameless, but the vine shall be burnt with fire since it was planted for good, and bore fruit unto evil of its own will. *For God*, according to the Preacher, *made man upright, and they have themselves sought out many inventions. For we are His workmanship*, says the Apostle, *created unto good works, which God afore prepared, that we should walk in them.* So then the Creator, being good, created for good works; but the creature turned of its own free will to wickedness. Sin then is, as we have said, a fearful evil, but not incurable; fearful for him who clings to it, but easy of cure for him who by repentance puts it from him.[1]

We saw above that Athanasius focused on the soul when he looked at human nature. As he deals with sin, he speaks of the soul as an entity that controls the whole person:

> She moves then, no longer according to virtue or so as to see God, but imagining false things, she makes a novel use of her power, abusing it as a means to the pleasures she has devised, since she is after all made with power over herself. For she is able, as on the one hand to incline to what is good, so on the other to reject it; but in rejecting the good she of course entertains the thought of what is opposed to it, for she cannot at all cease from movement, being, as I said before, mobile by nature. And knowing her own power over herself, she sees that she is able to use the members of her body in either direction, both toward what is, or toward what is not. But good is, while evil is not; by what is, then, I mean what is good, inasmuch as it has its pattern in God Who is. But by what is not I mean what is evil, in so far as it consists in a false imagination in the thoughts of men. For though the body has eyes so as to see Creation, and by its entirely harmonious construction to recognise the Creator; and ears to listen to the divine oracles and the laws of God; and hands both to perform works of necessity and to raise to God in prayer; yet the soul, departing from the contemplation of what is good and from moving in its sphere, wanders away and moves toward its contraries. Then seeing, as I said before, and abusing her power, she has perceived that she can move the members of the body also in an

1. Ibid., 2.1.

opposite way: and so, instead of beholding the Creation, she turns the eye to lusts, shewing that she has this power too; and thinking that by the mere fact of moving she is maintaining her own dignity, and is doing no sin in doing as she pleases; not knowing that she is made not merely to move, but to move in the right direction.[1]

Taking this wrong direction, Athanasius sees the soul creating a momentum towards evil that it becomes affected by:

> so the soul too, turning from the way toward God, and driving the members of the body beyond what is proper, or rather, driven herself along with them by her own doing, sins and makes mischief for herself, not seeing that she has strayed from the way, and has swerved from the goal of truth.[2]

The result is a corruption of the human person:

> Thus, then, God has made man, and willed that he should abide in incorruption; but men, having despised and rejected the contemplation of God, and devised and contrived evil for themselves . . . received the condemnation of death with which they had been threatened; and from thenceforth no longer remained as they were made, but were being corrupted according to their devices; and death had the mastery over them as king.[3]

John Chrysostom warns against accusing God for sin, writing:

> It is not so grievous to sin, as after the sin to accuse the Master. Take knowledge of the cause of the sin, and thou wilt find that it is none other than thyself who hast sinned. Everywhere there is a need of a good intention.[4]

Meanwhile, Basil of Caesarea deals with human responsibility both in his *Hexaemeron* and in his work *Against Eunomius*. The latter deals directly with where the blame lies:

> But darkness and death and weakness are classed with the ruler of this world, with 'the world rulers of the darkness' [Eph 6.12], with 'the spirits of wickedness' [Eph 6.12], and with every power that is an enemy of the divine nature. None of these have acquired opposition to the good according to their substance. If so, the blame would redound to the creator. It is by their own free will that they have fallen away into evil, depriving themselves of what is good.[5]

1. Athanasius, *Against the Heathen*, 4.
2. Ibid., 5.
3. Athanasius, *On the Incarnation of the Word*, 4.
4. Chrysostom, *Power of Demons*, 3.2.
5. Basil, *Against Eunomius*, 2.27.

The former work is more extensive in its treatment, taking as its foundation the good nature of humanity:

> Do not then go beyond yourself to seek for evil, and imagine that there is an original nature of wickedness. Each of us, let us acknowledge it, is the first author of his own vice. Among the ordinary events of life, some come naturally, like old age and sickness, others by chance like unforeseen occurrences, of which the origin is beyond ourselves, often sad, sometimes fortunate, as for instance the discovery of a treasure when digging a well, or the meeting of a mad dog when going to the market place. Others depend upon ourselves, such as ruling one's passions, or not putting a bridle on one's pleasures, to be master of our anger, or to raise the hand against him who irritates us, to tell the truth, or to lie, to have a sweet and well-regulated disposition, or to be fierce and swollen and exalted with pride. Here you are the master of your actions. Do not look for the guiding cause beyond yourself, but recognise that evil, rightly so called, has no other origin than our voluntary falls. If it were involuntary, and did not depend upon ourselves, the laws would not have so much terror for the guilty, and the tribunals would not be so without pity when they condemn wretches according to the measure of their crimes.[1]

Gregory of Nyssa provides one of the fullest treatments of this point, working along very similar lines to Basil but illuminating his thought with a number of very effective images. The passage comes, perhaps surprisingly, in his work *On Virginity*, a topic on which many of these writers produced treatises:

> This reasoning and intelligent creature, man, at once the work and the likeness of the Divine and Imperishable Mind (for so in the Creation it is written of him that 'God made man in His image'), this creature, I say, did not in the course of his first production have united to the very essence of his nature the liability to passion and to death. Indeed, the truth about the image could never have been maintained if the beauty reflected in that image had been in the slightest degree opposed to the Archetypal Beauty. Passion was introduced afterwards, subsequent to man's first organisation; and it was in this way. Being the image and the likeness, as has been said, of the Power which rules all things, man kept also in the matter of a Free-Will this likeness to Him whose Will is over all. He was enslaved to no outward necessity whatever; his feeling towards that which pleased him depended only on his own private judgement; he was free to choose whatever he liked; and so he was a free agent, though circumvented with cunning,

---

1. Basil, *Hexaemeron*, 2.

when he drew upon himself that disaster which now overwhelms humanity. He became himself the discoverer of evil, but he did not therein discover what God had made; for God did not make death. Man became, in fact, himself the fabricator, to a certain extent, and the craftsman of evil. All who have the faculty of sight may enjoy equally the sunlight; and any one can if he likes put this enjoyment from him by shutting his eyes: in that case it is not that the sun retires and produces that darkness, but the man himself puts a barrier between his eye and the sunshine; the faculty of vision cannot indeed, even in the closing of the eyes, remain inactive, and so this operative sight necessarily becomes an operative darkness rising up in the man from his own free act in ceasing to see. Again, a man in building a house for himself may omit to make in it any way of entrance for the light; he will necessarily be in darkness, though he cuts himself off from the light voluntarily. So the first man on the earth, or rather he who generated evil in man, had for choice the Good and the Beautiful lying all around him in the very nature of things; yet he wilfully cut out a new way for himself against this nature, and in the act of turning away from virtue, which was his own free act, he created the usage of evil. For, be it observed, there is no such thing in the world as evil irrespective of a will, and discoverable in a substance apart from that. Every creature of God is good, and nothing of His 'to be rejected'; all that God made was 'very good.' But the habit of sinning entered as we have described, and with fatal quickness, into the life of man; and from that small beginning spread into this infinitude of evil. Then that godly beauty of the soul which was an imitation of the Archetypal Beauty, like fine steel blackened with the vicious rust, preserved no longer the glory of its familiar essence, but was disfigured with the ugliness of sin. This thing so great and precious, as the Scripture calls him, this being man, has fallen from his proud birthright. As those who have slipped and fallen heavily into mud, and have all their features so besmeared with it, that their nearest friends do not recognise them, so this creature has fallen into the mire of sin and lost the blessing of being an image of the imperishable Deity; he has clothed himself instead with a perishable and foul resemblance to something else; and this Reason counsels him to put away again by washing it off in the cleansing water of this calling.[1]

Given the extent of this examination, Gregory adds little, although he does make an interesting extension in his work *Against Eunomius* in regards to speech:

---

1. Gregory of Nyssa, *On Virginity*, 12.

> Should any one say that I decline to be abusive only because I
> cannot pay him back in his own coin, let such an one consider
> in his own case what proneness there is to evil generally, what
> a mechanical sliding into sin, dispensing with the need of any
> practice. The power of becoming bad resides in the will; one act of
> wishing is often the sufficient occasion for a finished wickedness;
> and this ease of operation is more especially fatal in the sins of
> the tongue. Other classes of sins require time and occasion and
> co-operation to be committed; but the propensity to speak can sin
> when it likes.[1]

Lastly, we come to John of Damascus, writing over three hundred years later but with the same view of sin and the will:

> But God made him by nature sinless, and endowed him with free
> will. By sinless, I mean not that sin could find no place in him (for
> that is the case with Deity alone), but that sin is the result of the
> free volition he enjoys rather than an integral part of his nature; that
> is to say, he has the power to continue and go forward in the path
> of goodness, by co-operating with the divine grace, and likewise to
> turn from good and take to wickedness, for God has conceded this
> by conferring freedom of will upon him. For there is no virtue in
> what is the result of mere force.[2]

Later in the same work, John writes, 'By nature, therefore, all things are servants of the Creator and obey Him. Whenever, then, any of His creatures voluntarily rebels and becomes disobedient to his Maker, he introduces evil into himself. For evil is not any essence nor a property of essence, but an accident, that is, a voluntary deviation from what is natural into what is unnatural, which is sin.'[3] He follows this by looking at the devil as an example of a creation that voluntarily fell:

> Whence, then, comes sin? It is an invention of the free-will of
> the devil. Is the devil, then, evil? In so far as he was brought into
> existence he is not evil but good. For he was created by his Maker
> a bright and very brilliant angel, endowed with free-will as being
> rational. But he voluntarily departed from the virtue that is natural
> and came into the darkness of evil, being far removed from God,
> Who alone is good and can give life and light. For from Him every
> good thing derives its goodness, and so far as it is separated from
> Him in will (for it is not in place), it falls into evil.[4]

1. Gregory of Nyssa, *Against Eunomius*, 1.10.
2. John of Damascus, *Exposition of the Christian Faith*, 2.12.
3. Ibid., 4.20.
4. Ibid.

The existence of the devil and the angels who fell, as well as their continued involvement in creation, is naturally the next topic for discussion since this would seem to affect the human will and thus our responsibility for the sins we commit.

Devil, Demons and Sin

Given that John Chrysostom wrote a specific work on this issue, *On the Power of Demons*, it seems reasonable to give him the first word, drawing out the sections that most directly address the issue of human will and sin. Following this, the other writers' views will be presented thematically, from the nature of the devil through demonic influence on humans in suggesting sin and affecting human will to the nature of Christ's victory over the devil and the effects of this on humanity.

Chrysostom's work on the devil and demons is not long, about 35 pages, and so the reader is encouraged as always to look at the original work in full if this is a point of particular interest. There are three separate homilies that form this book, the first of which is against the idea that demons govern human affairs, focussing more on the sovereignty of God and his relationship to demons than on human interaction. This comes through more in the second homily where, in line with the previous section of this chapter, the focus is on the responsibility for sin lying with humans:

> I will state another solution of this question, in order that thou mayest learn, that the Devil does not injure, but their own slothfulness everywhere overthrows those who do not take heed. Let the Devil be allowed to be exceeding wicked, not by nature, but by choice and conviction . . . believing the Devil's slander, thou mayest learn that he gained strength, not owing to his own power but from that man's slothfulness and carelessness. . . . Let the Devil then be let alone, and let us bring forward the creation, in order that thou mayest learn that the Devil is not the cause of ills to us, if we would only take heed: in order that thou mayest learn that the weak in choice, and the unprepared, and slothful, even were there no Devil, falls, and casts himself into many a depth of evil.[1]

Shortly after this, he makes a similar point against those seeking absolution in reference to the devil:

> All these things have been now said by me, not in order that I may discharge the Devil from blame, but that I may free you from slothfulness. For he wishes extremely to attribute the cause of our

1. Chrysostom, *Power of Demons*, 2.2.

> sins to himself, in order that we being nourished by these hopes, and entering on all kinds of evil, may increase the chastening in our own case, and may meet with no pardon from having transferred the cause to him.[1]

The third homily begins by accepting that the devil has an influence but denying that this is the fundamental cause of sin, which would be committed by people regardless of the devil:

> Did the Devil pray deceive them? How did he not deceive you? you and they are men alike; I mean as regards your nature. You and they have the same soul, you have the same desires, so far as nature is concerned. How is it then that you and they were not in the same place? Because you and they have not the same purpose. On this account they indeed are under deception, but you beyond deception. I do not say these things again as discharging the Devil from accusation, but as desiring earnestly to free you from sins. The Devil is wicked; I grant this indeed, but he is wicked for himself not towards us if we are wary. For the nature of wickedness is of this kind. It is destructive to those alone who hold to it.[2]

The result, as in the second homily, is to challenge those who would claim that it was fated that they would sin and thus place sin within the providence of God:

> Do thou accordingly use this method of proof, and if thou seest a man living in wickedness, and exhibiting all kinds of evil; then blaming the providence of God, and saying that by the necessity of fortune and fate and through tyranny of Demons He gave us our nature, and on all sides shifting the cause from himself indeed, and transferring it to the creator who provides for all; silence his speech not by word, but by deed, shewing him another fellow servant living in virtue and forbearance.[3]

In this third homily, Chrysostom moves on to the question of purpose in the continued existence of the devil, firstly arguing that the need for a courageous response strengthens the believer:

> Let our argument also about the Devil be the same. For on this account He hath left him also to be here, in order that he might render thee the stronger, in order that he may make the athlete more illustrious, in order that the contests may be greater. When therefore any one says, why has God left the Devil here? say these words to him, because he not only does no harm to the wary and the heedful, but

1. Ibid., 2.5.
2. Ibid., 3.1.
3. Ibid.

even profits them, not owing to his own purpose (for that is wicked), but owing to their courage who have used that wickedness aright. Since he even fixed upon Job not on this account that he might make him more illustrious, but in order that he might upset him. On this account he is wicked both because of such an opinion and such a purpose. But notwithstanding he did no harm to the righteous man, but he rather rejoiced in the conflict as we accordingly shewed. Both the Demon shewed his wickedness and the righteous man his courage. But he does upset many says one: owing to their weakness, not owing to his own strength: for this too has been already proved by many examples. Direct thine own intention aright then, and thou shalt never receive harm from any, but shall get the greatest gain, not only from the good but even from the wicked.[1]

In the following section, he then goes on to talk about the difference between those who resist and those who succumb in terms of eternal judgement:

> On this account God places together servants and servants in order that the one set may judge the other, and that some being judged by the others may not be able for the future to accuse the master.... Both these and those are men. For what reason then are those indeed sheep but these kids? Not that thou mayest learn a difference in their nature, but the difference in their purpose. But for what reason are they who did not show compassion kids? ... How then was the end not the same? Because the purpose did not permit it. For this alone made the difference. On this account the one set went to Gehenna, but the other to the Kingdom. But if the Devil were the cause to them of their sins, these would not be destined to be chastened, when another sinned and drove them on. Dost thou see here both those who sin, and those who do good works? ... How then did some enter in, and others did not enter in? Because some indeed were churlish, and others were gentle and loving. Dost thou see again that the purpose determined the nature of the end, not the Devil? Dost thou see that the judgements were parallel, and that the verdict given proceeds from those who are like each other? ... Is there a Demon? a Devil? chance? or Fate? has not each become the cause to himself both of evil, and of virtue? For if they themselves were not to be liable to account, he would not have said that they shall judge this generation.[2]

There are further riches available in Chrysostom's work for those who wish to dig. A link to that, and all the other writings referred to, is available as always at the end of the chapter. We move on now to the

1. Ibid., 3.2.
2. Ibid., 3.3.

5. The Greek Fathers on Sin

views of the other writers, starting by looking at what they say about the devil himself. Gregory of Nazianzus provides the first quotation as he considers the nature of the angelic beings:

> But since this movement of self-contemplation alone could not satisfy Goodness, but Good must be poured out and go forth beyond Itself to multiply the objects of Its beneficence, for this was essential to the highest Goodness, He first conceived the Heavenly and Angelic Powers. And this conception was a work fulfilled by His Word, and perfected by His Spirit. And so the secondary Splendours came into being, as the Ministers of the Primary Splendour; whether we are to conceive of them as intelligent Spirits, or as Fire of an immaterial and incorruptible kind, or as some other nature approaching this as near as may be. I should like to say that they were incapable of movement in the direction of evil, and susceptible only of the movement of good, as being about God, and illumined with the first rays from God – for earthly beings have but the second illumination; but I am obliged to stop short of saying that, and to conceive and speak of them only as difficult to move because of him, who for his splendour was called Lucifer, but became and is called Darkness through his pride.[1]

John of Damascus takes up this last point in looking at the rebellion of the devil:

> He who from among these angelic powers was set over the earthly realm, and into whose hands God committed the guardianship of the earth, was not made wicked in nature but was good, and made for good ends, and received from his Creator no trace whatever of evil in himself. But he did not sustain the brightness and the honour which the Creator had bestowed on him, and of his free choice was changed from what was in harmony to what was at variance with his nature, and became roused against God Who created him, and determined to rise in rebellion against Him: and he was the first to depart from good and become evil. For evil is nothing else than absence of goodness, just as darkness also is absence of light. For goodness is the light of the mind, and, similarly, evil is the darkness of the mind.[2]

This rebellion as an act of will on the part of the devil, making him the author of sin, is also found in Chrysostom's lectures on the Catechism:

> The devil then is the first author of sin, and the father of the wicked: and this is the Lord's saying, not mine, *that the devil sinneth from the beginning:* none sinned before him. But he sinned, not as having

---

1. Gregory of Nazianzus, *Oration 38*.
2. John of Damascus, *Exposition*, 2.4.

received necessarily from nature the propensity to sin, since then the cause of sin is traced back again to Him that made him so; but having been created good, he has of his own free will become a devil, and received that name from his action. For being an Archangel he was afterwards called a devil from his slandering: from being a good servant of God he has become rightly named Satan; for 'Satan' is interpreted *the adversary*.

The role of the devil in the fall of Adam and Eve is limited to a counselling role, upholding again the importance of the human decision. Athanasius writes of Adam:

> For he also, as long as he kept his mind to God, and the contemplation of God, turned away from the contemplation of the body. But when, by counsel of the serpent, he departed from the consideration of God, and began to regard himself, then they not only fell to bodily lust, but knew that they were naked, and knowing, were ashamed.[1]
>
> But men, having rejected things eternal, and, by counsel of the devil, turned to the things of corruption, became the cause of their own corruption in death, being, as I said before, by nature corruptible, but destined, by the grace following from partaking of the Word, to have escaped their natural state, had they remained good.[2]

Cyril of Jerusalem extends this a little further, writing about the method the devil used to tempt Adam through Eve:

> A wooden image of an earthly king is held in honour; how much more a rational image of God? But when this the greatest of the works of creation was disporting himself in Paradise, the envy of the Devil cast him out. The enemy was rejoicing over the fall of him whom he had envied: wouldest thou have had the enemy continue to rejoice? Not daring to accost the man because of his strength, he accosted as being weaker the woman, still a virgin.[3]

He goes on to assert that the devil continues to prompt us to sin however it can be resisted:

> Yet thou art not the sole author of the evil, but there is also another most wicked prompter, the devil. He indeed suggests, but does not get the mastery by force over those who do not consent. Therefore saith the Preacher, *If the Spirit of him that hath power rise up against thee, quit not thy place*. Shut thy door, and put him far from thee, and

1. Athanasius, *Against the Heathen*, 3.
2. Athanasius, *On the Incarnation of the Word*, 5.
3. Cyril of Jerusalem, *Catechetical Lectures*, 12.5.

5. The Greek Fathers on Sin

> he shall not hurt thee. But if thou indifferently admit the thought of lust, it strikes root in thee by its suggestions, and enthrals thy mind, and drags thee down into a pit of evils.[1]

John Chrysostom picks up on the method of the devil, in the context of omens in the following passage, with an exhortation to love one's neighbour despite one's fear of the potential consequences:

> Often when going forth from his own house he has seen a one-eyed or lame man, and has shunned him as an omen. This is a pomp of Satan. For meeting the man does not make the day turn out ill, but to live in sin. When thou goest forth, then, beware of one thing – that sin does not meet thee. For this it is which trips us up. And without this the devil will be able to do us no harm. What sayest thou? Thou seest a man, and shunnest him as an omen, and dost not see the snare of the devil, how he sets thee at war with him who has done thee no wrong, how he makes thee the enemy of thy brother on no just pretext; but God has bidden us love our enemies; but thou art turned away from him who did thee no wrong, having nothing to charge him with, and dost not consider how great is the absurdity, how great the shame, rather how great is the danger?[2]

Chrysostom writes to Theodore about the continuing role the devil plays in tempting those wills that struggle with righteousness:

> For this assuredly it is which, like some strong cord suspended from the heavens, supports our souls, gradually drawing towards that world on high those who cling firmly to it, and lifting them above the tempest of the evils of this life. If any one then becomes enervated, and lets go this sacred anchor, straightway he falls down, and is suffocated, having entered into the abyss of wickedness. And the Evil One knowing this, when he perceives that we are ourselves oppressed by the consciousness of evil deeds, steps in himself and lays upon us the additional burden, heavier than lead, of anxiety arising from despair; and if we accept it, it follows of necessity that we are forthwith dragged down by the weight, and having been parted from that cord, descend into the depth of misery where thou thyself art now, having forsaken the commandments of the meek and lowly Master and executing all the injunctions of the cruel tyrant, and implacable enemy of our salvation; having broken in pieces the easy yoke, and cast away the light burden, and having put on the iron collar instead of these things, yea, having hung the ponderous millstone from thy neck.[3]

1. Ibid., 2.3.
2. Chrysostom, *Instructions to Catechumens*, 2.5.
3. Chrysostom, *Letter to Theodore*, 1.

Athanasius also teaches about the continuing role of the devil's deceit:

> For where all were smitten and confused in soul from demoniacal deceit, and the vanity of idols, how was it possible for them to win over man's soul and man's mind – whereas they cannot even see them?[1]

This passage is from his work *On the Incarnation of the Word*, in which he shows that the fall of humans, aided by the work of the devil and demons, is not the final word on sin, as one then moves on to the role of Christ in restoring humans to the image of God:

> So then, men having thus become brutalised, and demoniacal deceit thus clouding every place, and hiding the knowledge of the true God, what was God to do? To keep still silence at so great a thing, and suffer men to be led astray by demons and not to know God? And what was the use of man having been originally made in God's image? For it had been better for him to have been made simply like a brute animal, than, once made rational, for him to live the life of the brutes. Or where was any necessity at all for his receiving the idea of God to begin with? For if he be not fit to receive it even now, it were better it had not been given him at first. . . . Shall not God much more spare His own creatures, that they be not led astray from Him and serve things of nought? especially since such going astray proves the cause of their ruin and undoing, and since it was unfitting that they should perish which had once been partakers of God's image. What then was God to do? or what was to be done save the renewing of that which was in God's image, so that by it men might once more be able to know Him? But how could this have come to pass save by the presence of the very Image of God, our Lord Jesus Christ?[2]

Cyril of Jerusalem makes a similar point about the continued rule of God, even over the devil:

> But the Divine Scripture and the doctrines of the truth know but One God, who rules all things by His power, but endures many things of His will. For He rules even over the idolaters, but endures them of His forbearance: He rules also over the heretics who set Him at nought, but bears with them because of His long-suffering: He rules even over the devil, but bears with him of His long-suffering, not from want of power; as if defeated. For *he is the beginning of the Lord's creation, made to be mocked*, not by Himself, for that were unworthy of Him, but *by the Angels* whom He hath

---

1. Athanasius, *On the Incarnation of the Word*, 14.
2. Ibid., 13.

made. But He suffered him to live, for two purposes, that he might disgrace himself the more in his defeat, and that mankind might be crowned with victory. O all wise providence of God! which takes the wicked purpose for a groundwork of salvation for the faithful. For as He took the unbrotherly purpose of Joseph's brethren for a groundwork of His own dispensation, and, by permitting them to sell their brother from hatred, took occasion to make him king whom He would; so he permitted the devil to wrestle, that the victors might be crowned; and that when victory was gained, he might be the more disgraced as being conquered by the weaker, and men be greatly honoured as having conquered him who was once an Archangel.[1]

Effects of Sin

Having considered the teachings of the Greek Fathers on the responsibility for sin (which they argue lies firmly with humanity, while acknowledging that the devil and demons do play a role in temptation), we will now move on to examining the ongoing effects of sin in life. The fundamental concept here is a change in human identity as a consequence of sin, a change that is depicted in different ways. Gregory of Nyssa talks of a depravity into which human nature sinks, in 'the truth that humanity, having been sunk in depravity by reason of sin, is debarred from the title of "Good"';[2] while Gregory of Nazianzus describes it as a plague:

> Let us be assured that to do no wrong is really superhuman, and belongs to God alone. I say nothing about the Angels, that we may give no room for wrong feelings, nor opportunity for harmful altercations. Our unhealed condition arises from our evil and unsubdued nature, and from the exercise of its powers. Our repentance when we sin, is a human action, but an action which bespeaks a good man, belonging to that portion which is in the way of salvation.[3]

Two writers use an image of water to explain the effects of sin on the human self. Athanasius builds his image from a concept of idolatry:

> Accordingly, evil is the cause which brings idolatry in its train; for men, having learned to contrive evil, which is no reality in itself, in like manner feigned for themselves as gods beings that had no real existence. Just, then, as though a man had plunged into the deep, and no longer saw the light, nor what appears by light, because his

1. Cyril of Jerusalem, *Catechetical Lectures*, 8.4.
2. Gregory of Nyssa, *Against Eunomius*, 11.2.
3. Gregory of Nazianzus, *Oration 16*.

eyes are turned downwards, and the water is all above him; and, perceiving only the things in the deep, thinks that nothing exists beside them, but that the things he sees are the only true realities.[1]

Gregory of Nyssa, meanwhile, speaks of impurity that spreads through a person like waves from a stone:

> She knows that between all sins there is a single kinship of impurity, and that if she were to defile herself with but one, she could no longer retain her spotlessness. An illustration will show what we mean. Suppose all the water in a pool remaining smooth and motionless, while no disturbance of any kind comes to mar the peacefulness of the spot; and then a stone thrown into the pool; the movement in that one part will extend to the whole, and while the stone's weight is carrying it to the bottom, the waves that are set in motion round it pass in circles into others, and so through all the intervening commotion are pushed on to the very edge of the water, and the whole surface is ruffled with these circles, feeling the movement of the depths.[2]

This blurring that results from sin at its root comes from a change in the clarity of the image of God in humankind. Gregory of Nyssa again writes on this concept:

> But the other impulse is greater, as the tendency of sin is heavy and downward; for the ruling element of our soul is more inclined to be dragged downwards by the weight of the irrational nature than is the heavy and earthy element to be exalted by the loftiness of the intellect; hence the misery that encompasses us often causes the Divine gift to be forgotten, and spreads the passions of the flesh, like some ugly mask, over the beauty of the image.[3]

Athanasius examines this idea in more depth, again centring on the human soul as a key element:

> We repeat then what we said before, that just as men denied God, and worship things without soul, so also in thinking they have not a rational soul, they receive at once the punishment of their folly, namely, to be reckoned among irrational creatures: and so, since as though from lack of a soul of their own they superstitiously worship soulless gods, they are worthy of pity and guidance. But if they claim to have a soul, and pride themselves on the rational principle, and that rightly, why do they, as though they had no soul, venture to go against reason, and think not as they ought, but make themselves

1. Athanasius, *Against the Heathen*, 8.
2. Gregory of Nyssa, *On Virginity*, 14.
3. Gregory of Nyssa, *On the Making of Man*, 18.

> out higher even than the Deity? For having a soul that is immortal and invisible to them, they make a likeness of God in things visible and mortal. Or why, in like manner as they have departed from God, do they not betake themselves to Him again? For they are able, as they turned away their understanding from God, and feigned as gods things that were not, in like manner to ascend with the intelligence of their soul, and turn back to God again. But turn back they can, if they lay aside the filth of all lust which they have put on, and wash it away persistently, until they have got rid of all the foreign matter that has affected their soul, and can shew it in its simplicity as it was made, that so they may be able by it to behold the Word of the Father after Whose likeness they were originally made. For the soul is made after the image and likeness of God, as divine Scripture also shews, when it says in the person of God: 'Let us make man after our Image and likeness.' Whence also when it gets rid of all the filth of sin which covers it and retains only the likeness of the Image in its purity, then surely this latter being thoroughly brightened, the soul beholds as in a mirror the Image of the Father, even the Word, and by His means reaches the idea of the Father, Whose Image the Saviour is.[1]

Two other writers depict this change of identity in more radical terms. Chrysostom writes that, 'For to sin may be a merely human failing, but to continue in the same sin ceases to be human, and becomes altogether devilish.'[2] Gregory of Nyssa, working on similar lines to Athanasius, indicates that humans become animalistic as a result of sin, losing some of their unique created nature:

> Thus our love of pleasure took its beginning from our being made like to the irrational creation, and was increased by the transgressions of men, becoming the parent of so many varieties of sins arising from pleasure as we cannot find among the irrational animals. Thus the rising of anger in us is indeed akin to the impulse of the brutes; but it grows by the alliance of thought: for thence come malignity, envy, deceit, conspiracy, hypocrisy; all these are the result of the evil husbandry of the mind; for if the passion were divested of the aid it receives from thought, the anger that is left behind is short-lived and not sustained, like a bubble, perishing straightway as soon as it comes into being. Thus the greediness of swine introduces covetousness, and the high spirit of the horse becomes the origin of pride; and all the particular forms that proceed from the want of reason in brute nature become vice by the evil use of the mind.[3]

1. Athanasius, *Against the Heathen*, 34.
2. Chrysostom, *Letter to Theodore*, 1.
3. Gregory of Nyssa, *Making of Man*, 18.

There is some consideration given to the continued role of sin in the life of a Christian, since the experience is necessarily altered by the reception of grace. However, while holiness is certainly taught a great deal, perfection does not seem to be held out as a possibility:

> Let us be assured that to do no wrong is really superhuman, and belongs to God alone. I say nothing about the Angels, that we may give no room for wrong feelings, nor opportunity for harmful altercations. Our unhealed condition arises from our evil and unsubdued nature, and from the exercise of its powers. Our repentance when we sin, is a human action, but an action which bespeaks a good man, belonging to that portion which is in the way of salvation.[1]

Cyril of Jerusalem confronts the idea that since sin no longer reigns over a Christian one does not need to work hard against its influence:

> But perhaps thou sayest, I am a believer, and lust does not gain the ascendant over me, even if I think upon it frequently. Knowest thou not that a root breaks even a rock by long persistence? Admit not the seed, since it will rend thy faith asunder: tear out the evil by the root before it blossom, lest from being careless at the beginning thou have afterwards to seek for axes and fire. When thine eyes begin to be diseased, get them cured in good time, lest thou become blind, and then have to seek the physician.[2]

On a similar theme, John Chrysostom indicates that there are lifestyles that aid one in avoiding sin, such as being a recluse, while others seem to involve an environment in which resisting temptation is particularly difficult:

> It would be, therefore, in no wise excessively surprising to us, that the recluse, living as he does by himself, is undisturbed and does not commit many and great sins. For he does not meet with things which irritate and excite his mind. But if any one who has devoted himself to whole multitudes, and has been compelled to bear the sins of many, has remained steadfast and firm, guiding his soul in the midst of the storm as if he were in a calm, he is the man to be justly applauded and admired of all, for he has shown sufficient proof of personal manliness.[3]

The last part of this quotation is talking about the priesthood, a subject to which Chrysostom devotes a lengthy work. When discussing the role of the priest in relation to sin, Chrysostom indicates that there is a communal nature to sin, both in the bishop's mediation for the sins of others and in the responsibility of those who appoint bishops for the sins they then commit:

1. Gregory of Nazianzus, *Oration 16*.
2. Cyril of Jerusalem, *Catechetical Lectures*, 2.3.
3. Chrysostom, *On the Priesthood*, 6.7.

> For it is not possible for inexperience to be urged as an excuse, nor to take refuge in ignorance, nor for the plea of necessity or force to be put forward. Yea, if it were possible, one of those under their charge could more easily make use of this refuge for his own sins than bishops in the case of the sins of others. Dost thou ask why? Because he who has been appointed to rectify the ignorance of others, and to warn them beforehand of the conflict with the devil which is coming upon them, will not be able to put forward ignorance as his excuse. . . .[1]
>
> For though they who ordain him share his punishment, for any sins which he may commit in his office, yet so far from escaping vengeance he will even pay a greater penalty than they – save only if they who chose him acted from some worldly motive contrary to what seemed justifiable to themselves. For if they should be detected so doing, and knowing a man to be unworthy have brought him forward on some pretext or other, the amount of their punishment shall be equivalent to his, nay perhaps the punishment shall be even greater for them who appointed the unfit man. For he who gives authority to any one who is minded to destroy the Church, would be certainly to blame for the outrages which that person commits.[2]

Lastly in looking at the effects of sin, there is some discussion of the effects of Adam's sin on the whole human race. Gregory of Nyssa speaks of a 'similarity of will' between Adam and humanity, and thus humanity suffers an exile from God that is the consequence of receiving human nature from Adam:

> But since, by the wiles of him that sowed in us the tares of disobedience, our nature no longer preserved in itself the impress of the Father's image, but was transformed into the foul likeness of sin, for this cause it was engrafted by virtue of similarity of will into the evil family of the father of sin: so that the good and true God and Father was no longer the God and Father of him who had been thus outlawed by his own depravity. . . . Since, then, this was the sum of our calamity, that humanity was exiled from the good Father, and was banished from the Divine oversight and care, for this cause He Who is the Shepherd of the whole rational creation, left in the heights of heaven His unsinning and supramundane flock, and, moved by love, went after the sheep which had gone astray, even our human nature.[3]

1. Ibid., 6.1.
2. Ibid., 4.2.
3. Gregory of Nyssa, *Against Eunomius*, 12.1.

Just as Gregory puts this in the context of the work of Christ, so Cyril of Alexandria writes about the fallen nature of humanity that we inherited from Adam when discussing the importance of the incarnation:

> For if He had not been born as we according to the flesh, if He had not taken *part like* us *of the same,* He would not have freed the nature of man from the blame [contracted] in Adam, nor would He have driven away from our bodies the decay, nor would the might of the curse have ceased which we say came on the first woman; for it was said to her, *In sorrows shalt thou bring forth children.* But the nature of man hath fallen into the disease of disobedience in Adam, it has become now approved in Christ through the utter obedience.[1]

The link between Adam's sin and that of succeeding generations is not discussed at length by the Greek Fathers, but is certainly present in their teaching. The concentration on the nature of the human soul, as we have seen in Athanasius and the perfection of each soul's creation means that the focus of the teaching on sin and righteousness is on the individual rather than something that is inherited. The clearest example of this is Gregory of Nyssa's treatise, *On Infants' Early Deaths*, which discusses whether or not an infant that dies is condemned. This is another short work, about seventeen pages, that is well worth reading. Gregory begins by acknowledging that the reader would not want an infant to be condemned, before raising objections to this view; however, he ultimately concludes that an infant does receive a future life. Below is a lengthy quotation collected from the central core of the work:

> It is one of your anxieties to know, amongst the other intentions of each detail of the Divine government, wherefore it is that, while the life of one is lengthened into old age, another has only so far a portion of it as to breathe the air with one gasp, and die. If nothing in this world happens without God, but all is linked to the Divine will, and if the Deity is skilful and prudential, then it follows necessarily that there is some plan in these things bearing the mark of His wisdom, and at the same time of His providential care.
>
> What are we to think about him? How are we to feel about such deaths? Will a soul such as that behold its Judge? Will it stand with the rest before the tribunal? Will it undergo its trial for deeds done in life? Will it receive the just recompense by being purged, according to the Gospel utterances, in fire, or refreshed with the dew of blessing? But I do not see how we can imagine that, in the case of such a soul. The word 'retribution' implies that something must have been previously given; but he who has not lived at all has

---

1. Cyril of Alexandria, *Against Nestorius*, 1.

been deprived of the material from which to give anything. There being, then, no retribution, there is neither good nor evil left to expect. 'Retribution' purports to be the paying back of one of these two qualities; but that which is to be found neither in the category of good nor that of bad is in no category at all; for this antithesis between good and bad is an opposition that admits no middle; and neither will come to him who has not made a beginning with either of them. What therefore falls under neither of these heads may be said not even to have existed. But if some one says that such a life does not only exist, but exists as one of the good ones, and that God gives, though He does not repay, what is good to such, we may ask what sort of reason he advances for this partiality; how is justice apparent in such a view; how will he prove his idea in concordance with the utterances in the Gospels?

But in this case there is no act of doing or of willing beforehand, and so what occasion is there for saying that these will receive from God any expected recompense? If one unreservedly accepts a statement such as that, to the effect that any so passing into life will necessarily be classed amongst the good, it will dawn upon him then that not partaking in life at all will be a happier state than living, seeing that in the one case the enjoyment of good is placed beyond a doubt even with barbarian parentage, or a conception from a union not legitimate; but he who has lived the span ordinarily possible to Nature gets the pollution of evil necessarily mingled more or less with his life, or, if he is to be quite outside this contagion, it will be at the price of much painful effort

So that one of two probations must be the inevitable fate of him who has had the longer lease of life; either to combat here on Virtue's toilsome field, or to suffer there the painful recompense of a life of evil. But in the case of infants prematurely dying there is nothing of that sort; but they pass to the blessed lot at once, if those who take this view of the matter speak true. It follows also necessarily from this that a state of unreason is preferable to having reason, and virtue will thereby be revealed as of no value: if he who has never possessed it suffers no loss, so, as regards the enjoyment of blessedness, the labour to acquire it will be useless folly; the unthinking condition will be the one that comes out best from God's judgement.

We may speak, then, in this way also as regards this question of the infants: we may say that the enjoyment of that future life does indeed belong of right to the human being, but that, seeing the plague of ignorance has seized almost all now living in the flesh, he who has purged himself of it by means of the necessary courses of treatment receives the due reward of his diligence, when he enters on the life that is truly natural; while he who refuses Virtue's purgatives and renders that plague of ignorance, through the pleasures he has been entrapped by, difficult in his case to cure, gets himself into an unnatural state, and so is estranged from the truly natural life, and has no share in the existence which of right belongs to us and is congenial to us. Whereas the innocent babe has no such plague before its soul's eyes obscuring its measure of light, and so it continues to exist in that natural life; it does not need the soundness which comes from purgation, because it never admitted the plague into its soul at all.[1]

Purpose of Sin

This short final section on sin looks at indications in the writings of the Greek Fathers of the last future for humankind in salvation or condemnation. There are many passages that look at the effects of the Christ event on humanity, but here we will focus on those that directly apply to the existence of sin in creation.

Chrysostom takes this right back to creation and the effects of the Fall, which allowed God to show his love in a way that would not otherwise have been possible:

> The woman suffered expulsion from Paradise, but by means of her ejection she was led to a knowledge of God, so that she found a greater thing than she lost. And if it were profitable, says one, to suffer expulsion from Paradise, for what cause did God give Paradise at the beginning? This turned out profitably to man, on account of our carelessness, since, if at least, they had taken heed to themselves, and had acknowledged their master, and had known how to be self-restrained, and to keep within bounds, they would have remained in honour. But when they treated the gifts which had been given them with insolence, then it became profitable, that they should be ejected. For what cause then did God give at first? In order that he might shew forth his own loving kindness, and because He himself was prepared to bring us even to greater honour.[2]

John of Damascus focuses more on the honour that God does humankind in giving them the choice to do good or evil and on the justice of God in giving to each their just deserts:

> God in His goodness brought what exists into being out of nothing, and has foreknowledge of what will exist in the future. If, therefore, they were not to exist in the future, they would neither be evil in the future nor would they be foreknown. For knowledge is of what exists and foreknowledge is of what will surely exist in the future.

1. Gregory of Nyssa, *On Infants' Early Deaths*.
2. Chrysostom, *On the Power of Demons*, 1.3.

> For simple being comes first and then good or evil being. But if the very existence of those, who through the goodness of God are in the future to exist, were to be prevented by the fact that they were to become evil of their own choice, evil would have prevailed over the goodness of God. Wherefore God makes all His works good, but each becomes of its own choice good or evil. Although, then, the Lord said, *Good were it for that man that he had never been born*, He said it in condemnation not of His own creation but of the evil which His own creation had acquired by his own choice and through his own heedlessness.[1]

The final quotation concerns the issue of assurance in terms of future destiny. Given the issue of responsibility that has consistently arisen, it is perhaps unsurprising that Gregory of Nazianzus challenges the idea of assurance of salvation if sin continues to hold onto a person:

> Do not again become dead, nor live with those who dwell in the tombs; nor bind yourself with the bonds of your own sins; for it is uncertain whether you will rise again from the tomb till the last and universal resurrection, which will bring every work into judgement, not to be healed, but to be judged, and to give account of all which for good or evil it has treasured up.[2]

Conclusion

While the concentration of the Greek Fathers may have been on upholding a correct view of God, because of the theological climate in which they were working, this chapter has shown clear and common strands of thought on sin. The dominant theme is that of the responsibility of humankind for sin against those who may place this with God in creation or with the devil in temptation. The nature and role of human will are thus key aspects of the teaching. Even the corruption of human nature that results from sin does not seem to mitigate against this central thought.

If you would like to read more of the background and thought of these writers, the best introduction is still Adrian Fortescue's *The Greek Fathers* (originally published in 1908 but continually reprinted, most recently by Aeterna Press in 2015). The only writer absent from this work is Gregory of Nyssa, but there are many other works on the Cappadocian Fathers (Basil and the two Gregorys) that include him, such as Anthony Meredith's *The Cappadocians* (London: Geoffrey Chapman, 1995).

1. John of Damascus, *Exposition*, 4.21.
2. Gregory of Nazianzus, *Oration 40*.

Most of the original writings can be found at www.ccel.org as part of the Ante-Nicene and Post-Nicene Fathers collection. Basil of Caesarea's work *Against Eunomius* has been published by the Catholic University of America Press (tr. Mark DelCogliano, 2011), while Cyril of Alexandria's works (and many of those by other writers mentioned in this chapter) are available at www.tertullian.org/fathers.

6.
The Greek Fathers on Grace

In the previous chapters, we have seen writers use grace in a variety of contexts without a sense of a strong doctrine. To a certain extent, this continues into the writings of the Greek Fathers, for whom grace remains first and foremost an experience, but the references are more numerous and one is able to trace stronger themes of grace across the various authors. Two areas that receive much greater attention than we have seen previously are the relationships between grace and nature and between grace and baptism, as well as discussion on the means of receiving grace. We begin this chapter with the former, which involves the role of grace in the whole of creation. We will then look at the means by which grace is communicated to creation. Following this, the three key areas of application that have been perceived in earlier writings – salvation, sanctification and gifts of grace – are again found in the Greek Fathers, with the salvific role of grace heavily illuminated in connections made to baptismal grace.

Grace and Nature

The fundamental idea present in this connection is that all that exists does so by the grace of God, separating out creation from God who exists by virtue of his own being. Basil of Caesarea shows how far this grace extends by applying it to the angels in his *On the Holy Spirit*. We see in these writings an element that was picked up in earlier chapters, the link between the Holy Spirit and grace:

> How could the Seraphim cry 'Holy, Holy, Holy,' were they not taught by the Spirit how often true religion requires them to lift their voice in this ascription of glory? Do 'all His angels' and 'all His hosts' praise God? It is through the co-operation of the Spirit. Do 'thousand thousand' of angels stand before Him, and 'ten thousand times ten thousand' ministering spirits? They are

blamelessly doing their proper work by the power of the Spirit. All the glorious and unspeakable harmony of the highest heavens both in the service of God, and in the mutual concord of the celestial powers, can therefore only be preserved by the direction of the Spirit. Thus with those beings who are not gradually perfected by increase and advance, but are perfect from the moment of the creation, there is in creation the presence of the Holy Spirit, who confers on them the grace that flows from Him for the completion and perfection of their essence.[1]

As the angels receive their essence from grace, so the holiness that is the core of their being is received by grace:

> Moreover, from the things created at the beginning may be learnt the fellowship of the Spirit with the Father and the Son. The pure, intelligent, and supermundane powers are and are styled holy, because they have their holiness of the grace given by the Holy Spirit.[2]

In looking at human nature and grace, the focus is on the soul, which John of Damascus states:

> is immortal, not by nature but by grace. For all that has had beginning comes also to its natural end. . . . Through the Word, therefore, all the angels were created, and through the sanctification by the Holy Spirit were they brought to perfection, sharing each in proportion to his worth and rank in brightness and grace.[3]

Later in the same work, he writes:

> The soul, accordingly, is a living essence, simple, incorporeal, invisible in its proper nature to bodily eyes, immortal, reasoning and intelligent, formless, making use of an organised body, and being the source of its powers of life, and growth, and sensation, and generation, mind being but its purest part and not in any wise alien to it; (for as the eye to the body, so is the mind to the soul); further it enjoys freedom and volition and energy, and is mutable, that is, it is given to change, because it is created. All these qualities according to nature it has received of the grace of the Creator, of which grace it has received both its being and this particular kind of nature.[4]

---

1. Basil, *On the Holy Spirit*, 16. When we look at the means of grace, we see a greater role for Christ than was indicated previously, yet still a focus on the Holy Spirit.
2. Ibid.
3. John of Damascus, *Exposition*, 2.3.
4. Ibid., 2.12.

6. The Greek Fathers on Grace

John Chrysostom makes a distinction between the limits of body and soul, with the basis and nature of the latter allowing a greater freedom for the soul:

> For corporeal beauty indeed God has confined within the limits of nature, but grace of soul is released from the constraint and bondage arising from that cause inasmuch as it is far superior to any bodily symmetry: and it depends entirely upon ourselves and the grace of God. For our Master, being merciful has in this special way honoured our race, that He has entrusted to the necessity of nature the inferior things which contribute nothing much to our advantage, and in their issue are matters of indifference, but of the things which are really noble He has caused us to be ourselves the artificers.[1]

Gregory of Nyssa is slightly more holistic in his approach, writing of humans as the image of God, although there is some focus on the mind and reason:

> Now since our Maker has bestowed upon our formation a certain Godlike grace, by implanting in His image the likeness of His own excellences, for this reason He gave, of His bounty, His other good gifts to human nature; but mind and reason we cannot strictly say that He *gave*, but that He *imparted* them, adding to the image the proper adornment of His own nature. Now since the mind is a thing intelligible and incorporeal, its grace would have been incommunicable and isolated, if its motion were not manifested by some contrivance.[2]

This idea of the image of God is picked up in reflections of human identity after the Fall, with clear indications that this grace has been retained. Gregory of Nyssa picks up on this image to teach the continuing ability for discernment in humankind:

> We declare, then, that the speculative, critical, and world-surveying faculty of the soul is its peculiar property by virtue of its very nature, and that thereby the soul preserves within itself the image of the divine grace; since our reason surmises that divinity itself, whatever it may be in its inmost nature, is manifested in these very things – universal supervision and the critical discernment between good and evil.[3]

Gregory does, however, allow for some change in human nature as a result of sin when he writes:

1. Chrysostom, *Letter to Theodore*, 1.13.
2. Gregory of Nyssa, *Making of Man*, 9.
3. Gregory of Nyssa, *On the Soul and Resurrection*.

so also the company of all the angels worships Him Who comes in the name of the First-begotten, in their rejoicing over the restoration of men, wherewith, by becoming the first-born among us, He restored us again to the grace which we had at the beginning.[1]

Athanasius has a similar idea on the rejection of grace:

> But men once more in their perversity having set at nought, in spite of all this, the grace given them, so wholly rejected God, and so darkened their soul, as not merely to forget their idea of God, but also to fashion for themselves one invention after another', with the possibility of restoration in Christ, 'so that by such grace perceiving the Image, that is, the Word of the Father, they may be able through Him to get an idea of the Father, and knowing their Maker, live the happy and truly blessed life.[2]

The remainder of this chapter looks at grace after the loss of this image of God in man; a situation that results from a decision not to hold onto the grace given at creation:

> But knowing once more how the will of man could sway to either side, in anticipation He secured the grace given them by a law and by the spot where He placed them. For He brought them into His own garden, and gave them a law: so that, if they kept the grace and remained good, they might still keep the life in paradise without sorrow or pain or care besides having the promise of incorruption in heaven; but that if they transgressed and turned back, and became evil, they might know that they were incurring that corruption in death which was theirs by nature: no longer to live in paradise, but cast out of it from that time forth to die and to abide in death and in corruption.[3]

Means of Grace

Given the theological climate noted in the previous chapter, marked deeply by disputes about the nature of God and Trinity, it is unsurprising that these discussions overflow into the work of the godhead and thus the means by which grace is given to people. The earliest of the writers, Athanasius, was closely focused on the Son in response to Arianism, and thus he contends that it is from the Son that we receive grace:

> For though He had no need, nevertheless He is said to have received what He received humanly, that on the other hand, inasmuch as the Lord has received, and the grant is lodged with Him, the grace may

1. Gregory of Nyssa, *Against Eunomius*, 4.3.
2. Athanasius, *On the Incarnation of the Word*, 11.
3. Ibid., 3.

> remain sure. For while mere man receives, he is liable to lose again (as was shewn in the case of Adam, for he received and he lost), but that the grace may be irrevocable, and may be kept sure by men, therefore He Himself appropriates the gift; and He says that He has received power, as man, which He ever had as God, and He says, 'Glorify Me,' who glorifies others, to shew that He hath a flesh which has need of these things. If then (as has many times been said) the Word has not become man, then ascribe to the Word, as you would have it, to receive, and to need glory, and to be ignorant; but if He has become man (and He has become), and it is man's to receive, and to need, and to be ignorant, wherefore do we consider the Giver as receiver, and the Dispenser to others do we suspect to be in need, and divide the Word from the Father as imperfect and needy, while we strip human nature of grace?[1]

This work of the Son is part of Athanasius' defence of the full divinity of the Son, with frequent references back to Scripture, where grace is given by both Father and Son:

> Since He is God's Word and own Wisdom, and being His Radiance, is ever with the Father, therefore it is impossible, if the Father bestows grace, that He should not give it in the Son, for the Son is in the Father as the radiance in the light. . . . And the grace given is one, given from the Father in the Son, as Paul writes in every Epistle, 'Grace unto you, and peace from God our Father and the Lord Jesus Christ.'[2]
>
> Therefore also, as we said just now, when the Father gives grace and peace, the Son also gives it, as Paul signifies in every Epistle, writing, 'Grace to you and peace from God our Father and the Lord Jesus Christ.' For one and the same grace is from the Father in the Son, as the light of the sun and of the radiance is one, and as the sun's illumination is effected through the radiance; and so too when he prays for the Thessalonians, in saying, 'Now God Himself even our Father, and the Lord Jesus Christ, may He direct our way unto you,' he has guarded the unity of the Father and of the Son. For he has not said, 'May they direct,' as if a double grace were given from two Sources, This and That, but 'May He direct,' to shew that the Father gives it through the Son; – at which these irreligious ones will not blush, though they well might.[3]

This faculty of giving grace is then used to defend the eternal nature of Christ and his worth of worship, which is key to establishing his divinity:

1. Athanasius, *Against the Arians*, 3.27.
2. Ibid., 2.18.
3. Ibid., 3.25.

And how did we receive it 'before the world was,' when we were not yet in being, but afterwards in time, but that in Christ was stored the grace which has reached us? Wherefore also in the Judgement, when every one shall receive according to his conduct, He says, 'Come, ye blessed of My Father, inherit the kingdom prepared for you from the foundation of the world.' How then, or in whom, was it prepared before we came to be, save in the Lord who 'before the world' was founded for this purpose; that we, as built upon Him, might partake, as well-compacted stones, the life and grace which is from Him?[1]

And to whom the affections are ascribed, such namely as to be condemned, to be scourged, to thirst, and the cross, and death, and the other infirmities of the body, of Him too is the triumph and the grace. For this cause then, consistently and fittingly such affections are ascribed not to another, but to the Lord; that the grace also may be from Him, and that we may become, not worshippers of any other, but truly devout towards God, because we invoke no originate thing, no ordinary man, but the natural and true Son from God, who has become man, yet is not the less Lord and God and Saviour.[2]

The person of the Holy Spirit is not a key factor in these discussions with the Arians, the clearest evidence for which is found in the creed that was promulgated at Nicaea in 325 CE. This creed has a lengthy statement on the nature, procession and work of the Son, but only comments perfunctorily on the third part of the Trinity ('And in the Holy Spirit'), with no further information about the Spirit's role in the godhead or in creation.

The later writers do not have the same limitations in focus, and thus all extend the mechanics of grace beyond the Son to the Holy Spirit, whilst not denying the importance of the Christ event. Cyril of Alexandria does have a short discussion of the nature of Christ from a comparison of his experience of the grace of prophecy:

> A: Let them tell then, for I will ask: Would the grace of Prophecy or the being vouchsafed apostolic prerogative, and being called High Priest too, be an honour to a man?
> B: Yes.
> A: Yet they would say that to Christ in that He is conceived of as God these things are petty and not worthy of receiving, even though through these very things He is seen emptied and receiving them with the manhood. But as being God by Nature and Lord in truth, He

1. Ibid., 2.22.
2. Ibid., 3.26.

> took bondman's form, made therein and assuming our estate, so, both giving the Spirit of Prophecy and ordaining Apostles and establishing Priests, He was *made like in all things to His brethren:* for thus was He named, Prophet, Apostle, High Priest.
> B: But even though they grant that He was a Prophet, they say that He was not so as one of the Prophets, but that He was placed far above their measure. For they had the grace meted to them and accruing to them in time, He was full of the Godhead even straightway from His very Birth, for the Word being God was with Him.
> A: It was then in the amount of grace and in length of time that Christ has surpassed the holy Prophets which were before Him, and it is this which is His special privilege.[1]

Later in this work, Cyril moves on from the Son to the Spirit:

> For He being God by Nature and out of God and from above, hath come down in our estate, in an unwonted and strange way, MADE offspring of the Spirit according to the flesh, in order that WE too as He might remain holy and undecaying, the grace descending upon us as from out a second beginning and root, i.e., Him.[2]

He has a clearer extension to the role of the Spirit in his work against Nestorius: 'But *they* are operated upon by the Spirit and have a measured grace, *He,* as God in-worketh, and through His own Spirit achieveth without toil the things whereby He is marvelled at.'[3]

Basil of Caesarea is one of the key figures in the history of Christian thought on the Holy Spirit; yet he also first deals with grace in the context of the Son:

> For whenever we are contemplating the majesty of the nature of the Only Begotten, and the excellence of His dignity, we bear witness that the glory is *with* the Father; while on the other hand, whenever we bethink us of His bestowal on us of good gifts, and of our access to, and admission into, the household of God, we confess that this grace is effected for us *through* Him and *by* Him.[4]

Basil's work on the Holy Spirit bases much of its elevation of the Spirit on the relative roles played by the Father, Son and Spirit in a common action and the grace and gifts that Christians received form one theme that is used in this task:

1. Cyril of Alexandria, *Christ is One*, 1.
2. Ibid.
3. Cyril of Alexandria, *Against Nestorius*, 4.
4. Basil, *On the Holy Spirit*, 7.

> In relation to the originate, then, the Spirit is said to *be in* them 'in divers portions and in divers manners,' while in relation to the Father and the Son it is more consistent with true religion to assert Him not to *be in* but to *be with*. For the grace flowing from Him when He dwells in those that are worthy, and carries out His own operations, is well described as existing in those that are able to receive Him. On the other hand His essential existence before the ages, and His ceaseless abiding with Son and Father, cannot be contemplated without requiring titles expressive of eternal conjunction. . . . Where on the other hand the grace flowing from the Spirit naturally comes and goes, it is properly and truly said to exist *in*, even if on account of the firmness of the recipients' disposition to good the grace abides with them continually. Thus whenever we have in mind the Spirit's proper rank, we contemplate Him as being *with* the Father and the Son, but when we think of the grace that flows from Him operating on those who participate in it, we say that the Spirit is *in* us. And the doxology which we offer 'in the Spirit' is not an acknowledgement of His rank; it is rather a confession of our own weakness, while we shew that we are not sufficient to glorify Him of ourselves, but our sufficiency is in the Holy Spirit. Enabled in, [or by,] Him we render thanks to our God for the benefits we have received, according to the measure of our purification from evil, as we receive one a larger and another a smaller share of the aid of the Spirit, that we may offer 'the sacrifice of praise to God.' According to one use, then, it is thus that we offer our thanksgiving, as the true religion requires, in the Spirit; although it is not quite unobjectionable that any one should testify of himself 'the Spirit of God is in me, and I offer glory after being made wise through the grace that flows from Him.'[1]

Cyril of Jerusalem, who as we will see devotes a large amount of material to grace and baptism, consistently brings the different persons of the godhead into relationship in our experience of grace. Reflecting on the words of Jesus, he writes:

> For He says, *Except a man be born of water and of the Spirit, he cannot enter into the kingdom of God*. And that this grace is from the Father, He thus states, *How much more shall your heavenly Father give the Holy Spirit to them that ask him*.[2]

Likewise when looking at the death of Jesus:

1. Ibid., 26.
2. Cyril of Jerusalem, *Catechetical Lectures*, 17.11.

> For He who, as Mark relates, was crucified at the third hour, now at the third hour sent down His grace. For His grace is not other than the Spirit's grace, but He who was then crucified, who also gave the promise, made good that which He promised.[1]

Finally, Cyril equates the Holy Spirit with the grace of Christ in the gift of the Spirit both in John's gospel and again at Pentecost:

> The fellowship of this Holy Spirit He bestowed on the Apostles; for it is written, *And when He had said this, He breathed on them, and saith unto them, Receive ye the Holy Ghost: whose soever sins ye remit, they are remitted unto them; and whose soever sins ye retain, they are retained.* This was the second time He breathed on man (His first breath having been stifled through wilful sins); that the Scripture might be fulfilled, *He went up breathing upon thy face, and delivering thee from affliction.* But whence went He up? From Hades; for thus the Gospel relates, that then after His resurrection He breathed on them. But though He bestowed His grace then, He was to lavish it yet more bountifully; and He says to them, 'I am ready to give it even now, but the vessel cannot yet hold it; for a while therefore receive ye as much grace as ye can bear; and look forward for yet more; *but tarry ye in the city of Jerusalem, until ye be clothed with power from on high*.[2]

Of all the writers, it is probably Gregory of Nyssa who is the most explicitly Trinitarian in his writings on the gift of grace. He highlights our experience of this through the Spirit but only in the context of the work of the Father and the Son:

> So that if these despisers and impugners of their very own life conceive of the gift as a little one, and decree accordingly to slight the Being who imparts the gift, let them be made aware that they cannot limit to one Person only their ingratitude, but must extend its profanity beyond the Holy Spirit to the Holy Trinity Itself. For like as the grace flows down in an unbroken stream from the Father, through the Son and the Spirit, upon the persons worthy of it, so does this profanity return backward, and is transmitted from the Son to the God of all the world, passing from one to the other. If, when a man is slighted, He Who sent him is slighted (yet what a distance there was between the man and the Sender!), what criminality is thereby implied in those who thus defy the Holy Spirit![3]

1. Ibid., 17.19.
2. Ibid., 17.12.
3. Gregory of Nyssa, *On the Holy Spirit*.

In a tract on the Holy Trinity written to Eustathius, Gregory writes:

> The Father, the Son, and the Holy Spirit alike give sanctification, and life, and light, and comfort, and all similar graces. And let no one attribute the power of sanctification in an especial sense to the Spirit, when he hears the Saviour in the Gospel saying to the Father concerning His disciples, 'Father, sanctify them in Thy name.' So too all the other gifts are wrought in those who are worthy alike by the Father, the Son, and the Holy Spirit: every grace and power, guidance, life, comfort, the change to immortality, the passage to liberty, and every other boon that exists, which descends to us. . . . But the order of things which is above us, alike in the region of intelligence and in that of sense (if by what we know we may form conjectures about those things also which are above us), is itself established within the operation and power of the Holy Spirit, every man receiving the benefit according to his own desert and need. For although the arrangement and ordering of things above our nature is obscure to our sense, yet one may more reasonably infer, by the things which we know, that in them too the power of the Spirit works, than that it is banished from the order existing in the things above us. For he who asserts the latter view advances his blasphemy in a naked and unseemly shape, without being able to support his absurd opinion by any argument. But he who agrees that those things which are above us are also ordered by the power of the Spirit with the Father and the Son, makes his assertion on this point with the support of clear evidence from his own life. For as the nature of man is compounded of body and soul, and the angelic nature has for its portion life without a body, if the Holy Spirit worked only in the case of bodies, and the soul were not capable of receiving the grace that comes from Him, one might perhaps infer from this, if the intellectual and incorporeal nature which is in us were above the power of the Spirit, that the angelic life too was in no need of His grace. But if the gift of the Holy Spirit is principally a grace of the soul, and the constitution of the soul is linked by its intellectuality and invisibility to the angelic life, what person who knows how to see a consequence would not agree, that every intellectual nature is governed by the ordering of the Holy Spirit?[1]

One final note on the means of grace extends beyond the work of the godhead to Scripture and the church, inspired by the Spirit, about which Basil of Caesarea writes: 'And here I do not wish to speak of the narrator's talent, but of the grace of Scripture, for the narrative is so naturally told that it pleases and delights all the friends of truth.'[2] Meanwhile, Cyril of Jerusalem states:

1. Gregory of Nyssa, *On the Trinity*.
2. Basil, *Hexaemeron*, 3.1.

that Elias said that a double portion in the Holy Spirit should be given to his holy disciple; but that Christ granted to His own disciples so great enjoyment of the grace of the Holy Ghost, as not only to have It in themselves, but also, by the laying on of their hands, to impart the fellowship of It to them who believed.[1]

Grace and Salvation

Having looked at the role of grace in created nature and the work of the Trinity in giving grace, we now move on to the experience of grace in fallen humanity, which begins with salvation. The Greek Fathers were in no doubt that they were saved by grace, as the following lengthy quotation from Basil of Caesarea shows:

> Moreover by any one who carefully uses his reason it will be found that even at the moment of the expected appearance of the Lord from heaven the Holy Spirit will not, as some suppose, have no functions to discharge: on the contrary, even in the day of His revelation, in which the blessed and only potentate will judge the world in righteousness, the Holy Spirit will be present with Him. For who is so ignorant of the good things prepared by God for them that are worthy, as not to know that the crown of the righteous is the grace of the Spirit, bestowed in more abundant and perfect measure in that day, when spiritual glory shall be distributed to each in proportion as he shall have nobly played the man? For among the glories of the saints are 'many mansions' in the Father's house, that is differences of dignities: for as 'star differeth from star in glory, so also is the resurrection of the dead.' They, then, that were sealed by the Spirit unto the day of redemption, and preserve pure and undiminished the first fruits which they received of the Spirit, are they that shall hear the words 'well done thou good and faithful servant; thou hast been faithful over a few things, I will make thee ruler over many things.' In like manner they which have grieved the Holy Spirit by the wickedness of their ways, or have not wrought for Him that gave to them, shall be deprived of what they have received, their grace being transferred to others; or, according to one of the evangelists, they shall even be wholly cut asunder – the cutting asunder meaning complete separation from the Spirit. The body is not divided, part being delivered to chastisement, and part let off; for when a whole has sinned it were like the old fables, and unworthy of a righteous judge, for only the half to suffer chastisement. Nor is the soul cut in two – that soul the whole of which possesses the sinful affection throughout, and works the wickedness in co-operation with the body. The cutting asunder, as I have observed, is the separation for aye of the soul from the Spirit. For now, although the Spirit does not

1. Cyril of Jerusalem, *Catechetical Lectures*, 14.25.

suffer admixture with the unworthy, He nevertheless does seem in a manner to be present with them that have once been sealed, awaiting the salvation which follows on their conversion; but then He will be wholly cut off from the soul that has defiled His grace.[1]

The ability to comprehend this grace is no longer guaranteed due to the impact of sin, as Basil states:

> For the carnal man, who has never trained his mind to contemplation, but rather keeps it buried deep in lust of the flesh, as in mud, is powerless to look up to the spiritual light of the truth. And so the world, that is life enslaved by the affections of the flesh, can no more receive the grace of the Spirit than a weak eye the light of a sunbeam. But the Lord, who by His teaching bore witness to purity of life, gives to His disciples the power of now both beholding and contemplating the Spirit.[2]

Rather, as Gregory of Nyssa shows, there is a need for a first move of grace:

> But since that which is by nature finite cannot rise above its prescribed limits, or lay hold of the superior nature of the Most High, on this account He, bringing His power, so full of love for humanity, down to the level of human weakness, so far as it was possible for us to receive it, bestowed on us this helpful gift of grace.[3]

There is less direct comparison between the law and grace than is found in the New Testament writings, given that the Christian message is now primarily aimed at the wider Roman world. There are some passages that engage in this area, however, such as this from Gregory of Nazianzus:

> Who is the man who has never beheld, as our duty is to behold it, the fair beauty of the Lord, nor has visited His temple, or rather, become the temple of God, and the habitation of Christ in the Spirit? Who is the man who has never recognised the correlation and distinction between figures and the truth, so that by withdrawing from the former and cleaving to the latter, and by thus escaping from the oldness of the letter and serving the newness of the spirit, he may clean pass over to grace from the law, which finds its spiritual fulfilment in the dissolution of the body.[4]

John Chrysostom makes comparisons between the effects of baptism and the cleansing rituals of the Old Testament: '[T]here is the Jewish laver, more honorable than the other, but far inferior to that of grace;

1. Basil, *On the Holy Spirit*, 16.
2. Ibid., 22.
3. Gregory of Nyssa, *Against Eunomius*, 2.
4. Gregory of Nazianzus, *Oration 2*.

6. The Greek Fathers on Grace

and it too wipes off bodily uncleanness but not simply uncleanness of body, since it even reaches to the weak conscience.'[1] He continues later in the same work:

> Such is the defilement from which the laver of the Jews cleansed. But the laver of grace, not such, but the real uncleanness which has introduced defilement into the soul as well as into the body. For it does not make those who have touched dead bodies clean, but those who have set their hand to dead works: and if any man be effeminate, or a fornicator, or an idolator, or a doer of whatever ill you please, or if he be full of all the wickedness there is among men: should he fall into this pool of waters, he comes up again from the divine fountain purer than the sun's rays.[2]

This salvation through grace grants a new identity, with two authors in particular picking up the idea of sonship strongly. Cyril of Alexandria focuses on unity with Christ when he writes:

> And if Emmanuel was son in the same way too as was Israel who was made so after the flesh, thou hast brought down among bondservants Him Who is in His own Nature Free, even though He became in the form of a bondman by reason of the flesh and the things thereto pertaining: thou hast set in equal measure with the sons by grace Him on account of whom they have been enriched with the grace of sonship: for He has been called first-born of us by reason of the manhood, yet even so hath remained Only-begotten as God.[3]

Athanasius also uses this concept in his work against the Arians: 'Reasonably then, we being servants, when He became as we, He too calls the Father Lord, as we do; and this He has so done from love to man, that we too, being servants by nature, and receiving the Spirit of the Son, might have confidence to call Him by grace Father, who is by nature our Lord.'[4] Shortly after this, Athanasius extends the teaching:

> But this is God's kindness to man, that of whom He is Maker, of them according to grace He afterwards becomes Father also; becomes, that is, when men, His creatures, receive into their hearts, as the Apostle says, 'the Spirit of His Son, crying, Abba, Father.' And these are they who, having received the Word, gained power from Him to become sons of God; for they could not become sons, being by nature creatures, otherwise than by receiving the Spirit of the natural and

1. Chrysostom, *Instructions to Catechumens*, 1.2.
2. Ibid., 1.3.
3. Cyril of Alexandria, *Against Nestorius*, 2.
4. Athanasius, *Against the Arians*, 2.19.

> true Son . . . but afterwards, on receiving the grace of the Spirit, we are said thenceforth to be begotten also; just as the great Moses in his Song with an apposite meaning says first 'He bought,' and afterwards 'He begat;' lest, hearing 'He begat,' they might forget their own original nature; but that they might know that from the beginning they are creatures, but when according to grace they are said to be begotten, as sons, still no less than before are men works according to nature. . . . If then we are by nature sons, then is He by nature creature and work; but if we become sons by adoption and grace, then has the Word also, when in grace towards us He became man, said, 'The Lord created me'. . . . But 'first-born' implied the descent to the creation; for of it has He been called first-born; and 'He created' implies His grace towards the works, for for them is He created.[1]

While salvation by grace is clearly taught, even in this area there is a role for the person in receiving and holding onto this grace. Gregory of Nyssa writes of the role of the will in prayer and faith in the mystery of grace:

> For if in the case of that other kind of man-formation the impulses of the parents, even though they do not invoke the Deity, yet by the power of God, as we have before said, mould the embryo, and if this power is withheld their eagerness is ineffectual and useless, how much more will the object be accomplished in that spiritual mode of generation, where both God has promised that He will be present in the process and, as we have believed, has put power from Himself into the work, and, besides, our own will is bent upon that object; supposing, that is, that the aid which comes through prayer has at the same time been duly called in? For as they who pray God that the sun may shine on them in no way blunt the promptitude of that which is actually going to take place, yet no one will say that the zeal of those who thus pray is useless on the ground that they pray God for what must happen, in the same way they who, resting on the truthfulness of His promise, are firmly persuaded that His grace is surely present in those who are regenerate in this mystical Dispensation, either themselves make an actual addition to that grace, or at all events do not cause the existing grace to miscarry. For that the grace is there is a matter of faith, on account of Him Who has promised to give it being Divine; while the testimony as to His Divinity comes through the Miracles.[2]

Cyril of Jerusalem takes a very interesting line in his *Catechetical Lectures*, indicating some kind of space between becoming a Christian and receiving grace. The first of these lectures opens with the following statement:

1. Ibid., 2.21.
2. Gregory of Nyssa, *The Great Catechism*, 34.

6. The Greek Fathers on Grace

> Disciples of the New Testament and partakers of the mysteries of Christ, as yet by calling only, but ere long by grace also, *make you a new heart and a new spirit*, that there may be gladness among the inhabitants of heaven.[1]

There is a similar concept in the Prologue, where those coming for instruction are told:

> If thou seest the believers ministering, and shewing no care, they enjoy security, they know what they have received, they are in possession of grace. But thou standest just now in the turn of the scale, to be received or not: copy not those who have freedom from anxiety, but cherish fear.[2]

Later in the lectures, he says:

> I do not mean before you have received the grace, for how could that be? since it is for remission of sins that ye have been called; but that, when the grace is to be given, your conscience being found uncondemned may concur with the grace.[3]

Given the strong link between baptism and grace that we will shortly examine in Cyril's work, this may be less surprising, but is still worthy of remark.

Once grace has been received, Cyril is keen to stress that the believer has a continuing role in relationship to it:

> As then it is His part to plant and to water, so it is thine to bear fruit: it is God's to grant grace, but thine to receive and guard it. Despise not the grace because it is freely given, but receive and treasure it devoutly.[4]

This command is accompanied by warnings for those who would treat God's grace lightly:

> For if any of those who are present should think to tempt God's grace, he deceives himself, and knows not its power. Keep thy soul free from hypocrisy, O man, because of Him *who searcheth hearts and reins*. For as those who are going to make a levy for war examine the ages and the bodies of those who are taking service, so also the Lord in enlisting souls examines their purpose: and if any has a secret hypocrisy, He rejects the man as unfit for His true service; but if He finds one worthy, to him He readily gives His grace. He gives not holy things to the dogs; but where He discerns the good conscience,

---

1. Cyril of Jerusalem, *Catechetical Lectures*, 1.1.
2. Ibid., Prologue, 13.
3. Ibid., 3.2.
4. Ibid., 1.4.

there He gives the Seal of salvation, that wondrous Seal, which devils tremble at, and Angels recognise; that the one may be driven to flight, and the others may watch around it as kindred to themselves. Those therefore who receive this spiritual and saving Seal, have need also of the disposition akin to it. For as a writing-reed or a dart has need of one to use it, so grace also has need of believing minds.[1]

Gregory of Nazianzus also writes of the need to respond to grace, rather than seeing it as something dormant:

But since to us grace has been given to flee from superstitious error and to be joined to the truth and to serve the living and true God, and to rise above creation, passing by all that is subject to time and to first motion; let us look at and reason upon God and things divine in a manner corresponding to this Grace given us.[2]

The last word here will be given to John Chrysostom, who sounds very Pauline in the following exhortation:

Having learned then the healing of our wounds, let us constantly apply these medicines, in order that we may return to health and enjoy the sacred table with assurance; and with much glory, reach Christ the king of glory, and attain to everlasting good by the grace, and compassion, and lovingkindness of our Lord Jesus Christ, by whom and with whom be glory, power, honour, to the Father, together with the all holy, and good and quickening Spirit, now and always and for ever and ever.[3]

Baptism and Grace

There are two writers who particularly concentrate on the connection between baptism and grace, Cyril of Jerusalem and Gregory of Nazianzus. We will look at these two first, before moving on to look at how the other writers talk about grace in the context of baptism.

As indicated above, Cyril of Jerusalem has a very high view of baptism, indicating in his lectures on the catechism that grace is conferred after one is called to be a Christian. Foundational to his thought on baptism is the model of Christ and his baptism:

Jesus sanctified Baptism by being Himself baptised. If the Son of God was baptised, what godly man is he that despiseth Baptism? But He was baptised not that He might receive remission of sins, for He was sinless; but being sinless, He was baptised, that He might

---

1. Ibid., 1.3.
2. Gregory of Nazianzus, *Oration*, 39.
3. Chrysostom, *On the Power of Demons*, 2.6.

> give to them that are baptised a divine and excellent grace. For *since the children are partakers of flesh and blood, He also Himself likewise partook of the same,* that having been made partakers of His presence in the flesh we might be made partakers also of His Divine grace: thus Jesus was baptised, that thereby we again by our participation might receive both salvation and honour.[1]

As Christ went from baptism to temptation, so Cyril draws a parallel between the grace a Christian receives at baptism and their readiness for struggles in life:

> Moreover, when thou hast been deemed worthy of the grace, He then giveth thee strength to wrestle against the adverse powers. For as after His Baptism He was tempted forty days (not that He was unable to gain the victory before, but because He wished to do all things in due order and succession), so thou likewise, though not daring before thy baptism to wrestle with the adversaries, yet after thou hast received the grace and art henceforth confident in *the armour of righteousness,* must then do battle, and preach the Gospel, if thou wilt.[2]

Cyril believes that water is a vital element, drawing on a range of Scriptures to defend the importance of this in baptism:

> But if any one wishes to know why the grace is given by water and not by a different element, let him take up the Divine Scriptures and he shall learn. For water is a grand thing, and the noblest of the four visible elements of the world. Heaven is the dwelling-place of Angels, but the heavens are from the waters: the earth is the place of men, but the earth is from the waters: and before the whole six days' formation of the things that were made, *the Spirit of God moved upon the face of the water.* The water was the beginning of the world, and Jordan the beginning of the Gospel tidings: for Israel deliverance from Pharaoh was through the sea, and for the world deliverance from sins *by the washing of water with the Word of God.* Where a covenant is made with any, there is water also.[3]

The baptismal water then is not merely symbolic for Cyril, but powerful in the life of the believer:

> For thou goest down into the water, bearing thy sins, but the invocation of grace, having sealed thy soul, suffereth thee not afterwards to be swallowed up by the terrible dragon. Having gone

1. Cyril of Jerusalem, *Catechetical Lectures,* 3.11.
2. Ibid., 3.13.
3. Ibid., 3.5.

down dead in sins, thou comest up quickened in righteousness. For if thou hast been *united with the likeness of the Saviour's death*, thou shalt also be deemed worthy of His Resurrection.[1]

Again he writes:

> Regard not the Laver as simple water, but rather regard the spiritual grace that is given with the water. For just as the offerings brought to the heathen altars, though simple in their nature, become defiled by the invocation of the idols, so contrariwise the simple water having received the invocation of the Holy Ghost, and of Christ, and of the Father, acquires a new power of holiness.[2]

However, simply because Scripture indicates that the Spirit works through the water of baptism does not mean that the water takes on independent magical properties. It instead rather depends on the attitude of the person coming to be baptised:

> But if thou persist in an evil purpose, the speaker is blameless, but thou must not look for the grace: for the water will receive, but the Spirit will not accept thee. If any one is conscious of his wound, let him take the salve; if any has fallen, let him arise. Let there be no Simon among you, no hypocrisy, no idle curiosity about the matter.[3]

Later in the lectures, Cyril teaches on this point:

> Yet He tries the soul. He casts not His pearls before swine; if thou play the hypocrite, though men baptise thee now, the Holy Spirit will not baptise thee. But if thou approach with faith, though men minister in what is seen, the Holy Ghost bestows that which is unseen. Thou art coming to a great trial, to a great muster, in that one hour, which if thou throw away, thy disaster is irretrievable; but if thou be counted worthy of the grace, thy soul will be enlightened, thou wilt receive a power which thou hadst not, thou wilt receive weapons terrible to the evil spirits; and if thou cast not away thine arms, but keep the Seal upon thy soul, no evil spirit will approach thee; for he will be cowed; for verily by the Spirit of God are the evil spirits cast out.[4]

Cyril even goes so far as to say that baptism in water is necessary for salvation because the whole body needs to receive grace:

> Neither doth he that is baptised with water, but not found worthy of the Spirit, receive the grace in perfection; nor if a man be virtuous in his deeds, but receive not the seal by water, shall he enter into

1. Ibid., 3.12.
2. Ibid., 3.3.
3. Ibid., Prologue, 4.
4. Ibid., 17.36.

> the kingdom of heaven. A bold saying, but not mine, for it is Jesus who hath declared it: and here is the proof of the statement from Holy Scripture. Cornelius was a just man, who was honoured with a vision of Angels, and had set up his prayers and alms-deeds as a good memorial before God in heaven. Peter came, and the Spirit was poured out upon them that believed, and they spake with other tongues, and prophesied: and after the grace of the Spirit the Scripture saith that Peter *commanded them to be baptised in the name of Jesus Christ*; in order that, the soul having been born again by faith, the body also might by the water partake of the grace.[1]

Gregory of Nazianzus wrote one of his great orations on baptism, with a position just as strong as that found in Cyril's lectures: 'Such is the grace and power of baptism; not an overwhelming of the world as of old, but a purification of the sins of each individual, and a complete cleansing from all the bruises and stains of sin.'[2] Gregory writes of three births: natural, baptism and resurrection. His introduction to the second, baptism, which is his topic in this Oration, is quite remarkable:

> Concerning two of these births, the first and the last, we have not to speak on the present occasion. Let us discourse upon the second, which is now necessary for us, and which gives its name to the Feast of the Lights. Illumination is the splendour of souls, the conversion of the life, the question put to the Godward conscience. It is the aid to our weakness, the renunciation of the flesh, the following of the Spirit, the fellowship of the Word, the improvement of the creature, the overwhelming of sin, the participation of light, the dissolution of darkness. It is the carriage to God, the dying with Christ, the perfecting of the mind, the bulwark of Faith, the key of the Kingdom of heaven, the change of life, the removal of slavery, the loosing of chains, the remodelling of the whole man. . . . And as Christ the Giver of it is called by many various names, so too is this Gift, whether it is from the exceeding gladness of its nature (as those who are very fond of a thing take pleasure in using its name), or that the great variety of its benefits has reacted for us upon its names. We call it, the Gift, the Grace, Baptism, Unction, Illumination, the Clothing of Immortality, the Laver of Regeneration, the Seal, and everything that is honourable. We call it the Gift, because it is given to us in return for nothing on our part; Grace, because it is conferred even on debtors; Baptism, because sin is buried with it in the water; Unction, as Priestly and Royal, for such were they who were anointed; Illumination, because of its splendour; Clothing, because it hides our shame; the Laver, because it washes us; the Seal because

1. Ibid., 3.4.
2. Gregory of Nazianzus, *Oration 40*.

it preserves us, and is moreover the indication of Dominion. In it the heavens rejoice; it is glorified by Angels, because of its kindred splendour. It is the image of the heavenly bliss. We long indeed to sing out its praises, but we cannot worthily do so.[1]

Gregory has some interesting things to say about the timing and procedure for baptism. Firstly, he warns against someone rushing into baptism:

> Who is He, and by whom is He baptised, and at what time? He is the All-pure; and He is baptised by John; and the time is the beginning of His miracles. What are we to learn and to be taught by this? To purify ourselves first; to be lowly minded; and to preach only in maturity both of spiritual and bodily stature. The first has a word especially for those who rush to Baptism off hand, and without due preparation, or providing for the stability of the Baptismal Grace by the disposition of their minds to good. For since Grace contains remission of the past (for it is a *grace*), it is on that account more worthy of reverence, that we return not to the same vomit again.[2]

He also writes about the policy of baptising children:

> Be it so, some will say, in the case of those who ask for Baptism; what have you to say about those who are still children, and conscious neither of the loss nor of the grace? Are we to baptise them too? Certainly, if any danger presses. For it is better that they should be unconsciously sanctified than that they should depart unsealed and uninitiated.[3]

Despite seeming contradictory to some degree, both uphold the principle of the importance of what happens at baptism.

Another area that is addressed by Gregory concerns the person baptising, where we see the focus on the importance of the work of the Spirit in the sacrament, rather than the minister:

> Detect the material in the wax, if you are so very clever. Tell me which is the impression of the iron ring, and which of the golden. And how do they come to be one? The difference is in the material and not in the seal. And so anyone can be your baptiser; for though one may excel another in his life, yet the grace of baptism is the same, and any one may be your consecrator who is formed in the same faith.[4]

Basil of Caesarea makes a similar point in reference to the water, rather than the minister:

1. Ibid.
2. Gregory of Nazianzus, *Oration 39*.
3. Gregory of Nazianzus, *Oration 40*.
4. Ibid.

6. The Greek Fathers on Grace

> This then is what it is to be born again of water and of the Spirit, the being made dead being effected in the water, while our life is wrought in us through the Spirit. In three immersions, then, and with three invocations, the great mystery of baptism is performed, to the end that the type of death may be fully figured, and that by the tradition of the divine knowledge the baptised may have their souls enlightened. It follows that if there is any grace in the water, it is not of the nature of the water, but of the presence of the Spirit.[1]

On a similar line of thought in relation to grace, this time in the context of the Eucharist rather than baptism, John Chrysostom writes of the need to focus on the work of the Spirit above all things:

> Now then pass from this scene to the rites which are celebrated in the present day; they are not only marvellous to behold, but transcendent in terror. There stands the priest, not bringing down fire from Heaven, but the Holy Spirit: and he makes prolonged supplication, not that some flame sent down from on high may consume the offerings, but that grace descending on the sacrifice may thereby enlighten the souls of all, and render them more refulgent than silver purified by fire. Who can despise this most awful mystery, unless he is stark mad and senseless? Or do you not know that no human soul could have endured that fire in the sacrifice, but all would have been utterly consumed, had not the assistance of God's grace been great.[2]

A final word in this section goes to Gregory of Nyssa, who begins in his work on the Catechism to move beyond the water of baptism to the life that follows, which is the subject of our next section in this chapter:

> Observe, then, that it is necessary for us to rehearse beforehand in the water the grace of the resurrection, to the intent that we may understand that, as far as facility goes, it is the same thing for us to be baptised with water and to rise again from death . . . but in saying this I do not regard the mere remoulding and refashioning of our composite body; for towards this it is absolutely necessary that human nature should advance, being constrained thereto by its own laws according to the dispensation of Him Who has so ordained, whether it have received the grace of the laver, or whether it remains without that initiation.[3]

1. Basil, *On the Holy Spirit*, 15.
2. Chrysostom, *On the Priesthood*, 3.4.
3. Gregory of Nyssa, *The Great Catechism*, 35.

Grace and Sanctification

Gregory unpacks this idea that the grace received at baptism must then lead into a holy life in two of his works. Firstly, later in his work on the Catechism, he states:

> But, as far as what has been already said, the instruction of this Catechism does not seem to me to be yet complete. For we ought, in my opinion, to take into consideration the sequel of this matter; which many of those who come to the grace of baptism overlook, being led astray, and self-deceived, and indeed only seemingly, and not really, regenerate. For that change in our life which takes place through regeneration will not be change, if we continue in the state in which we were. . . . If, then, the birth from above is a definite refashioning of the man, and yet these properties do not admit of change, it is a subject for inquiry what that is in him, by the changing of which the grace of regeneration is perfected. It is evident that when those evil features which mark our nature have been obliterated a change to a better state takes place.[1]

He delves into on the same subject during his work on the Holy Spirit:

> Then let us look to this too. In Holy Baptism, what is it that we secure thereby? Is it not a participation in a life no longer subject to death? I think that no one who can in any way be reckoned amongst Christians will deny that statement. What then? Is that life-giving power in the water itself which is employed to convey the grace of Baptism? Or is it not rather clear to every one that this element is only employed as a means in the external ministry, and of itself contributes nothing towards the sanctification, unless it be first transformed itself by the sanctification; and that what gives life to the baptised is the Spirit; as our Lord Himself says in respect to Him with His own lips, 'It is the Spirit that giveth life;' but for the completion of this grace He alone, received by faith, does not give life, but belief in our Lord must precede, in order that the lively gift may come upon the believer, as our Lord has spoken, 'He giveth life to whom He willeth.' But further still, seeing that this grace administered through the Son is dependent on the Ungenerate Source of all, Scripture accordingly teaches us that belief in the Father Who engendereth all things is to come first; so that this life-giving grace should be completed, for those fit to receive it, after starting from that Source as from a spring pouring life abundantly, through the Only-begotten Who is the True life, by the operation of the Holy Spirit.[2]

1. Ibid., 40.
2. Gregory of Nyssa, *On the Holy Spirit*.

6. The Greek Fathers on Grace

Cyril of Jerusalem links sanctification and grace in two warnings to his readers about their conduct. Firstly, he states that the experience of the Holy Spirit and grace is dependent on one actions:

> Cleanse thy vessel, that thou mayest receive grace more abundantly. For though remission of sins is given equally to all, the communion of the Holy Ghost is bestowed in proportion to each man's faith. If thou hast laboured little, thou receivest little; but if thou hast wrought much, the reward is great. Thou art running for thyself, see to thine own interest.[1]

Secondly, he warns that grace can be withheld from those who do not seek to live holy lives: 'For where there is wilful wickedness, there is also a withholding of grace.'[2]

Gregory of Nyssa writes about sanctification and a specific grace of virginity in his work on that subject in a passage that may seem removed from much of what the church says today, which many writers of this period devoted much teaching to:

> And if we must extol with laudations this gift from the great God, the words of His Apostle are sufficient in its praise; they are few, but they throw into the background all extravagant laudations; he only styles as 'holy and without blemish' her who has this grace for her ornament. . . . Many who write lengthy laudations in detailed treatises, with the view of adding something to the wonder of this grace, unconsciously defeat, in my opinion, their own end; the fulsome manner in which they amplify their subject brings its credit into suspicion. . . . A man who takes this theme for ambitious praise has the appearance of supposing that one drop of his own perspiration will make an appreciable increase of the boundless ocean, if indeed he believes, as he does, that any human words can give more dignity to so rare a grace; he must be ignorant either of his own powers or of that which he attempts to praise.[3]

Perhaps the most beautiful meditation on this theme comes from 'the golden-mouthed' preacher, John Chrysostom:

> This too he has bidden thee do according to thy power, with what has been entrusted to thee, to extend the holiness which thou hast received, and to make the righteousness which comes from the laver brighter, and the gift of grace more radiant; even as therefore Paul did, increasing all the good things which he received by his subsequent labours, and his zeal, and his diligence. And look at

1. Cyril of Jerusalem, *Catechetical Lectures*, 1.5.
2. Ibid., 6.28.
3. Gregory of Nyssa, *On Virginity*, 1.

the carefulness of God; neither did he give the whole to thee then, nor withhold the whole, but gave part, and promised part. And for what reason did he not give the whole then? In order that thou mightest show thy faith about Him, believing, on his promise alone, in what was not yet given. And for what reason again did he not there dispense the whole, but did give the grace of the Spirit, and righteousness and sanctification? In order that he might lighten thy labours for thee, and by what has been already given may also put thee in good hope for that which is to come. . . . Not so bright at least is the world, when the sunbeams come forth, as the soul shines and becomes brighter when it has received grace from the Spirit and learns more exactly the nature of the case. For when night prevails, and there is darkness, often a man has seen a coil of rope and has thought it was a serpent, and has fled from an approaching friend as from an enemy, and being aware of some noise, has become very much alarmed; but when the day has come, nothing of this sort could happen, but all appears just as it really is; which thing also occurs in the case of our soul. For when grace has come, and driven away the darkness of the understanding, we learn the exact nature of things, and what was before dreadful to us becomes contemptible. For we no longer fear death, after learning exactly, from this sacred initiation, that death is not death, but a sleep and a seasonable slumber; nor poverty nor disease, nor any other such thing, knowing that we are on our way to a better life, undefiled and incorruptible, and free from all such vicissitudes.[1]

From the grace of salvation, secured by the grace of baptism, the work of the Holy Spirit in sanctifying the believer through this ongoing grace is a key element of the teaching of the Greek Fathers. The grace that is received, however, is not simply about an inward transformation, but also about gifting for service and spreading the message of God.

Grace and Charismata

As with the previous writers in this volume, the gifts of grace are an important aspect of the Greek Fathers' teaching on the experience of grace. Sometimes the Pauline lists are referred to in this context, while occasionally it is individual gifts that are highlighted. Athanasius, writing to the bishops of Egypt, highlights power against demons as a fundamental part of the grace received alongside salvation and knowledge of God:

1. Chrysostom, *The Great Catechism*, 2.1.

6. The Greek Fathers on Grace

> Manifold indeed and beyond human conception are the instructions and gifts of grace which He has laid up in us; as the pattern of heavenly conversation, power against demons, the adoption of sons, and that exceeding great and singular grace, the knowledge of the Father and of the Word Himself, and the gift of the Holy Ghost. But the mind of man is prone to evil exceedingly; moreover, our adversary the devil, envying us the possession of such great blessings, goeth about seeking to snatch away the seed of the word which is sown within us.[1]

Elsewhere, Athanasius makes the gifts of the Spirit a key element of the reception of the Spirit from the Son in his work defending the identity of the Son against the Arians:

> As then in this place the Lord Himself, the Giver of the Spirit, does not refuse to say that through the Spirit He casts out demons, as man; in like manner He the same, the Giver of the Spirit, refused not to say, 'The Spirit of the Lord is upon Me, because He hath anointed Me,' in respect of His having become flesh, as John hath said; that it might be shewn in both these particulars, that we are they who need the Spirit's grace in our sanctification, and again who are unable to cast out demons without the Spirit's power. Through whom then and from whom behoved it that the Spirit should be given but through the Son, whose also the Spirit is? and when were we enabled to receive It, except when the Word became man? and, as the passage of the Apostle shews, that we had not been redeemed and highly exalted, had not He who exists in form of God taken a servant's form, so David also shews, that no otherwise should we have partaken the Spirit and been sanctified, but that the Giver of the Spirit, the Word Himself, hast spoken of Himself as anointed with the Spirit for us. And therefore have we securely received it, He being said to be anointed in the flesh; for the flesh being first sanctified in Him, and He being said, as man, to have received for its sake, we have the sequel of the Spirit grace, receiving 'out of His fulness.'[2]

Cyril of Alexandria also supports the nature of the Son from the gifts of grace through the Spirit in writing against Nestorius, comparing the Son's experience of giving the Spirit to the church receiving grace from the Spirit:

> For the God of all measured to the saints the grace through the Spirit, and to one He gave the *word of wisdom,* to another *the word of knowledge,* to another, *gifts of healing:* and this I think is that those who have the operation have power *of measure:* but our Lord Jesus

1. Athanasius, *Bishops of Egypt*, 1.
2. Athanasius, *Against the Arians*, 1.12.

Christ, putting forth the Spirit out of His own fulness, even as doth the Father Himself, gives It *not* as *of measure* to those who are worthy to receive It. Why then, most excellent sir, dost thou make Him Who giveth the Spirit *not of measure*, connumerate with those who have It in measure, saying that His glory has been cemented by the Spirit and that He has been operated on, like one of us, receiving as a grace support from Him, rather than working Divine signs through His own Spirit.[1]

Basil of Caesarea takes a similar approach to defending the Trinity from an experience of grace when dealing with the person of the Holy Spirit, linking Spirit, Son and gifting:

> Grant, they say, that He is to be glorified, but not with the Father and the Son. But what reason is there in giving up the place appointed by the Lord for the Spirit, and inventing some other? What reason is there for robbing of His share of glory Him Who is everywhere associated with the Godhead; in the confession of the Faith, in the baptism of redemption, in the working of miracles, in the indwelling of the saints, in the graces bestowed on obedience? For there is not even one single gift which reaches creation without the Holy Ghost; when not even a single word can be spoken in defence of Christ except by them that are aided by the Spirit, as we have learnt in the Gospels from our Lord and Saviour.[2]

An important basis for understanding the gifts of grace comes from the New Testament and the accounts of the Apostles, following on from the work of the Spirit in the Old Testament, as Athanasius indicates when he writes, 'Samuel too in the days of the harvest praying to God to grant rain, and the Apostles saying that not in their own power they did miracles but in the Lord's grace.'[3] John of Damascus writes of the link from the Apostles through their successors down to his day:

> The disciples of the Lord and His Apostles, made wise by the Holy Spirit and working wonders in His power and grace, took them captive in the net of miracles and drew them up out of the depths of ignorance to the light of the knowledge of God. In like manner also their successors in grace and worth, both pastors and teachers, having received the enlightening grace of the Spirit, were wont, alike by the power of miracles and the word of grace, to enlighten those walking in darkness and to bring back the wanderers into the way. But as for us who are not recipients either

---

1. Cyril of Alexandria, *Against Nestorius*, 4.
2. Basil, *On the Holy Spirit*, 24.
3. Athanasius, *Against the Arians*, 3.23.

6. The Greek Fathers on Grace

of the gift of miracles or the gift of teaching (for indeed we have rendered ourselves unworthy of these by our passion for pleasure), come, let us in connection with this theme discuss a few of those things which have been delivered to us on this subject by the expounders of grace, calling on the Father, the Son, and the Holy Spirit.[1]

In terms of the church and the gifts of grace from the Spirit, Cyril of Jerusalem expounds at length on this topic when discussing the Spirit in his lectures on the Catechism:

> And why did He call the grace of the Spirit water? Because by water all things subsist; because water brings forth grass and living things; because the water of the showers comes down from heaven; because it comes down one in form, but works in many forms. For one fountain watereth the whole of Paradise, and one and the same rain comes down upon all the world, yet it becomes white in the lily, and red in the rose, and purple in violets and hyacinths, and different and varied in each several kind: so it is one in the palm-tree, and another in the vine, and all in all things; and yet is one in nature, not diverse from itself; for the rain does not change itself, and come down first as one thing, then as another, but adapting itself to the constitution of each thing which receives it, it becomes to each what is suitable. Thus also the Holy Ghost, being one, and of one nature, and indivisible, divides to each His grace, *according as He will*: and as the dry tree, after partaking of water, puts forth shoots, so also the soul in sin, when it has been through repentance made worthy of the Holy Ghost, brings forth clusters of righteousness. And though He is One in nature, yet many are the virtues which by the will of God and in the Name of Christ He works. For He employs the tongue of one man for wisdom; the soul of another He enlightens by Prophecy; to another He gives power to drive away devils; to another He gives to interpret the divine Scriptures. He strengthens one man's self-command; He teaches another the way to give alms; another He teaches to fast and discipline himself; another He teaches to despise the things of the body; another He trains for martyrdom: diverse in different men, yet not diverse from Himself.

While John of Damascus looks at a range of gifts, at times writers focus more on particular gifts in the context of their discussions. For example, John Chrysostom, when writing on the priesthood, highlights a power from grace that those in this ministry should receive: 'The souls therefore of men elected to the priesthood ought to be endued with such power

---

1. John of Damascus, *Exposition*, 1.3.

as the grace of God bestowed on the bodies of those saints who were cast into the Babylonian furnace.'[1] Gregory of Nyssa discusses prophecy and understanding from the Old Testament through to the church:

> Rather let us say, that as we indicate to the deaf what we want them to do, by gestures and signs, not because we have no voice of our own, but because a verbal communication would be utterly useless to those who cannot hear, so, in as much as human nature is in a sense deaf and insensible to higher truths, we maintain that the grace of God at sundry times and in divers manners spake by the Prophets, ordering their voices conformably to our capacity and the modes of expression with which we are familiar, and that by such means it leads us, as with a guiding hand, to the knowledge of higher truths, not teaching us in terms proportioned to their inherent sublimity, (for how can the great be contained by the little?) but descending to the lower level of our limited comprehension. . . . But whatsoever of God's words are recorded by Moses or the Prophets, are indications of the Divine will, flashing forth, now in one way, now in another, on the pure intellect of those holy men, according to the measure of the grace of which they were partakers.[2]

Amount of Grace

There are two lengthy passages in the writings of the Greek Fathers that speak about the amount of grace received, and since these did not seem to fit naturally into any of the previous sections of this chapter, they receive this short addendum to themselves. Firstly, John Chrysostom compares the grace received in the New Covenant with that present before Christ when writing about Job:

> Because he indeed was before the day of grace and of the law, when there was not much strictness of life, when the grace of the Spirit was not so great, when sin was hard to fight against, when the curse prevailed and when death was terrible. But now our wrestlings have become easier, all these things being removed after the coming of Christ; so that we have no excuse, when we are unable to reach the same standard as he, after so long a time, and such advantage, and so many gifts given to us by God.[3]

Cyril of Jerusalem discusses the amount of grace in the context of the life and work of the Apostles, indicating that they had a greater degree of grace than has otherwise been present:

1. Chrysostom, *On the Priesthood*, 3.14.
2. Gregory of Nyssa, *Against Eunomius*, 2.
3. Chrysostom, *Power of Demons*, 3.7.

So great was the grace which wrought in all the Apostles together, that, out of the Jews, those crucifiers of Christ, this great number believed, and were baptised in the Name of Christ, and *continued steadfastly in the Apostles' doctrine and in the prayers*. And again in the same power of the Holy Ghost, *Peter and John went up into the Temple at the hour of prayer, which was the ninth hour*, and in the Name of Jesus healed the man at the Beautiful gate, who had been lame from his mother's womb for forty years; that it might be fulfilled which was spoken, *Then shall the lame man leap as an hart*. And thus, as they captured in the spiritual net of their doctrine five thousand believers at once, so they confuted the misguided rulers of the people and chief priests, and that, not through their own wisdom, for *they were unlearned and ignorant men*, but through the mighty power of the Holy Ghost; for it is written, *Then Peter filled with the Holy Ghost said to them*. So great also was the grace of the Holy Ghost, which wrought by means of the Twelve Apostles in them who believed, that *they were of one heart and of one soul*, and their enjoyment of their goods was common, the possessors piously offering the prices of their possessions, and no one among them wanting aught; while Ananias and Sapphira, who attempted to lie to the Holy Ghost, underwent their befitting punishment.

And by the hands of the Apostles were many signs and wonders wrought among the people. And so great was the spiritual grace shed around the Apostles, that gentle as they were, they were the objects of dread; for *of the rest durst no man join himself to them; but the people magnified them; and multitudes were added of those who believed on the Lord, both of men and women*; and the streets were filled with the sick on their beds and couches, *that as Peter passed by, at least his shadow might overshadow some of them*. And *the multitude also of the cities round about came* unto this holy Jerusalem, *bringing sick folk, and them that were vexed with unclean spirits, and they were healed every one* in this power of the Holy Ghost.[1]

Conclusion

The key themes that have developed the doctrine of grace in the writings of the Greek Fathers, compared to the previous chapters, derive from their involvement in the developing doctrine of the Trinity. There is more discussion of grace and nature, coming as part of the debate over the nature of the Son and his role as the image of the Father, and, similarly, much more material on the means of receiving grace from both Son and Spirit. The dominant role of the Spirit remains clear throughout these

1. Cyril of Jerusalem, *Catechetical Lectures*, 17.21-2.

works, with the later sections of this chapter mirroring the major themes that have been seen previously in salvation, sanctification and gifting. There is little here on whether one can lose the grace that is received, although Basil does mention this when he writes, 'For the one divinised by grace possesses a nature subject to change and falls away from the better state whenever he is careless.'[1]

For further reading and the primary sources, see the conclusion to the previous chapter.

---

1. Basil, *Against Eunomious*, 3.5.

7.
The Greek Fathers on Free Will

Whereas ideas related to free will were rife in the earlier chapters on Tertullian, Irenaeus and Origen, the Cappadocian Fathers gave much more attention to the concept of grace, largely in light of the kind of Trinitarian thought noted in the previous chapter. The sheer volume of material on the godhead means that there is consequently less on the nature of humanity in places where one would expect to find passages discussing the freedom of the will. Most writers have very little developed thought on this theme independent of their thought on sin (we saw earlier how human free will was key to establishing responsibility for sin), but both Gregory of Nyssa and John of Damascus do engage with the concept, particularly in their work on the Catechism.

This chapter will start by looking at free will and human nature, of which the ability to sin is a key element in the teaching. From this basis, we will then discuss how John of Damascus views human life in light of the Fall in retaining human free will and then examine the role of the will in salvation. Finally, we will explore the nature of Divine Providence and the resulting impact on human free will as part of an analysis of the relationship between divine knowledge and human action.

Free Will and Nature

We start by noting an interesting line taken by John of Damascus in discussing the nature of angels and their free will as created beings. The first quotation seems rather removed from humanity, looking solely at angelic nature, but the implications will become important as John continues his thought:

> An angel, then, is an intelligent essence, in perpetual motion, with free-will, incorporeal, ministering to God, having obtained by grace an immortal nature: and the Creator alone knows the

form and limitation of its essence. . . . The angel's nature then is rational, and intelligent, and endowed with free-will, changeable in will, or fickle. For all that is created is changeable, and only that which is un-created is unchangeable. Also all that is rational is endowed with free-will. As it is, then, rational and intelligent, it is endowed with free-will: and as it is created, it is changeable, having power either to abide or progress in goodness, or to turn towards evil.[1]

One particular aspect is the nature of evil and sin in the angels:

> Note also that the angels, being rational, are endowed with free-will, and, inasmuch as they are created, are liable to change. This in fact is made plain by the devil who, although made good by the Creator, became of his own free-will the inventor of evil, and by the powers who revolted with him, the demons, and by the other troops of angels who abode in goodness.[2]

Later in the work, John develops the free will of angels in relation to free will in God and humanity, placing angelic freedom in an intermediary state:

> It is to be observed further, that freedom of will is used in several senses, one in connection with God, another in connection with angels, and a third in connection with men. For used in reference to God it is to be understood in a superessential manner, and in reference to angels it is to be taken in the sense that the election is concomitant with the state, and admits of the interposition of no interval of time at all: for while the angel possesses free-will by nature, he uses it without let or hindrance, having neither antipathy on the part of the body to overcome nor any assailant. Again, used in reference to men, it is to be taken in the sense that the state is considered to be anterior in time to the election. For man is free and has free-will by nature, but he has also the assault of the devil to impede him and the motion of the body: and thus through the assault and the weight of the body, election comes to be later than the state.[3]

Moving onto passages that focus more narrowly on human free will, we begin by continuing through the thought of John of Damascus. One area that he addresses early on in *Exposition of the Christian Faith* is astrological determinism, which contends that our lives are ruled by the movement of the stars. Against this he writes:

1. John of Damascus, *Exposition*, 2.3.
2. Ibid., 2.27.
3. Ibid., 3.14.

> Now the Greeks declare that all our affairs are controlled by the rising and setting and collision of these stars, viz., the sun and moon: for it is with these matters that astrology has to do. But we hold that we get from them signs of rain and drought, cold and heat, moisture and dryness, and of the various winds, and so forth, but no sign whatever as to our actions. For we have been created with free wills by our Creator and are masters over our own actions. Indeed, if all our actions depend on the courses of the stars, all we do is done of necessity: and necessity precludes either virtue or vice. But if we possess neither virtue nor vice, we do not deserve praise or punishment, and God, too, will turn out to be unjust, since He gives good things to some and afflicts others. Nay, He will no longer continue to guide or provide for His own creatures, if all things are carried and swept along in the grip of necessity. And the faculty of reason will be superfluous to us: for if we are not masters of any of our actions, deliberation is quite superfluous. Reason, indeed, is granted to us solely that we might take counsel, and hence all reason implies freedom of will.[1]

Cyril of Jerusalem also addresses this area of thought in his work on the Catechism:

> Next to the knowledge of this venerable and glorious and all-holy Faith, learn further what thou thyself art: that as man thou art of a two-fold nature, consisting of soul and body; and that, as was said a short time ago, the same God is the Creator both of soul and body. Know also that thou hast a soul self-governed, the noblest work of God, made after the image of its Creator: immortal because of God that gives it immortality; a living being, rational, imperishable, because of Him that bestowed these gifts: having free power to do what it willeth. For it is not according to thy nativity that thou sinnest, nor is it by the power of chance that thou committest fornication, nor, as some idly talk, do the conjunctions of the stars compel thee to give thyself to wantonness. Why dost thou shrink from confessing thine own evil deeds, and ascribe the blame to the innocent stars?[2]

Moving on from this reactive thought to a more constructive position on the nature of humanity, John of Damascus starts by appealing to the image of God as a basis for freedom:

> Now this being the case, He creates with His own hands man of a visible nature and an invisible, after His own image and likeness: on the one hand man's body He formed of earth, and on the other his

---

1. Ibid., 2.7.
2. Cyril of Jerusalem, *Catechetical Lectures*, 4.18.

> reasoning and thinking soul He bestowed upon him by His own inbreathing, and this is what we mean by 'after His image.' For the phrase 'after His image' clearly refers to the side of his nature which consists of mind and free will, whereas 'after His likeness' means likeness in virtue so far as that is possible.[1]

Reason is an important factor in the thought of John of Damascus, and it remains key as he builds his doctrine of humanity in combination with the different elements that comprise the human person:

> The forces again, inherent in a living creature are, it should be noted, partly psychical, partly vegetative, partly vital. The psychical forces are concerned with free volition, that is to say, impulsive movement and sensation. Impulsive movement includes change of place and movement of the body as a whole, and phonation and respiration. For it is in our power to perform or refrain from performing these acts. The vegetative and vital forces, however, are quite outside the province of will.[2]

John also deals with the differences between humanity and creatures in separating basic appetites from the use of reason, heavily emphasising the scope of freedom that the latter allows:

> In the case, however, of creatures without reason, as soon as appetite is roused for anything, straightway arises impulse to action. For the appetite of creatures without reason is irrational, and they are ruled by their natural appetite. Hence, neither the names of will or wish are applicable to the appetite of creatures without reason. For will is rational, free and natural desire, and in the case of man, endowed with reason as he is, the natural appetite is ruled rather than rules. For his actions are free, and depend upon reason, since the faculties of knowledge and life are bound up together in man. He is free in desire, free in wish, free in examination and investigation, free in deliberation, free in judgement, free in inclination, free in choice, free in impulse, and free in action where that is in accordance with nature.[3]

The developed aspects of reason in speculation and contemplation increase the capability, but also the responsibility, of humankind, meaning that they are judged on the basis of their actions while other creatures are not:

> We hold, therefore, that free-will comes on the scene at the same moment as reason, and that change and alteration are congenital to all that is produced. For all that is produced is also subject to change.

1. John of Damascus, *Exposition*, 2.12.
2. Ibid.
3. Ibid., 2.22.

> For those things must be subject to change whose production has its origin in change. And change consists in being brought into being out of nothing, and in transforming a substratum of matter into something different. Inanimate things, then, and things without reason undergo the aforementioned bodily changes, while the changes of things endowed with reason depend on choice. For reason consists of a speculative and a practical part. The speculative part is the contemplation of the nature of things, and the practical consists in deliberation and defines the true reason for what is to be done. The speculative side is called mind or wisdom, and the practical side is called reason or prudence. Every one, then, who deliberates does so in the belief that the choice of what is to be done lies in his hands, that he may choose what seems best as the result of his deliberation, and having chosen may act upon it. And if this is so, free-will must necessarily be very closely related to reason. For either man is an irrational being, or, if he is rational, he is master of his acts and endowed with free-will. Hence also creatures without reason do not enjoy free-will: for nature leads them rather than they nature, and so they do not oppose the natural appetite, but as soon as their appetite longs after anything they rush headlong after it. But man, being rational, leads nature rather than nature him, and so when he desires aught he has the power to curb his appetite or to indulge it as he pleases. Hence also creatures devoid of reason are the subjects neither of praise nor blame, while man is the subject of both praise and blame.[1]

Later on in his *Exposition*, John returns to the same theme:

> For the Creator hath implanted even in the unreasoning brutes natural appetite to compel them to sustain their own nature. For devoid of reason, as they are, they cannot guide their natural appetite but are guided by it. And so, as soon as the appetite for anything has sprung up, straightway arises also the impulse for action. And thus they do not win praise or happiness for pursuing virtue, nor punishment for doing evil. But the rational nature, although it does possess a natural appetite, can guide and train it by reason wherever the laws of nature are observed. For the advantage of reason consists in this, the free-will, by which we mean natural activity in a rational subject. Wherefore in pursuing virtue it wins praise and happiness, and in pursuing vice it wins punishment.[2]

If these consequences are incumbent on the decisions that the will makes, it is unsurprising that John of Damascus maintains that the will cannot be constrained by any necessity:

1. Ibid., 2.27.
2. Ibid., 3.18.

> While, however, we assert that will is natural, we hold not that it is dominated by necessity, but that it is free. For if it is rational, it must be absolutely free. For it is not only the divine and uncreated nature that is free from the bonds of necessity, but also the intellectual and created nature. And this is manifest: for God, being by nature good and being by nature the Creator and by nature God, is not all this of necessity. For who is there to introduce this necessity?[1]

Gregory of Nyssa is the other Cappadocian Father who has written extensively on free will as a key part of humanity. He also bases this in the image of God, as arguing that free will not only originates in God but also finds its end in the beauty that comes from God:

> We distinctly remember what in the course of our argument we said in the commencement of this treatise; namely, that man was fashioned in imitation of the Divine nature, preserving his resemblance to the Deity as well in other excellences as in possession of freedom of the will, yet being of necessity of a nature subject to change. For it was not possible that a being who derived his origin from an alteration should be altogether free from this liability . . . since, then, by reason of this impulse and movement of changeful alteration it is not possible that the nature of the subject of this change should remain self-centred and unmoved, but there is always something towards which the will is tending, the appetency for moral beauty naturally drawing it on to movement, this beauty is in one instance really such in its nature, in another it is not so, only blossoming with an illusive appearance of beauty; and the criterion of these two kinds is the mind that dwells within us.[2]

The idea of purpose in created nature is also present in his work *On the Soul and Resurrection*:

> The All-creating Wisdom fashioned these souls, these receptacles with free wills, as vessels as it were, for this very purpose, that there should be some capacities able to receive His blessings and become continually larger with the inpouring of the stream.[3]

In another work, *On the Making of Man*, Gregory highlights the exalted nature of humanity in comparison with the rest of creation on the basis of this freedom of the will:

> For as in our own life artificers fashion a tool in the way suitable to its use, so the best Artificer made our nature as it were a formation fit for the exercise of royalty, preparing it at once by superior advantages

1. Ibid., 3.14.
2. Gregory of Nyssa, *On the Catechism*, 21.
3. Gregory of Nyssa, *On the Soul and Resurrection*.

> of soul, and by the very form of the body, to be such as to be adapted for royalty: for the soul immediately shows its royal and exalted character, far removed as it is from the lowliness of private station, in that it owns no lord, and is self-governed, swayed autocratically by its own will; for to whom else does this belong than to a king?
>
> Thus there is in us the principle of all excellence, all virtue and wisdom, and every higher thing that we conceive: but pre-eminent among all is the fact that we are free from necessity, and not in bondage to any natural power, but have decision in our own power as we please; for virtue is a voluntary thing, subject to no dominion: that which is the result of compulsion and force cannot be virtue.[1]

Before we look at created nature in relation to sin, it is worth noting an interesting passage by Gregory of Nazianzus in one of his *Orations* on the concept of eunuchs. Here he allows for humans to possess free will, but also notes that certain people have a particular aptitude for good (or, by implication, for bad):

> There are, He says, some eunuchs which were so born from their mother's womb; and there are some eunuchs which were made eunuchs of men; and there be eunuchs which have made themselves eunuchs for the Kingdom of Heaven's sake. He that is able to receive it, let him receive it. I think that the discourse would sever itself from the body, and represent higher things by bodily figures; for to stop the meaning at bodily eunuchs would be small and very weak, and unworthy of the Word; and we must understand in addition something worthy of the Spirit. Some, then, seem by nature to incline to good. And when I speak of nature, I am not slighting free will, but supposing both – an aptitude for good, and that which brings the natural aptitude to effect. And there are others whom reason cleanses, by cutting them off from the passions. These I imagine to be meant by those whom men have made Eunuchs, when the word of teaching distinguishing the better from the worse and rejecting the one and commanding the other (like the verse, Depart from evil and do good), works spiritual chastity. This sort of making eunuchs I approve; and I highly praise both teachers and taught, that the one have nobly effected, and the other still more nobly endured, the cutting off.[2]

Free Will and Sin

As has been indicated, some of the Greek Fathers' views in this area were presented in the chapter on sin. The passages quoted below focus more on a nature that is *able* to sin, rather than the engagement of the

1. Gregory of Nyssa, *On the Making of Man*, 4, 16.
2. Gregory of Nazianzus, *Oration 37*.

will in performing sin. John of Damascus notes that, in giving free will to humankind, God necessarily set up guidance on the right use of the will that would lead to blessing and improper use that must be punished:

> When therefore He had furnished his nature with free-will, He imposed a law on him, not to taste of the tree of knowledge. Concerning this tree, we have said as much as is necessary in the chapter about Paradise, at least as much as it was in our power to say. And with this command He gave the promise that, if he should preserve the dignity of the soul by giving the victory to reason, and acknowledging his Creator and observing His command, he should share eternal blessedness and live to all eternity, proving mightier than death: but if forsooth he should subject the soul to the body, and prefer the delights of the body, comparing himself in ignorance of his true dignity to the senseless beasts, and shaking off His Creator's yoke, and neglecting His divine injunction, he will be liable to death and corruption, and will be compelled to labour throughout a miserable life. For it was no profit to man to obtain incorruption while still untried and unproved, lest he should fall into pride and under the judgement of the devil. For through his incorruption the devil, when he had fallen as the result of his own free choice, was firmly established in wickedness, so that there was no room for repentance and no hope of change: just as, moreover, the angels also, when they had made free choice of virtue became through grace immoveably rooted in goodness.[1]

Gregory of Nyssa devotes three extended passages to the fact that evil is a necessary possibility in the creation of humanity without God being in any way responsible for the wrong use that humans make of their free will. When writing about the Catechism, Gregory states:

> For He who made man for the participation of His own peculiar good, and incorporated in him the instincts for all that was excellent, in order that his desire might be carried forward by a corresponding movement in each case to its like, would never have deprived him of that most excellent and precious of all goods; I mean the gift implied in being his own master, and having a free will. For if necessity in any way was the master of the life of man, the 'image' would have been falsified in that particular part, by being estranged owing to this unlikeness to its archetype. How can that nature which is under a yoke and bondage to any kind of necessity be called an image of a Master Being? Was it not, then, most right that that which is in every detail made like the Divine should possess in its nature a self-ruling and independent principle, such as to enable the participation of good to be the reward of its virtue? Whence, then, comes it, you

1. John of Damascus, *Exposition*, 2.30.

will ask, that he who had been distinguished throughout with most excellent endowments exchanged these good things for the worse? The reason of this also is plain. No growth of evil had its beginning in the Divine will. Vice would have been blameless were it inscribed with the name of God as its maker and father. But the evil is, in some way or other, engendered from within, springing up in the will at that moment when there is a retrocession of the soul from the beautiful. For as sight is an activity of nature, and blindness a deprivation of that natural operation, such is the kind of opposition between virtue and vice. It is, in fact, not possible to form any other notion of the origin of vice than as the absence of virtue. For as when the light has been removed the darkness supervenes, but as long as it is present there is no darkness, so, as long as the good is present in the nature, vice is a thing that has no inherent existence; while the departure of the better state becomes the origin of its opposite. Since then, this is the peculiarity of the possession of a free will, that it chooses as it likes the thing that pleases it, you will find that it is not God Who is the author of the present evils, seeing that He has ordered your nature so as to be its own master and free; but rather the recklessness that makes choice of the worse in preference to the better.[1]

A very similar approach is taken in *On the Soul and Resurrection*:

Therefore it is by that fact clearly proved that vice is not prior in time to the act of beginning to live, and that our nature did not thence derive its source, but that the all-disposing wisdom of God was the Cause of it: in short, that the soul issues on the stage of life in the manner which is pleasing to its Creator, and then (but not before), by virtue of its power of willing, is free to choose that which is to its mind, and so, whatever it may wish to be, becomes that very thing. We may understand this truth by the example of the eyes. To see is their natural state; but to fail to see results to them either from choice or from disease. This unnatural state may supervene instead of the natural, either by wilful shutting of the eyes or by deprivation of their sight through disease. With the like truth we may assert that the soul derives its constitution from God, and that, as we cannot conceive of any vice in Him, it is removed from any necessity of being vicious; that nevertheless, though this is the condition in which it came into being, it can be attracted of its own free will in a chosen direction, either wilfully shutting its eyes to the Good, or letting them be damaged by that insidious foe whom we have taken home to live with us, and so passing through life in the darkness of error; or, reversely, preserving undimmed its sight of the Truth and keeping far away from all weaknesses that could darken it.[2]

1. Gregory of Nyssa, *On the Catechism*, 5.
2. Gregory of Nyssa, *On the Soul and Resurrection*.

Earlier in the same work, when discussing a free will that allows for evil, there is an indication of a more constructive line that evil can end in a strengthening of character:

> But since, according to the view which we have just enunciated, it is not possible for this reasoning faculty to exist in the life of the body without existing by means of sensations, and since sensation is already found subsisting in the brute creation, necessarily as it were, by reason of this one condition, our soul has touch with the other things which are knit up with it; and these are all those phænomena within us that we call 'passions'; which have not been allotted to human nature for any bad purpose at all (for the Creator would most certainly be the author of evil, if in *them*, so deeply rooted as they are in our nature, any necessities of wrong-doing were found), but according to the use which our free will puts them to, these emotions of the soul become the instruments of virtue or of vice. They are like the iron which is being fashioned according to the volition of the artificer, and receives whatever shape the idea which is in his mind prescribes, and becomes a sword or some agricultural implement. Supposing, then, that our reason, which is our nature's choicest part, holds the dominion over these imported emotions (as Scripture allegorically declares in the command to men to rule over the brutes), none of them will be active in the ministry of evil; fear will only generate within us obedience, and anger fortitude, and cowardice caution; and the instinct of desire will procure for us the delight that is Divine and perfect. But if reason drops the reins and is dragged behind like a charioteer who has got entangled in his car, then these instincts are changed into fierceness, just as we see happens amongst the brutes. For since reason does not preside over the natural impulses that are implanted in them, the more irascible animals, under the generalship of their anger, mutually destroy each other; while the bulky and powerful animals get no good themselves from their strength, but become by their want of reason slaves of that which has reason.[1]

Free Will and Experience

Moving on from the created nature, John Chrysostom addresses the role of the will in the context of demonic activity, drawing a parallel between continuing human freedom to determine our movement with the movement of nature that is not impeded by demonic activity:

> But nevertheless some dare to say that Demons administer our affairs. What can I do? Thou hast a loving Master. He chooses rather to be blasphemed by thee through these words, than to

1. Ibid.

> commit thine affairs to the Demons and persuade thee by the reality how Demons administer.... If Demons were to arrange affairs, we should be in no better condition than possessed men, yea rather we should be worse than they. For God did not give them over entirely to the tyranny of the Demons, otherwise they would suffer far worse things than these which they now suffer. And I would ask this of those who say these things, what kind of disorder they behold in the present, that they set down all our affairs to the arrangement of Demons? And yet we behold the sun for so many years proceeding day by day in regular order, a manifold band of stars keeping their own order, the courses of the moon unimpeded, an invariable succession of night and day, all things, both above and below, as it were in a certain fitting harmony, yea rather even far more, and more accurately each keeping his own place, and not departing from the order which God who made them ordained from the beginning.[1]

Again it is John of Damascus who has the most material on the continuing role of the will in human life. The following lengthy quotation responds to questions about various modes of determinism, defending the freedom of the will. There are mentions of providence here, but extended treatment of that aspect will come at the end of the chapter:

> The first enquiry involved in the consideration of free-will, that is, of what is in our own power, is whether anything is in our power: for there are many who deny this. The second is, what are the things that are in our power, and over what things do we have authority? The third is, what is the reason for which God Who created us endued us with free-will? So then we shall take up the first question, and firstly we shall prove that of those things which even our opponents grant, some are within our power. And let us proceed thus.
>
> Of all the things that happen, the cause is said to be either God, or necessity, or fate, or nature, or chance, or accident. But God's function has to do with essence and providence: necessity deals with the movement of things that ever keep to the same course: fate with the necessary accomplishment of the things it brings to pass (for fate itself implies necessity): nature with birth, growth, destruction, plants and animals; chance with what is rare and unexpected. For chance is defined as the meeting and concurrence of two causes, originating in choice but bringing to pass something other than what is natural: for example, if a man finds a treasure while digging a ditch: for the man who hid the treasure did not do so that the other might find it, nor did the finder dig with the purpose of

1. Chrysostom, *Power of Demons*, 1.6.

> finding the treasure: but the former hid it that he might take it away when he wished, and the other's aim was to dig the ditch: whereas something happened quite different from what both had in view. Accident again deals with casual occurrences that take place among lifeless or irrational things, apart from nature and art. This then is their doctrine. Under which, then, of these categories are we to bring what happens through the agency of man, if indeed man is not the cause and beginning of action? for it would not be right to ascribe to God actions that are sometimes base and unjust: nor may we ascribe these to necessity, for they are not such as ever continue the same: nor to fate, for fate implies not possibility only but necessity: nor to nature, for nature's province is animals and plants: nor to chance, for the actions of men are not rare and unexpected: nor to accident, for that is used in reference to the casual occurrences that take place in the world of lifeless and irrational things. We are left then with this fact, that the man who acts and makes is himself the author of his own works, and is a creature endowed with free-will.
>
> Further, if man is the author of no action, the faculty of deliberation is quite superfluous: for to what purpose could deliberation be put if man is the master of none of his actions? for all deliberation is for the sake of action. But to prove that the fairest and most precious of man's endowments is quite superfluous would be the height of absurdity. If then man deliberates, he deliberates with a view to action. For all deliberation is with a view to and on account of action.[1]

Following on from this, John recognises that when we talk about freedom of the will, there needs to be a recognition that circumstances mean that humans cannot necessarily do what they will:

> Of events, some are in our hands, others are not. Those then are in our hands which we are free to do or not to do at our will, that is all actions that are done voluntarily (for those actions are not called voluntary the doing of which is not in our hands), and in a word, all that are followed by blame or praise and depend on motive and law. Strictly all mental and deliberative acts are in our hands. Now deliberation is concerned with equal possibilities: and an 'equal possibility' is an action that is itself within our power and its opposite, and our mind makes choice of the alternatives, and this is the origin of action. The actions, therefore, that are in our hands are these equal possibilities: e.g. to be moved or not to be moved, to hasten or not to hasten, to long for unnecessaries or not to do so, to tell lies or not to tell lies, to give or not to give, to rejoice or not to rejoice as fits the occasion, and all such actions as

1. John of Damascus, *Exposition*, 2.25.

> imply virtue or vice in their performance, for we are free to do or not to do these at our pleasure. Amongst equal possibilities also are included the arts, for we have it in our power to cultivate these or not as we please.[1]

Later in the work, he addresses another question against human free will in relation to Scriptures that seem to indicate that God actively prevents people from responding. Even here John is determined that the active agent is the human person, with God permitting what they have freely decided:

> Wherefore this passage that we have quoted and this, *God hath concluded them all in unbelief*, and this, *God hath given them the spirit of slumber, eyes that they should not see, and ears that they should not hear*, all these must be understood not as though God Himself were energising, but as though God were permitting, both because of free-will and because goodness knows no compulsion.[2]

This is an interesting interpretation that seems to go against a surface reading of the text, and shows how strongly John of Damascus held to the importance of free will. We will see more on this theme in the final section of the chapter that looks at providence and free will.

Free Will and Salvation

The role of the will in sin is key for these writers, who also have a persistent high view of the role of the will in life since the Fall. It is interesting to see how the Cappadocian Fathers appeal to the human and the divine nature in terms of the human sinful predicament and the means of gaining salvation.

John of Damascus starts with the nature of God, desiring that all be saved but that those who are sinners be justly punished. This seems to be God's unchanging position, with God's will always being that people do what is right without seeking to compel this:

> Also one must bear in mind that God's original wish was that all should be saved and come to His Kingdom. For it was not for punishment that He formed us but to share in His goodness, inasmuch as He is a good God. But inasmuch as He is a just God, His will is that sinners should suffer punishment.
>
> The first then is called God's antecedent will and pleasure, and springs from Himself, while the second is called God's consequent will and permission, and has its origin in us. And the latter is two-

1. Ibid., 2.26.
2. Ibid., 4.19.

fold; one part dealing with matters of guidance and training, and having in view our salvation, and the other being hopeless and leading to our utter punishment, as we said above. And this is the case with actions that are not left in our hands.

But of actions that are in our hands the good ones depend on His antecedent goodwill and pleasure, while the wicked ones depend neither on His antecedent nor on His consequent will, but are a concession to free-will. For that which is the result of compulsion has neither reason nor virtue in it. God makes provision for all creation and makes all creation the instrument of His help and training, yea often even the demons themselves, as for example in the cases of Job and the swine.[1]

Two writers, Gregory of Nyssa and Cyril of Jerusalem, paint pictures of human inability to achieve salvation for themselves and the need for a divine work. They balance this with the need for the human will to respond to that which is offered. Gregory of Nyssa writes:

> In fact this likeness to the divine is not our work at all; it is not the achievement of any faculty of man; it is the great gift of God bestowed upon our nature at the very moment of our birth; human efforts can only go so far as to clear away the filth of sin, and so cause the buried beauty of the soul to shine forth again. This truth is, I think, taught in the Gospel, when our Lord says, to those who can hear what Wisdom speaks beneath a mystery, that 'the Kingdom of God is within you.' That word points out the fact that the Divine good is not something apart from our nature, and is not removed far away from those who have the will to seek it; it is in fact within each of us, ignored indeed, and unnoticed while it is stifled beneath the cares and pleasures of life, but found again whenever we can turn our power of conscious thinking towards it.[2]

Cyril of Jerusalem places sinful humanity in a very similar position to Gregory, calling on people not to give in to their condition because of the hope held out by Christ:

> What then? some one will say. We have been beguiled and are lost. Is there then no salvation left? We have fallen: Is it not possible to rise again? We have been blinded: May we not recover our sight? We have become crippled: Can we never walk upright? In a word, we are dead: May we not rise again? He that woke Lazarus who was four days dead and already stank, shall He not, O man, much more easily raise thee who art alive? He who shed His precious blood for us, shall Himself deliver us from sin. Let us not despair of ourselves,

1. Ibid., 2.29.
2. Gregory of Nyssa, *On Virginity*, 12.

brethren; let us not abandon ourselves to a hopeless condition. For it is a fearful thing not to believe in a hope of repentance. For he that looks not for salvation spares not to add evil to evil: but to him that hopes for cure, it is henceforth easy to be careful over himself. The robber who looks not for pardon grows desperate; but, if he hopes for forgiveness, often comes to repentance. What then, does the serpent cast its slough, and shall not we cast off our sin? Thorny ground also, if cultivated well, is turned into fruitful; and is salvation to us irrecoverable? Nay rather, our nature admits of salvation, but the will also is required.[1]

John Chrysostom defines a much more active role for humanity in *On the Priesthood*, arguing that one who is sick cannot be cured against their will:

For neither has authority of this kind for the restraint of sinners been given us by law, nor, if it had been given, should we have any field for the exercise of our power, inasmuch as God rewards those who abstain from evil by their own choice, not of necessity. Consequently much skill is required that our patients may be induced to submit willingly to the treatment prescribed by the physicians, and not only this, but that they may be grateful also for the cure. For if any one when he is bound becomes restive (which it is in his power to be), he makes the mischief worse; and if he should pay no heed to the words which cut like steel, he inflicts another wound by means of this contempt, and the intention to heal only becomes the occasion of a worse disorder. For it is not possible for any one to cure a man by compulsion against his will.[2]

There thus seems to be at least a symbiotic element to salvation, with movement required both from God and humankind in order to uphold the nature of God and humanity as free, rather than creating an imposition. This leads us to a discussion of the Providence of God and the extent to which God's foreknowledge and action affect human free will.

Free Will and Providence

It is John of Damascus who again provides a focussed passage for us to study towards the end of book two of *Exact Exposition of the Orthodox Faith*. His initial position looks only at the nature of God and thus establishes an elevated view of providence that is linked to God's work as the Creator of all things:

1. Cyril of Jerusalem, *Catechetical Lectures*, 2.5.
2. Chrysostom, *On the Priesthood*, 2.3.

> But if Providence is God's will, according to true reasoning all things that come into being through Providence must necessarily be both most fair and most excellent, and such that they cannot be surpassed. For the same person must of necessity be creator of and provider for what exists: for it is not meet nor fitting that the creator of what exists and the provider should be separate persons. For in that case they would both assuredly be deficient, the one in creating, the other in providing. God therefore is both Creator and Provider, and His creative and preserving and providing power is simply His good-will. For *whatsoever the Lord pleased that did He in heaven and in earth*, and *no one resisted His will*. He willed that all things should be and they were. He wills the universe to be framed and it is framed, and all that He wills comes to pass.[1]

However, when he deals with the outworking of providence in creation, John clarifies God's perspective by establishing categories of will and permission, with the former being the basis of all that is good and the latter allowing for human will:

> Now the works of Providence are partly according to the good-will (of God) and partly according to permission. Works of good-will include all those that are undeniably good, while works of permission are [. . .] For Providence often permits the just man to encounter misfortune in order that he may reveal to others the virtue that lies concealed within him, as was the case with Job. At other times it allows something strange to be done in order that something great and marvellous might be accomplished through the seemingly-strange act, as when the salvation of men was brought about through the Cross.[2]

The result, for John of Damascus, is a concentration on the foreknowledge of God rather than the predestining action of God, with providence thus referring more to the existence and responsibility of human free will than to God supplying a determining element to our actions:

> Moreover, it is to be observed that the choice of what is to be done is in our own hands: but the final issue depends, in the one case when our actions are good, on the cooperation of God, Who in His justice brings help according to His foreknowledge to such as choose the good with a right conscience, and, in the other case when our actions are to evil, on the desertion by God, Who again in His justice stands aloof in accordance with His foreknowledge.[3]

1. John of Damascus, *Exposition*, 2.29.
2. Ibid. There is a gap in the reliable manuscripts in the middle of this quotation, hence the bracketed ellipsis.
3. Ibid.

This teaching is developed further in the next chapter of John's work:

> We ought to understand that while God knows all things beforehand, yet He does not predetermine all things. For He knows beforehand those things that are in our power, but He does not predetermine them. For it is not His will that there should be wickedness nor does He choose to compel virtue. So that predetermination is the work of the divine command based on fore-knowledge. But on the other hand God predetermines those things which are not within our power in accordance with His prescience. For already God in His prescience has prejudged all things in accordance with His goodness and justice.[1]

This view of the role of humanity is then immediately clarified with the recognition that all we have is from God and that there is an important co-operative element in goodness:

> Bear in mind, too, that virtue is a gift from God implanted in our nature, and that He Himself is the source and cause of all good, and without His co-operation and help we cannot will or do any good thing. But we have it in our power either to abide in virtue and follow God, Who calls us into ways of virtue, or to stray from paths of virtue, which is to dwell in wickedness, and to follow the devil who summons but cannot compel us. For wickedness is nothing else than the withdrawal of goodness, just as darkness is nothing else than the withdrawal of light. While then we abide in the natural state we abide in virtue, but when we deviate from the natural state, that is from virtue, we come into an unnatural state and dwell in wickedness.... For having been endowed with reason and mind, and free-will after the image of God, he was fitly entrusted with dominion over earthly things by the common Creator and Master of all.[2]

Outside these passages, the concept of providence is not developed at length by the Greek Fathers, although the sovereignty of God is undoubtedly recognised. Cyril of Jerusalem seems to almost attribute irony to the Providence of God when discussing the heretic Manes' change of name from Cubricus:

> Then, lest the name of slavery might be a reproach, instead of Cubricus he called himself Manes, which in the language of the Persians signifies discourse. For as he thought himself something of a disputant, he surnamed himself Manes, as it were an excellent master of discourse. But though he contrived for himself an honourable title according to the language of the Persians, yet

1. Ibid., 2.30.
2. Ibid.

the providence of God caused him to become a self-accuser even against his will, that through thinking to honour himself in Persia, he might proclaim himself among the Greeks by name a maniac.

Conclusion

While there are few significant, lengthy discussions about human free will present in the writings of the Greek Fathers, there are sufficient indications present to build up a solid picture of their general philosophy. These centre on the nature of created humanity, the results of improper use of this will in sin and the continuing role of the will in life and salvation in relationship to the nature of God as the fount of all good. There is one last quotation for this chapter from Gregory of Nyssa, left until last because it encompasses most of the elements that have been looked at here:

> For they assert that God, if He had been so pleased, might have forcibly drawn those, who were not inclined to yield, to accept the Gospel message. But where then would have been their free will? Where their virtuous merit? Where their meed of praise from their moral directors? It belongs only to inanimate or irrational creatures to be brought round by the will of another to his purpose; whereas the reasoning and intelligent nature, if it lays aside its freedom of action, loses at the same time the gracious gift of intellect. For upon what is he to employ any faculty of thought, if his power of choosing anything according to his inclination lies in the will of another? But then, if the will remains without the capacity of action, virtue necessarily disappears, since it is shackled by the enforced quiescence of the will. Then, if virtue does not exist, life loses its value, reason moves in accordance with fatalism, the praise of moral guardians is gone, sin may be indulged in without risk, and the difference between the courses of life is obliterated. For who, henceforth, could with any reason condemn profligacy, or praise sobriety? Since every one would have this ready answer, that nothing of all the things we are inclined to is in our own power, but that by some superior and ruling influence the wills of men are brought round to the purpose of one who has the mastery over them. The conclusion, then is that it is not the goodness of God that is chargeable with the fact that the Faith is not engendered in all men, but rather the disposition of those by whom the preaching of the Word is received.[1]

For further reading on the Greek Fathers and information about accessing their works, see the final paragraph in the chapter on the Greek Fathers and sin.

1. Gregory of Nyssa, *On the Catechism*, 31.

8.
Early Augustine

Augustine of Hippo (354-430 CE) is the most influential theologian in the history of the western church. This is due to the range and volume of his writings and because of his place in the history of western thought. In the early centuries of Christianity, it was Eastern thought and the Greek language that dominated theological reflection, while those writing in Latin focused more on the nature of the church in their writing – men such as Cyprian of Carthage and Ambrose of Milan.[1] The clearest manifestation of this supremacy of Greek thought in the church were the great councils at Nicaea (325), Constantinople (381), Ephesus (431) and Chalcedon (451), where the major defining statements of Christian belief were debated, agreed and presented in Greek.

Into this context, Augustine's theological contributions are like a great weight added to the western side of the scales. Covering a wide range of key areas, they form the foundation for Latin engagement with the Christian faith, but, due largely to historical factors, they became more defining than foundational. Several centuries passed before with a tradition developed to engage with them, by which time they had achieved an unquestioned authority. By the fifth century, the western Roman Empire was well into decline and would shortly fragment politically, creating an environment with little room for intellectual exploits and little novel thought until peace and stability began to settle in the eleventh and twelfth centuries.[2] Given the lack

1. This does not mean that theology was absent in the West, and it is important to recognise the contributions of these writers and Hilary of Poitiers to the discipline. Early Church theology, however, was dominated by the Greek churches.
2. This is not to say that there were no important contributions in this period, and Boethius (480-524 CE) and Gregory the Great (540-604 CE) were certainly deep and influential thinkers. In addition to these, there was a

of familiarity with Greek for several centuries, the resources available to the Western church were severely limited beyond the Bible and the works of Augustine.

Augustine himself is a fascinating character. Born to a Christian mother, he was schooled in the Christian faith, but after moving to Carthage for his studies he began a hedonistic lifestyle, devoting himself to pleasure. He took up a career in rhetoric and found a love of philosophy, all of which culminated in him becoming a Manichean. The Manicheans valued the natural sciences, which intrigued Augustine, and sought to solve the problem of evil by positing two sources of being – one good and one evil – to allow the true God to be removed from any suggestion of involvement in sin and evil. Gradually Augustine began to mistrust the teachings of the Manicheans. About ten years after he had identified himself with their philosophy, he moved to Milan and came under the influence of Bishop Ambrose, who would lead Augustine to accept the Christian faith.

The concepts of will and grace are key elements in many of Augustine's writings but his views develop and even change during the course of his life, largely in light of teachings that he was seeking to refute. His early work focuses on the Manichean teaching that was rather fatalistic, against which Augustine argues in support of human will and responsibility. The later work, particularly that against the Pelagians, concentrates more on the importance of divine action and grace, earning Augustine the title, 'The Doctor of Grace'. There is no single moment of change that is readily discernible but it seems to happen around the end of the fourth century at least partly through the influence of Simplicianus, Ambrose's successor as Bishop of Milan, to whom Augustine wrote a letter in 397 CE. For the purposes of this work, and because there needs to be some split in the presentation of Augustine's work, this first chapter will look at his writings up to this point, while the second, longer chapter will present his writings from 398 onwards.

This chapter will start by looking at Augustine's early views on sin and evil, which confront the Manichean dualist idea that good is from God and evil from some other source. In this, there is some engagement with the human will, and this will act as a bridge to a fuller examination of that concept founded on Augustine's *On Free Choice of the Will*. Finally, we will look at the material on grace in Augustine's early works, although this is rather limited.

---

minor renaissance under Charlemagne – the Carolingian Renaissance – that will be recognised in the brief examination of Erigena in the final chapter of this volume.

Sin

The first point that Augustine stresses about sin is that no blame for it can be laid at God's door:

> For God is not the author, but He is the controller of sin; so that sinful actions, which are sinful because they are against nature, are judged and controlled, and assigned to their proper place and condition, in order that they may not bring discord and disgrace on universal nature.[1]

He was against the idea that, as the creator of all things, God has a responsibility for what that creation does. Augustine teaches that sins result from the will of creatures, even angels:

> But because evil angels also were not constituted evil by God, but were made evil by sinning, Peter in his epistle says: 'For if God spared not angels when they sinned, but casting them down into the dungeons of smoky hell, He delivered them to be reserved for punishment in judgment.' Hence Peter shows that there is still due to them the penalty of the last judgment, concerning which the Lord says: 'Go ye into everlasting fire, which has been prepared for the Devil and his angels.'[2]

The purity of God, when brought alongside God as the fount of all being, requires that an answer be given to the question of evil, and Augustine provides this in the following quote in a work discussing the morals of the Manicheans, in which he argues that sin and evil are the opposite of being:

> You ask me, Whence is evil? I ask you in return, What is evil? Which is the more reasonable question? Are those right who ask whence a thing is, when they do not know what it is; or he who thinks it necessary to inquire first what it is, in order to avoid the gross absurdity of searching for the origin of a thing unknown? Your answer is quite correct, when you say that evil is that which is contrary to nature; for no one is so mentally blind as not to see that, in every kind, evil is that which is contrary to the nature of the kind. But the establishment of this doctrine is the overthrow of your heresy. For evil is no nature, if it is contrary to nature. Now, according to you, evil is a certain nature and substance. Moreover, whatever is contrary to nature must oppose nature and seek its destruction. For nature means nothing else than that which anything is conceived of as being in its own kind. Hence is the new word which we now use derived from the word for being – essence namely, or, as we usually say, substance – while before these words

1. Augustine, *Against Faustus*, 22.78.
2. Augustine, *Nature of Good*, 33.

> were in use, the word nature was used instead. Here, then, if you will consider the matter without stubbornness, we see that evil is that which falls away from essence and tends to non-existence.[1]

This allows Augustine to make a clear distinction between God and evil:

> Accordingly, when the Catholic Church declares that God is the author of all natures and substances, those who understand this understand at the same time that God is not the author of evil. For how can He who is the cause of the being of all things be at the same time the cause of their not being, – that is, of their falling off from essence and tending to non-existence? For this is what reason plainly declares to be the definition of evil.[2]

Given this basis, Augustine teaches heavily on the role of the will in the nature and action of sin, which can be clearly seen in another definition of sin found in *On Two Souls*:

> Permit me first also to define sin, which, every mind reads divinely written in itself, cannot exist apart from will. Sin therefore is the will to retain and follow after what justice forbids, and from which it is free to abstain. Although if it be not free, it is not will. But I have preferred to define more roughly than precisely. Should I not also have carefully examined those obscure books, whence I might have learned that no one is worthy of blame or punishment who either wills what justice does not prohibit him from willing, or does not do what he is not able to do? . . . But if no one is worthy of blame and condemnation, who either does not act against the prohibition of justice, or who does not do what he cannot do, yet every sin is blameworthy and condemnable, who doubts then that it is sin, when willing is unjust, and not willing is free. And hence that definition is both true and easy to understand, and not only now but then also could have been spoken by me: Sin is the will of retaining or of obtaining, what justice forbids, and whence it is free to abstain?[3]

Augustine's teaching on sin is closely linked to the human will and becomes something of a subsection of that area of thought. Following the passage just quoted, Augustine writes:

> But by nature souls can in no way be evil. Whence do we teach this. From the above definitions of will and sin. For to speak of souls, and that they are evil, and that they do not sin, is full of madness; but to say that they sin without will, is great craziness, and to hold any one guilty of sin for not doing what he could not do, belongs to the height of

1. Augustine, *Morals of Manicheans*, 2.
2. Ibid., 3.
3. Augustine, *On Two Souls*, 11.

8. Early Augustine

> iniquity and insanity. Wherefore whatever these souls do, if they do it by nature not by will, that is, if they are wanting in a movement of mind free both for doing and not doing, if finally no power of abstaining from their work is conceded to them; we cannot hold that the sin is theirs.[1]

The concept of consequence for sins requiring a free act of will is an important element of Augustine's thought at this stage. He questions whether someone sins if, while they sleep, another person should use their hand to write something disgraceful? To this he answers, '[W]hoever has done anything evil by means of one unconscious or unable to resist, the latter can by no means be justly condemned.'[2] The role of compulsion and its effect on the will and sin is then addressed:

> Sinning therefore takes place only by exercise of will. But our will is very well known to us; for neither should I know that I will, if I did not know what will itself is. Accordingly, it is thus defined: will is a movement of mind, no one compelling, either for not losing or for obtaining something. . . . For every one also who does a thing unwillingly is compelled, and every one who is compelled, if he does a thing, does it only unwillingly. It follows that he that is willing is free from compulsion, even if any one thinks himself compelled.[3]

One factor that is brought in to support this teaching is the punishment that is contingent on the use of this will. This appears repeatedly in Augustine's writings against Fortunatus:

> Evils have their being by the voluntary sin of the soul, to which God gave free will. Which free will if God had not given, there could be no just penal judgment, nor merit of righteous conduct, nor divine instruction to repent of sins, nor the forgiveness of sins itself which God has bestowed upon us through our Lord Jesus Christ. Because he who sins not voluntarily, sins not at all. This I suppose to be open and perspicuous to all.[4]

> I say it is not sin, if it be not committed by one's own will; hence also there is reward, because of our own will we do right. Or if he who sins unwillingly deserves punishment, he who unwillingly does well ought to deserve reward. But who doubts that reward is only bestowed upon him who does something of good will? From which we know that punishment also is inflicted upon him who does something of ill will.[5]

1. Ibid., 12.
2. Ibid., 10.
3. Ibid.
4. Augustine, *Against Fortunatus*, 2.20.
5. Ibid., 2.21.

From this, Augustine is able to distinguish between evil that is sin and caused by humans, and evil that is not sin, but the penalty for sin, which comes from God:

> For God made all things good, and ordered them well; but He did not make sin, and our voluntary sin is the only thing that is called evil. There is another kind of evil, which is the penalty of sin. Since therefore there are two kinds of evil, sin and the penalty of sin, sin does not pertain to God; the penalty of sin pertains to the avenger. For as God is good who constituted all things, so He is just in taking vengeance on sin. Since therefore all things are ordered in the best possible way, which seem to us now to be adverse, it has deservedly happened to fallen man who was unwilling to keep the law of God. For God gave free will to the rational soul which is in man. For thus it would have been possible to have merit, if we should be good voluntarily and not of necessity. Since therefore it behooves us to be good not of necessity but voluntarily, it behooved God to give to the soul free will. But to this soul obeying His laws, He subjected all things without adversity, so that the rest of the things that God made should serve it, if also the soul itself had willed to serve God. But if it should refuse to serve God, those things that served it should be converted into its punishment.[1]

There is one final point to be made in this section on sin, which comes from Augustine's work against Faustus. In this he indicates the effects of Adam's sin on all humanity, both in death and in the corruption of the human person:

> Thus we are informed by the sure Word of God of Adam's sin; and Scripture truly declares that in him all die, and that by him sin entered into the world, and death by sin. And our experience gives abundant evidence, that in punishment for this sin our body is corrupted, and weighs down the soul, and the clay tabernacle clogs the mind in its manifold activity; and we know that we can be freed from this punishment only by gracious interposition.
>
> By the old man the apostle simply means the old life, which is a life in sin, and is after the manner of Adam, of whom it is said, 'By one man sin entered into the world, and death by sin; and so death passed upon all men, in that all have sinned.' Thus the whole of this man, both the inner and the outer part, has become old because of sin, and liable to the punishment of mortality.[2]

---

1. Ibid., 1.15.
2. Augustine, *Against Faustus*, 22.78, 24.2. In 22.22 of this work, there is an extended engagement with a Manichean view of sin that removes responsibility from the human will by creating being of evil that is the root

Free Will

Once Augustine has established the purity of God, he focusses very closely on the role of human will in sin. It is therefore a natural progression to move onto discussing more widely what Augustine had to say in his early writings about free will. This task is made easier by the fact that Augustine wrote a book called *On Free Choice of the Will*, which is well worth a read in full. Extracts will be presented here to convey the thread of teaching on free will that runs through that work.

Augustine starts the book by looking at God and evil along similar lines to those seen above:

> We are accustomed to talk of two modes of evil in two senses: one when we say that someone has done an evil thing; the other, when something of evil has been suffered. . . . But if you know or believe that God is good, for it is not right to believe anything else, he does not do evil. Again, if we admit that God is just, for it is sacrilegious to deny this, there is a reward to the good and punishment for the evil. . . . For which reason if no one suffers unjust punishment, which it is necessary that we believe since we believe that divine providence rules this universe, God is the author of that second type of evil, but in no way of the first kind.[1]

The result is the cause of evil is the will: 'Nothing can come into being without an author. But if you ask what is the cause of that [evil], I cannot say; for there is not one cause, but each evil person is the cause of their own evil.'[2] Following this, there is an extended discussion of the root of all sins, which Augustine states is lust or desire. A good will is then defined as that 'by which we seek to live rightly and honourably and to come to the highest wisdom'.[3]

Augustine then makes a statement that shows how high an opinion of human will he has:

> Therefore you see that, as it seem, it is in the constitution of our will that we are able to enjoy or to be lacking in so great and such a true good. For what is so much in the will as that will itself? Indeed, whoever has a good will, that which he has is preferred more than all rule in the world and all desires of the flesh. But

---

of all sin. This is not quoted here due to issues of space and because it focuses more on Manichean teaching than Augustine's own ideas, but is worth a read if you wish to go into this subject more deeply.
1. Augustine, *On Free Choice of the Will*, 1.1.
2. Ibid.
3. Ibid., 1.12.

> whoever does not have it is certainly lacking in that thing which is more excellent than all the goods that are not in our power, which the will alone can give through itself.[1]

Human will decides what kind of life is lived:

> What therefore is the cause why we doubt, even if we were never wise before, that it is by the will that we merit and live a laudable and blessed life or a shameful and unhappy life?[2]

Again: 'Whoever wants to live rightly and honestly, if his will for this overcomes that for temporal goods, he achieves so great a thing with such ease that nothing else is needed to have that will but to will it.'[3] This first part of the book concludes:

> That which each man chooses to follow and to love is placed in nature of his will; and that the mind cannot be deposed from the place of dominance or from right ordering unless by the will. And it is clear no things themselves are responsible when they are used for evil, but those are blamed who use them for evil.[4]

The second part of the work considers whether it was right for God to give humans a free will that could lead to sin. It is written as a debate between Augustine and Evodius, a common structure that allowed writers to set up contrary positions to which they could reply. The second book begins with the following discussion:

> **Evodius:** Now, if it is possible, explain to me why God gave people free choice of the will: since if he had not accepted it, he would not be able to sin.
> **Augustine:** For now have you certainly understood that God gave to humans what you think ought not to have been given?
> **E:** As far as I was able to understand the discussion in the previous book, we both have freedom of will, and without it were not able to sin.
> **A:** I also remember that this became clear to us. But now I have asked whether you know this which we have and by which it is clear that we sin is given to us by God.[5]

The first stage of response to this from Augustine is that while free will gives us the capacity to sin, this was not why free will was given to us:

1. Ibid.
2. Ibid., 1.13.
3. Ibid.
4. Ibid., 1.16.
5. Ibid., 2.1.

8. Early Augustine

> For we must not believe that, because it is through that [free will] that we sin, God gave us for that reason. It is enough for our cause to know why it ought to have been given, since without that it would not be possible for a person to live rightly. That it was given for this can be understood since if anyone were to use it for sinning, he receives divine punishment. This would be unjust, if free will had been given not only in order that man might live rightly, but even that he might sin. For in what way can there be a just punishment for a person who used the will for that for which it was given? Now indeed when God punishes a sinner, what else does this seem to say to you unless, 'Why did you not use free will for that which I gave it, which is to act rightly'?[1]

A large section of book two is then taken up by discussions of the bodily sense, reason, wisdom and truth, all of which seek to show that good things can be given but could then be used for bad purposes. Free will is one example:

> If therefore we find in the good body anything that a man is able use wrongly, we cannot however say on that account that it should not have been given, since it was given for good; what is the wonder if there are certain goods in the soul which even if we are able to use the for that which is not right, yet because they are good were not able to given except by him from whom are all good things? For you see how great a good is lacking to a body that has no hands, but however the evils with hands uses them for cruel or shameful deeds. . . . Therefore just as you approve those goods in the body and, do not consider those who use these for evil, you praise him who gave these good things: in the same way for free will, without which no one is able to live rightly, it is right that this is good, and divinely given, and you should grant that those who use this for evil will be damned, rather than arguing that it ought not to have been given by he who gave it.[2]

There remains the question of why a will designed for good should ever turn to evil, to which Augustine responds that this is the result of an evil desire rising up in the will that can be resisted:

> But perhaps you may be asking, since the will is moved when it turns from an unchanging good to a mutable good, from where this motion exists; this is certainly evil, although the free will (without which it is not possible to live rightly) is numbered in the good. For if that motion, which is against the will of the Lord God, is without doubt a sin, surely we are able to say that God is the author

1. Ibid.
2. Ibid., 2.18.

of sin? Therefore this motion is not from God. Then where is it from? . . . However, since this defect is voluntary, it is placed within our power. For if you fear this, it is needful that you not desire it; but if you do not desire it, it will not exist. Therefore, what is more secure than to be in that life where it is not possible for something to happen to you if you do not want it to? But since a man who has fallen freely cannot in the same way freely rise, let us hold firmly with faith to the right hand of God, that is our Jesus Christ our Lord, which is stretched out to us from above.[1]

The task of book two is accomplished in upholding the good purpose of the will and the responsibility of a person for the wrong use of that will, as Evodius the student avows at the beginning of book three:

There is nothing my opinion is so firm and resolved on as that I have a will, that I move to the enjoyment of something; that of anything I say is mine, I find nothing more completely mine, if it is not my will by which I want or reject anything: On account of this, if I do anything evil through that, to whom can this be attributed if not to me? For since a good God made me, I can do no good if not by my will, from which it is quite clear it was rightly given by a good God. But the movement by which the will is turned this way and that, if it were not voluntary and within our power, a man could neither be praised when we seek higher things, nor blamed when seeking lower ones, twisted as if on a pivot; nor should anyone be admonished that they should neglect the temporal and reach for the eternal, and that they should not want to live in an evil way, but live well.[2]

This in turn leads Evodius to ask another question, this time about the God who created this will:

I am unspeakably moved to know in what way it is possible that, since God foreknows all future things, it is not also necessary that we sin. For whoever would say that something can happen than that which God foreknows, undertakes the most insane impiety in destroying the foreknowledge of God. On this account, if God foreknows that the first man will sin, which is necessarily conceded to me by anyone who admits God's foreknowledge of all future things; if therefore this is the case, I do not say that God should not have made him, for he made him good, and the sin of the him whom God made good cannot hurt God; on the contrary, he showed his goodness in that which he made, showing justice even in punishment and in freeing him by his mercy; Therefore I do not say that God should not have made him; but I do

1. Ibid., 2.20.
2. Ibid., 3.1.

8. Early Augustine

say this, that since he foreknew that he would sin, it was necessary that he did this, because God foreknew what would happen. Therefore how is there be free will where there is such inevitable necessity?[1]

Augustine clarifies the issues raised by the question:

> For certain this is what moves you, this makes you wonder, how it is not contradictory and repugnant that both God should foreknow all of the future, and we do not act necessarily, but sin voluntarily. For if God has foreknowledge, you say, when people sin, it is necessary that they sin: but if it is necessary, therefore there is no choice of the will in sin, but rather it is inevitable and a fixed necessity. This reasoning it seems you fear should not be confessed, since either God's foreknowledge of all future things is impiously negated, or if we are not able to reject this, we must say that sin is not voluntary but necessary.[2]

In creating a response, Augustine conducts a rather lengthy exercise into happiness, and the reasons why a person is happy. This demonstrates that the root of happiness is in God, and yet a person is not happy against their will because of this. He concludes this example:

> Although God foreknows our future will, it should not be concluded from that that we want anything involuntarily. For as regards blessedness, you said that you do not achieve this of yourself, as if I would deny it. But I say that, when you will to be blessed, this is not against your will, but on account of your future will. When therefore God foreknows that you will be blessed in the future, nothing can be other than what he foreknows or there would be no foreknowledge; not however, that we are forced to believe from this that you do not want a blessed future, which is most absurd and is a long way from the truth. But just as the foreknowledge of God does not take away from you the will for blessedness, when you begin to be blessed, since today it is certain of tomorrow's happiness; so even a will that is culpable, which will be in your future, is nonetheless a will, since God foreknew that it would be in the future.[3]

From this, Augustine seeks to establish the principle that foreknowledge does not entail coercion on God's part and thus his punishment remains just:

> God makes no one to sin, however he foreknows those who will sin through their own will. Why therefore does it seem that he is not just, since he did not force what he foreknew? For just as your memory of things does not make what happened occur; in the same

1. Ibid., 3.2.
2. Ibid., 3.3.
3. Ibid.

way the foreknowledge of God does not make happen what will be in the future. And just as you remember certain things that you have done, but have not done all the things that you remember, in the same way God foreknows all those things of which he is the author, but however he is not the author of all that he foreknows. For he is not evil author of these things, but he is the just punisher. From this now you can understand by what justice God punishes since, since he knows the future but does not make it: For if it is right should he ought not to exact punishment on sinners, because he foresees that they will sin, neither is it right that he ought to give rewards for right actions, since he foresaw nevertheless that they would act rightly. On the contrary, we should admit that it pertains to his foreknowledge that nothing should be hidden in the future, and that it pertains to his justice that sin, which is committed voluntarily, should not be unpunished by his judgement, just as it was not forced to be committed by his foreknowledge.[1]

It is the creation of a nature with a free will, even with the capacity to sin, that emphasises both the excellence and the perfection of creation:

> God did not withhold his great goodness in not making that creature, whom God foreknew would not only sin, but even remain in voluntary sin. . . therefore that create is more excellent who sins through his free will than he who does not sin because he does not have a free will.[2]

> It is not sin or unhappiness that is necessary to the perfection of the universe, but souls inasmuch as they are souls; these, if they will to sin, they sin; if they have sinned, they become unhappy. For if unhappiness continued after these sins had been taken away, or even preceded sin, it would rightly be said that the order and administration of the universe is deformed. Again, if there were sins and no unhappiness, then iniquity would violate order.[3]

Augustine is therefore arguing that God was right to create the best that he could, even if this involved the possibility of sin: 'He [God] did not make them so that they might sin, but that they might adorn the universe whether they willed to sin or whether they do not will to sin.'[4]

The last part of book three moves onto areas that affect how free a will is. The devil is briefly addressed, with a clarity that this is persuasive influence rather than control:

1. Ibid., 3.4.
2. Ibid., 3.5.
3. Ibid., 3.9.
4. Ibid., 3.11.

8. Early Augustine

> Neither was man denied the power of that devil, to whom he had made himself subject through evil persuasion. For it would be unjust if man were not dominated by the one who had captured him. . . . Those whom the devil has persuaded to persevere in unbelief he justly has as consorts in eternal damnation. In this way it was that the devil did not snatch away man by force, but caught him by persuasion.[1]

However, the effects of the sin of Adam are fundamental to the discussion, since ingrained sin leads to ignorance and difficulty that affect a person's ability to do what they ought:

> It should not be surprising that, because of his ignorance, man does not have free choice of will to choose what he should rightly do; or that in resisting the carnal habit, which is naturally increased by that violence that comes from his mortality, he sees that he ought to do right, and wants to, and yet is unable. For that is a most just penalty for sin that each loses that which he does not want to use well, when he could have it without difficult if he willed. This is why one who knows right and does not do it loses the knowledge of what is right; and he who does not do what is right, when he is able, loses the ability when he wills to do it. For there are truly two penalties for all sinful souls, ignorance and difficulty. From ignorance, error disgraces, from difficulty pain afflicts. But to approve false things as true, so one unwillingly errs, and the lack of power to resist lust because of the opposition and torments of the bondage of the flesh, these are not in the created nature of man, but are the penalties of the damned. But when we speak of the will that is free to do right, we speak of that natural will with which man was made.[2]

This results in a type of sin that is not purely generated by the will:

> For that which is not done right, and that which is not able to be done with a right will, these are called sins because they come from the origin of a free will . . . so we call sin not only that which is properly called sin, for it is committed by a free will and in knowledge; but even that which now must follow from the punishment of sin.[3]

Finally, Augustine writes about the inheritance of sin from Adam in a discussion of the soul, clarifying that he does not know where souls come from – whether they come from the parents or are immediately created.[4]

1. Ibid., 3.10.
2. Ibid., 3.18.
3. Ibid., 3.19.
4. Augustine discusses the various possibilities and the need to recognise that we do not know the source of the soul for sure in 3.21.

There is a certain affirmation of the communal nature of humankind in the good nature and the presence of evil:

> Then, if one soul was made, from which all human souls derive their birth, who is able to say that he has not sinned, when that first soul sinned? But if each soul is made individually in a birth, it is not wrong, rather it is most suitable and in order, that the evil earned by the former should be in the nature of the latter; and the good earned by the latter be in the nature of the former.[1]

The themes of ignorance and difficulty that were discussed above are also attributed to the sin of Adam, with a purpose held out that salvation is revealed through these effects:

> It pleased God, the most just ruler of the universe, that those who are from the first union be born with ignorance, difficult and mortality, since they were cast into sin and error and hardship and death; so that the justice of punishment might appear in the birth of people, and the mercy of liberation be seen in their progress.[2]

Even given this inheritance, Augustine does not want to leave a person helpless in sin, but instead allows for the will to be involved in continuing to sin or seeking release from this:

> Because this is the case, ignorance and difficulty will not be punishment of sin for souls being born, but warnings for advancement and for the beginning of perfection. . . . Because if the person is not willing to act, he will hold onto sins justly, since he has not put to good use the faculty which he received. For although he was born in ignorance and difficulty, he was not compelled by necessity to be permanently in that state in which it was born.[3]

Much of the rest of Augustine's early teaching on free will has already been highlighted in the section above on sin. There is clearly a strong emphasis on this continued element of humanity even in its fallen state:

> Thus, when rational souls fall away from God, although they possess the greatest amount of free-will, He ranks them in the lower grades of creation, where their proper place is. So they suffer misery by the divine judgment, while they are ranked suitably to their deserts.[4]

1. Ibid., 3.20.
2. Ibid.
3. Ibid.
4. Augustine, *Morals of Manicheans*, 7.

8. Early Augustine

Through this, we can see the context in which Augustine was writing in his experience of Manicheanism, which held to evil as an entity that severely restricted the nature of the human will and its freedom. In the changing context of his later writings, against the Donatists and Pelagians, we will see a shift in his emphasis on the human predicament.

Grace

Augustine does not teach against salvation by grace, nor the work of the Spirit in a person's life, but these themes are less to the fore in his books and so there is less to discuss in this chapter. The passage quoted here is from his work against Faustus and concentrates on the relationship between law and grace and the effects of this grace on the Christian identity.

The first element of teaching that should be noted is the presence of grace in the Old Testament, with indications that there was sufficient grace presence for the people of Israel to have resisted sins:

> If Cain had obeyed God when He said, 'Be content, for to thee shall be its reference, and thou shalt rule over it,' he would have referred his sin to himself, by taking the blame of it, and confessing it to God; and so assisted by supplies of grace, he would have ruled over his sin, instead of acting as the servant of sin in killing his innocent brother. So also the Jews, of whom all these things are a figure, if they had been content, instead of being turbulent, and had acknowledged the time of salvation through the pardon of sins by grace, and heard Christ saying, 'They that are whole need not a physician, but they that are sick; I came not to call the righteous, but sinners to repentance;' and, 'Every one that committeth sin is the servant of sin;' and, 'If the Son make you free, ye shall be free indeed' – they would in confession have referred their sin to themselves, saying to the Physician, as it is written in the Psalm, 'I said, Lord, be merciful to me; heal my soul, for I have sinned against Thee.' And being made free by the hope of grace, they would have ruled over sin as long as it continued in their mortal body.[1]

Later in the work, Augustine moves on to comparisons of law and grace, writing of the Spirit and the Letter, a theme he would return to in his later work. In this quote, we see Augustine interweaving the two together, although there is an emphasis on the efficient role that grace plays in comparison to the law:

---

1. Augustine, *Against Faustus*, 12.9.

> The true bride of Christ, whom thou hast the audacity to taunt with the stone tablets, knows the difference between the letter and the spirit, or in other words, between law and grace; and serving God no longer in the oldness of the letter, but in newness of spirit, she is not under the law, but under grace. . . . Not that the law is sin, though it cannot give life without grace, but rather increases the guilt; for 'where there is no law, there is no transgression.' The letter without the spirit, the law without grace, can only condemn. . . . So the letter when joined with the spirit, and the law when joined with grace, is no longer the letter and the law in the same sense as when by itself it kills by abounding sin. In this sense the law is even called the strength of sin, because its strict prohibitions increase the fatal pleasure of sin. . . . The bride of Christ, then, is dead to the law, that is, to sin, which abounds more from the prohibition of the law; for the law apart from grace commands, but does not enable. . . . The same law which was given by Moses becomes through Jesus Christ grace and truth; for the Spirit is joined to the letter, that the righteousness of the law might begin to be fulfilled, which when unfulfilled only added the guilt of transgression. . . . The law is always good: whether it hurts those who are destitute of grace, or benefits those who are filled with grace, itself is always good; as the sun is always good, for every creature of God is good, whether it hurts weak eyes or gladdens the sight of the healthy. Grace fits the mind for keeping the law, as health fits the eyes for seeing the sun. And as healthy eyes die not to the pleasure of seeing the sun, but to that painful effect of the rays which beat upon the eye so as to increase the darkness; so the mind, healed by the love of the spirit, dies not to the justice of the law, but to the guilt and transgression which followed on the law in the absence of grace.[1]

We thus see that grace is the basis of salvation, even in the giving of the law:

> The law itself, by being fulfilled, becomes grace and truth. Grace is the fulfilment of love, and truth is the accomplishment of the prophecies. And as both grace and truth are by Christ, it follows that He came not to destroy the law, but to fulfil it; not by supplying any defects in the law, but by obedience to what is written in the law.[2]

Later in the same book, Augustine writes of the effects of this grace on the Christian in the new identity that is attained as sons of God and members of the church, the bride of Christ:

1. Ibid., 15.8.
2. Ibid., 17.6.

> Again, when it is said that the Church is the sister of Christ, not by the mother but by the father, we learn the excellence of the relation, which is not of the temporary nature of earthly descent, but of divine grace, which is everlasting. By this grace we shall no longer be a race of mortals when we receive power to be called and to become sons of God. This grace we obtain not from the synagogue, which is the mother of Christ after the flesh, but from God the Father.[1]
>
> The other relationship, in which Christ and all the saints are brethren by divine grace and not by earthly consanguinity, or by the father and not by the mother, is more easily expressed in words, and more easily understood. For the same grace makes all the saints to be also brethren of one another; while in their society no one is the bridegroom of all the rest.[2]

There is little of note in this and perhaps the greatest lesson is how little explicit material there is in the early writings, given how important the concept of grace becomes in his later work.

Conclusion

Augustine, more than any other Early Church writer, is a difficult figure to approach through modern sources because of the volume of his work, the wide range of issues covered, and his conflicts with several different groups over a long period of time, all of which requires context. This makes a balanced presentation an incredibly difficult task. Augustine seems to encourage extreme responses from his readers, who love him or hate him, which means that reading Augustine himself, rather than through the eyes of others, is highly recommended. For those who want a basic introduction to the changing context in which Augustine worked, Henry Chadwick's *Augustine of Hippo: A Life* (Oxford: OUP, 2010) is a solid start by an excellent historian.

In terms of the original works, that most quoted in this chapter is *On Free Choice of the Will*, which is not freely available and the translations here are my own from the Latin in the *Patrologia Latina*. There is a recent edition by Peter King under the title *Augustine: On the Free Choice of the Will, On Grace and Free Choice, and Other Writings* (Cambridge: CUP, 2010). The remaining early works are available in Series 1, Volume 4 of the Nicene and Post-Nicene Fathers series,

1. Ibid., 22.39.
2. Ibid., 22.40.

which is available at www.ccel.org. This influential series, referenced in previous chapters, is rather strange in its presentation of Augustine's work, which is far from chronological in its order. A list by date can be found under the Augustine tab at www.augnet.org.

9.
Late Augustine

This chapter poses perhaps the greatest challenge in compiling these volumes, given the sheer amount of writing on these subjects by Augustine in the second phase of his Christian work. They are also highly influential teachings for the Western church, even in the present day. There is still a primary target for Augustine, but this has now shifted from the fatalist Manicheans, his former friends, to the Pelagians, grouped around the first influential British Christian who arrived in Rome around 400 CE. Pelagius, who taught a very high view of humanity and the will, and seems to have believed that a sinless life is theoretically possible because of the purity of humans at birth, supported by references to characters like Enoch in the Bible.[1] For Pelagius, grace is primarily, if not exclusively, an external aid to the human will, since this allows responsibility for sin and the response to salvation to be placed solely with humans against any sense of determinism.

It is in this context that Augustine writes strongly on the effects of Adam's original sin on the whole of humanity, sin in the corruption of the human person, and on the role of grace and the will in salvation in this changed identity. This chapter will begin, as others have done, by looking at the nature and effects of sin in humanity. It will then move on to free will and grace, recognising that the two are often intertwined. This can only provide an indicative, rather than an exhaustive, presentation of Augustine's work in these areas and the reader is, as always, encouraged to go back to the original books for a fuller investigation of Augustine's developing thought.

1. None of the works of Pelagius survive, so we do not know precisely what he taught, but Augustine does quote him at length in his responses. In addition, Pelagius was brought to trial for heresy, and the deliberations that took place at those trials are again used by Augustine to discuss Pelagius' teachings.

Sin

In looking at Augustine's later views on sin, we will begin with the nature of sin and what it constitutes before examining its origins in the human will, following the pattern of previous chapters. There is then more material on the role of Adam in sin and the effects of this on human nature, exemplified in Augustine's discussions of the position of infants and the significance of baptism. Moving further into Augustine's teachings, there is a question about degrees of sin and whether all sins should be considered the same, before finally a look at the effects of sin on humanity and the question, raised by Pelagius, of whether a sinless life is possible.

The clearest definitions of sin and evil come in *Enchiridion*, sometimes called *Faith, Hope and Love*. In the first quotation, Augustine uses an analogy from medicine to build his case that evil is the opposite, a privation, of the good that comes from God:

> For what is that which we call evil but the absence of good? In the bodies of animals, disease and wounds mean nothing but the absence of health; for when a cure is effected, that does not mean that the evils which were present – namely, the diseases and wounds – go away from the body and dwell elsewhere: they altogether cease to exist; for the wound or disease is not a substance, but a defect in the fleshly substance – the flesh itself being a substance, and therefore something good, of which those evils – that is, privations of the good which we call health – are accidents. Just in the same way, what are called vices in the soul are nothing but privations of natural good.[1]

A couple of chapters later, Augustine continues this argument by stating that all being is good, and therefore all evil is a detraction from being, a defect:

> Accordingly, there is nothing of what we call evil, if there be nothing good. But a good which is wholly without evil is a perfect good. A good, on the other hand, which contains evil is a faulty or imperfect good; and there can be no evil where there is no good. From all this we arrive at the curious result: that since every being, so far as it is a being, is good, when we say that a faulty being is an evil being, we just seem to say that what is good is evil, and that nothing but what is good can be evil, seeing that every being is good, and that no evil can exist except in a being.... Now, what is evil man but an evil being? for a man is a being. Now, if a man

---

1. Augustine, *Enchiridion*, 11.

is a good thing because he is a being, what is an evil man but an evil good? Yet, when we accurately distinguish these two things, we find that it is not because he is a man that he is an evil, or because he is wicked that he is a good; but that he is a good because he is a man, and an evil because he is wicked. Whoever, then, says, 'To be a man is an evil,' or, 'To be wicked is a good,' falls under the prophetic denunciation: 'Woe unto them that call evil good, and good evil!' For he condemns the work of God, which is the man, and praises the defect of man, which is the wickedness. Therefore every being, even if it be a defective one, in so far as it is a being is good, and in so far as it is defective is evil.[1]

In the first of these quotes, Augustine states that sin is not a substance, separating it from all that has been created by God. He makes the same point in other works:

> Since, then, we have already learnt that sin is not a substance, do we not consider, not to mention any other example, that not to eat is also not a substance? . . . In the same way sin is not a substance; but God is a substance, yea the height of substance and only true sustenance of the reasonable creature.[2]

> And I inquired what iniquity was, and ascertained it not to be a substance, but a perversion of the will, bent aside from Thee, O God, the Supreme Substance, towards these lower things, and casting out its bowels, and swelling outwardly.[3]

There are some passages that seek to clarify questions concerning what constitutes a sin. In *Enchiridion*, Augustine contrasts errors with sins, so when we mistake rough for smooth we are not sensing the truth, but we are not sinning:

> When, in the case of sensible objects themselves, we mistake rough for smooth, or bitter for sweet, or think that putrid matter has a good smell; or when we mistake the passing of a carriage for thunder; or mistake one man for another, the two being very much alike, as often happens in the case of twins (hence our great poet calls it 'a mistake pleasing to parents') – whether these, and other mistakes of this kind, ought to be called sins. . . . In the case of these and other false impressions of the same kind, we are indeed deceived, but our faith in God remains secure. We go astray, but we do not leave the way that leads us to Him. But yet these errors, though they are not sinful, are to be reckoned among the evils of

---

1. Ibid., 13.
2. Augustine, *On Nature and Grace*, 22.
3. Augustine, *Confessions*, 7.16.

> this life which is so far made subject to vanity, that we receive what is false as if it were true, reject what is true as if it were false, and cling to what is uncertain as if it were certain.[1]

Another area that Augustine looks at is ignorance and whether deeds committed in ignorance are sins. In the following two quotes, he argues that this is a sin, although there is slight mitigation in comparison with sins of weakness and unwillingness to know:

> There are two causes that lead to sin: either we do not yet know our duty, or we do not perform the duty that we know. The former is the sin of ignorance, the latter of weakness. . . . In the latter case we are not only sinners, for we are so even when we err through ignorance, but we are also transgressors of the law; for we leave undone what we know we ought to do, and we do what we know we ought not to do.[2]

> It is one thing to be ignorant, and another thing to be unwilling to know. . . . But even the ignorance, which is not theirs who refuse to know, but theirs who are, as it were, simply ignorant, does not so far excuse any one as to exempt him from the punishment of eternal fire, though his failure to believe has been the result of his not having at all heard what he should believe; but probably only so far as to mitigate his punishment.[3]

Finally in this regard, in his book *On Lying*, Augustine queries whether one is ever right to lie and thus avoids sinning in this respect. One example that he gives of a person being absolved is when something is done to them that would make them defiled or unclean:

> One must conclude then that the sins of others, be they what they may, those always excepted which defile him on whom they are committed, a man must not seek to avoid by sin of his own, either for himself or for any other, but rather he must put up with them, and suffer bravely; and if by no sins of his own he ought to avoid them, therefore not by a lie: but those which by being committed upon a man do make him unclean, these we are bound to avoid even by sinning ourselves; and for this reason those things are not to be called sins, which are done for the purpose of avoiding that uncleanness.[4]

1. Augustine, *Enchiridion*, 20-21.
2. Ibid., 81.
3. Augustine, *On Grace and Free Will*, 5.
4. Augustine, *On Lying*, 15. What constitutes defilement is stated by Augustine, but is rather disgusting and so is left out here. I recognise that for some this may prove a form of inspiration to go back to the original texts to see for themselves, and thus the aim of this book would be accomplished!

A last word on the nature of sin is a famous comparison from *On Rebuke and Grace* concerning the nature of humanity in this creation and the next, comparing Adam's ability not to sin with the inability to sin in the new creation:

> For the first man was able not to sin, was able not to die, was able not to forsake good. Are we to say that he who had such a free will could not sin? Or that he to whom it was said, 'If thou shalt sin thou shalt die by death,' could not die? Or that he could not forsake good, when he would forsake this by sinning, and so die? Therefore the first liberty of the will was *to be able not to sin*, the last will be much greater, *not to be able to sin;* the first immortality was to be able not to die, the last will be much greater, not to be able to die; the first was the power of perseverance, to be able not to forsake good – the last will be the felicity of perseverance, not to be able to forsake good.[1]

The next theme that will be examined is the origin of sin and here there is continuation with what has come before in removing responsibility from God and placing it firmly on the human will. As other writers had done, Augustine extends this defence to the fall of the angels: '[I]t is hard to believe that they were not all from the beginning on an equal footing, until these who are now evil did of their own will fall away from the light of goodness.'[2] 'Accordingly, He caused the devil (good by God's creation, wicked by his own will) to be cast down from his high position, and to become the mockery of His angels.'[3]

In his *Confessions*, Augustine narrates this origin of evil in man as one of the great struggles in his movement towards Christianity:

> And I directed my attention to discern what I now heard, that free will was the cause of our doing evil, and Thy righteous judgement of our suffering it. But I was unable clearly to discern it. So, then, trying to draw the eye of my mind from that pit, I was plunged again therein, and trying often, was as often plunged back again.[4]

The most consistent treatment of this theme comes in *The City of God*, which repeatedly returns to this idea. The following quote shows the essence of the problem as Augustine faces it, which is the fact that evil must come from a being inherently good:

1. Augustine, *On Rebuke and Grace*, 33.
2. Augustine, *City of God*, 11.13.
3. Ibid., 11.17.
4. Augustine, *Confessions*, 7.3.

> How, then, can a good thing be the efficient cause of an evil will? How, I say, can good be the cause of evil? For when the will abandons what is above itself, and turns to what is lower, it becomes evil – not because that is evil to which it turns, but because the turning itself is wicked. Therefore it is not an inferior thing which has made the will evil, but it is itself which has become so by wickedly and inordinately desiring an inferior thing. . . . However minutely we examine the case, therefore, we can discern nothing which caused the will of the one to be evil. For if we say that the man himself made his will evil, what was the man himself before his will was evil but a good nature created by God, the unchangeable good? Here are two men who, before the temptation, were alike in body and soul, and of whom one yielded to the tempter who persuaded him, while the other could not be persuaded to desire that lovely body which was equally before the eyes of both. Shall we say of the successfully tempted man that he corrupted his own will, since he was certainly good before his will became bad? Then, why did he do so? Was it because his will was a nature, or because it was made of nothing? We shall find that the latter is the case. For if a nature is the cause of an evil will, what else can we say than that evil arises from good or that good is the cause of evil? And how can it come to pass that a nature, good though mutable, should produce any evil – that is to say, should make the will itself wicked?[1]

As Augustine works through this issue, he is resolved that the origin of corruption lies in a first movement of the will:

> The good will, then, is the work of God; for God created him with it. But the first evil will, which preceded all man's evil acts, was rather a kind of falling away from the work of God to its own works than any positive work. And therefore the acts resulting were evil, not having God, but the will itself for their end; so that the will or the man himself, so far as his will is bad, was as it were the evil tree bringing forth evil fruit.[2]

He defends this position against a range of excuses that he has come across which might seem to absolve humans from responsibility. In his work on the Catechism, Augustine addresses both God's foreknowledge of sin and the role of the devil in temptation:

> Why, then, should God not make man, although He foreknew that he would sin, when He might crown him if he stood, and set him right if he fell, and help him if he rose, Himself being always and everywhere glorious in goodness, righteousness, and clemency?

---

1. Augustine, *City of God*, 12.6.
2. Ibid., 14.11.

9. Late Augustine

> ... For He who gave freedom of will to men, in order that they might worship God not of slavish necessity but with ingenuous inclination.... Consequently, neither did the devil in any manner harm God, whether in falling himself, or in seducing man to death; nor did man himself in any degree impair the truth, or power, or blessedness of His Maker, in that, when his partner was seduced by the devil, he of his own deliberate inclination consented unto her in the doing of that which God had forbidden.[1]

In *On Grace and Free Will*, Augustine writes of those who plead temptation or divine providence that they sin, but responding with quotations from the books of James and Ecclesiasticus, he concludes: 'Observe how very plainly is set before our view the free choice of the human will.'[2] One last case that Augustine notes is those who blame their actions on fate in the movement of the stars, of which idea Augustine is rather scornful:

> And some indeed, who are used to excuse their own sins, complain that they are driven to sin by fate, as though the stars had decreed this, and heaven had first sinned by decreeing such, in order that man should after sin by committing such, and thus had rather impute their sin to fortune: who think that all things are driven to and fro by chance accidents, and yet contend that this their wisdom and assertion is not of chance rashness, but of ascertained reason. What madness then is it, to lay to reason their discussions, and to make their actions subject to accidents![3]

While Adam's sin has been important to previous writers presented in this book, Augustine devotes greater attention to both the event of sin and the consequences that those previously studied. For Augustine, pride was the central cause of Adam's fall:

> Our first parents fell into open disobedience because already they were secretly corrupted; for the evil act had never been done had not an evil will preceded it. And what is the origin of our evil will but pride? For 'pride is the beginning of sin.' And what is pride but the craving for undue exaltation? And this is undue exaltation, when the soul abandons Him to whom it ought to cleave as its end, and becomes a kind of end to itself. This happens when it becomes its own satisfaction.... The devil, then, would not have ensnared man

---

1. Augustine, *On Catechising Beginners*, 18.
2. Augustine, *On Grace and Free Will*, 3. Ecclesiasticus is one of the books known as the Apocrypha, and would have been included in Augustine's edition of the Old Testament.
3. Augustine, *On Continence*, 14.

in the open and manifest sin of doing what God had forbidden, had man not already begun to live for himself. It was this that made him listen with pleasure to the words, 'Ye shall be as gods,' which they would much more readily have accomplished by obediently adhering to their supreme and true end than by proudly living to themselves. For created gods are gods not by virtue of what is in themselves, but by a participation of the true God. By craving to be more, man becomes less; and by aspiring to be self-sufficing, he fell away from Him who truly suffices him.[1]

The beginning of sin is not the sole importance of Adam for Augustine, since that which comes from Adam inherits the sin in some way through propagation. Thus humans do not simply replicate Adam's sin, but are born sinful:

> No doubt all they imitate Adam who by disobedience transgress the commandment of God; but he is one thing as an example to those who sin because they choose; and another thing as the progenitor of all who are born with sin.[2]

This idea is worked through more thoroughly in *The City of God*:

> But as man the parent is, such is man the offspring. In the first man, therefore, there existed the whole human nature, which was to be transmitted by the woman to posterity, when that conjugal union received the divine sentence of its own condemnation; and what man was made, not when created, but when he sinned and was punished, this he propagated, so far as the origin of sin and death are concerned. For neither by sin nor its punishment was he himself reduced to that infantine and helpless infirmity of body and mind which we see in children.... To this infantine imbecility the first man did not fall by his lawless presumption and just sentence; but human nature was in his person vitiated and altered to such an extent, that he suffered in his members the warring of disobedient lust, and became subject to the necessity of dying. And what he himself had become by sin and punishment, such he generated those whom he begot; that is to say, subject to sin and death.[3]

The result is a fundamental flaw in human nature from this time onwards:

> Man's nature, indeed, was created at first faultless and without any sin; but that nature of man in which every one is born from Adam, now wants the Physician, because it is not sound. All good

1. Augustine, *City of God*, 14.13.
2. Augustine, *On Merits and Forgiveness of Sins*, 1.10.
3. Augustine, *City of God*, 13.3.

qualities, no doubt, which it still possesses in its make, life, senses, intellect, it has of the Most High God, its Creator and Maker. But the flaw, which darkens and weakens all those natural goods, so that it has need of illumination and healing, it has not contracted from its blameless Creator – but from that original sin, which it committed by free will. Accordingly, criminal nature has its part in most righteous punishment.[1]

This leads to all coming under the same punishment as that prescribed for the first humans:

> Thence, after his sin, he was driven into exile, and by his sin the whole race of which he was the root was corrupted in him, and thereby subjected to the penalty of death. And so it happens that all descended from him, and from the woman who had led him into sin, and was condemned at the same time with him – being the offspring of carnal lust on which the same punishment of disobedience was visited – were tainted with the original sin, and were by it drawn through divers errors and sufferings into that last and endless punishment which they suffer in common with the fallen angels, their corrupters and masters, and the partakers of their doom.[2]

One result of Augustine's focus on Adam is a greater concentration on the nature and state of infants, with corresponding teaching on baptism. Whereas Gregory of Nyssa in *On Infants' Early Deaths* argues that they will see the resurrection, Augustine argues that they are under judgement. The title of one chapter in his book, *On the Merit and Forgiveness of Sins*, begins with the strange-sounding phrase 'Unbaptised Infants Damned, But Most Lightly'. This chapter states:

> It may therefore be correctly affirmed, that such infants as quit the body without being baptised will be involved in the mildest condemnation of all. That person, therefore, greatly deceives both himself and others, who teaches that they will not be involved in condemnation.[3]

This is confirmed in *The City of God*, in which Augustine argues that the whole human race was present in the first humans who sinned:

> For God, the author of natures, not of vices, created man upright; but man, being of his own will corrupted, and justly condemned, begot corrupted and condemned children. For we all were in that

---

1. Augustine, *On Nature and Grace*, 3.
2. Augustine, *Enchiridion*, 26.
3. Augustine, *On Merit and Forgiveness of Sins*, 1.21.

one man, since we all were that one man, who fell into sin by the woman who was made from him before the sin. For not yet was the particular form created and distributed to us, in which we as individuals were to live, but already the seminal nature was there from which we were to be propagated; and this being vitiated by sin, and bound by the chain of death, and justly condemned, man could not be born of man in any other state.[1]

The word that Augustine most often uses for this sinfulness and inclination to sin is 'concupiscence', which in its root Latin form indicates a desire. For Augustine, since the fall of Adam, the innate desires of humankind have been corrupted, with a change of state to one under judgement:

> Concupiscence, therefore, as the law of sin which remains in the members of this body of death, is born with infants. In baptised infants, it is deprived of guilt, is left for the struggle [of life], but pursues with no condemnation, such as die before the struggle. Unbaptised infants it implicates as guilty and as children of wrath, even if they die in infancy, draws into condemnation.[2]

It is this concupiscence and the presence of what is termed Original Sin, transmitted down from Adam, which is overcome for Augustine in the baptismal waters. Augustine writes in his *Confessions* about being disappointed that he was not baptised in childhood as his mother could not convince his father to allow it:

> How much better, then, had it been for me to have been cured at once; and then, by my own and my friends' diligence, my soul's restored health had been kept safe in Your keeping, who gavest it! Better, in truth. But how numerous and great waves of temptation appeared to hang over me after my childhood! These were foreseen by my mother; and she preferred that the unformed clay should be exposed to them rather than the image itself.[3]

The grace of baptism is thus seen as overcoming the guilt that is passed down from parents to children:

> You must not be surprised at what I have said, that although the law of sin remains with its concupiscence, the guilt thereof is done away through the grace of the sacrament. For as wicked deeds, and words, and thoughts have already passed away, and cease to exist, so far as regards the mere movements of the mind and the body, and yet their guilt remains after they have passed away and no longer exist,

---

1. Augustine, *City of God*, 13.14.
2. Augustine, *On Merits and Forgiveness of Sins*, 2.4.
3. Augustine, *Confessions*, 1.11.

> unless it be done away by the remission of sins; so, contrariwise, in this law of concupiscence, which is not yet done away but still remains, its guilt is done away, and continues no longer, since in baptism there takes place a full forgiveness of sins. Indeed, if a man were to quit this present life immediately after his baptism, there would be nothing at all left to hold him liable, inasmuch as all which held him is released.[1]

There is thus the union with Christ established in baptism that allows an infant to be saved:

> But what can be plainer than the many weighty testimonies of the divine declarations, which afford to us the clearest proof possible that without union with Christ there is no man who can attain to eternal life and salvation; and that no man can unjustly be damned – that is, separated from that life and salvation – by the judgement of God? The inevitable conclusion from these truths is this, that, as nothing else is effected when infants are baptised except that they are incorporated into the church, in other words, that they are united with the body and members of Christ, unless this benefit has been bestowed upon them, they are manifestly in danger of damnation. Damned, however, they could not be if they really had no sin. Now, since their tender age could not possibly have contracted sin in its own life, it remains for us, even if we are as yet unable to understand, at least to believe that infants inherit original sin.[2]

This does not mean that those who are baptised no longer sin, but that sins that separate the believer from God can and should be avoided. We are introduced to the idea of differing degrees of sins and a divide between sins that can be pardoned through prayer (venial sins) and those that separate a person from God (mortal sins):

> When ye have been baptised, hold fast a good life in the commandments of God, that ye may guard your Baptism even unto the end. I do not tell you that ye will live here without sin; but they are venial, without which this life is not. For the sake of all sins was Baptism provided; for the sake of light sins, without which we cannot be, was prayer provided. What hath the Prayer? 'Forgive us our debts, as we also forgive our debtors.' Once for all we have washing in Baptism, every day we have washing in prayer. Only, do not commit those things for which ye must needs be separated from Christ's body: which be far from you! For those whom ye have seen doing penance, have committed heinous things, either

1. Augustine, *On Merits and Forgiveness of Sins*, 2.46.
2. Ibid., 3.7.

> adulteries or some enormous crimes: for these they do penance. Because if theirs had been light sins, to blot out these daily prayer would suffice.[1]

These venial sins, 'which do not hinder the righteous man from the attainment of eternal life, and which are unavoidable in this life',[2] are to be confronted through prayer and through almsgiving in order to keep the Christian clean and moving towards perfection:

> He, however, is not unreasonably said to walk blamelessly, not who has already reached the end of his journey, but who is pressing on towards the end in a blameless manner, free from damnable sins, and at the same time not neglecting to cleanse by almsgiving such sins as are venial. For the way in which we walk, that is, the road by which we reach perfection, is cleansed by clean prayer. That, however, is a clean prayer in which we say in truth, 'Forgive us, as we ourselves forgive.' So that, as there is nothing censured when blame is not imputed, we may hold on our course to perfection without censure, in a word, blamelessly; and in this perfect state, when we arrive at it at last, we shall find that there is absolutely nothing which requires cleansing by forgiveness.[3]

Augustine appeals to Scripture for a demonstration of what constitutes a venial or a mortal sin:

> Now, what sins are trivial and what heinous is not a matter to be decided by man's judgement, but by the judgement of God. For it is plain that the Apostles themselves have given an indulgence in the case of certain sins.[4]

But the fact that such a distinction in sins can be discerned should not lead these venial sins to be treated lightly, and some seem to have sought to excuse themselves and even to deny that their deeds were truly sinful, which Augustine condemns:

> But in all our doings, even good men are very greatly embarrassed in the matter of compensative sins; so that these are not esteemed to be sins, if they have such causes for the which they be done, and in the which it may seem to be rather sin, if they be left undone. And chiefly as concerning lies hath it come to this pass in the opinion of men that those lies are not accounted sins, nay rather are believed to be rightly done, when one tells a lie for the benefit of him for whom it is expedient to be deceived, or lest a person

1. Augustine, *On the Creed*, 15.
2. Augustine, *Spirit and the Letter*, 48.
3. Augustine, *On Perfection in Righteousness*, Chapter 9.
4. Augustine, *Enchiridion*, 78.

> should hurt others, who seems likely to hurt unless he be got rid of by lies. In defense of these kinds of lies, very many examples from holy Scripture are accounted to lend their support.[1]

Augustine also warns against those who become accustomed to these 'trivial' sins, which can become so commonplace as to be acceptable even in public:

> Add to this, that sins, however great and detestable they may be, are looked upon as trivial, or as not sins at all, when men get accustomed to them; and so far does this go, that such sins are not only not concealed, but are boasted of, and published far and wide. . . . And so in our own times: many forms of sin, though not just the same as those of Sodom and Gomorrah, are now so openly and habitually practised, that not only dare we not excommunicate a layman, we dare not even degrade a clergyman, for the commission of them.[2]

We must also consider the current state of humankind under sin. While the devil was not responsible for sin, there is now a power that he possesses as a result of that sin:

> By the justice of God in some sense, the human race was delivered into the power of the devil; the sin of the first man passing over originally into all of both sexes in their birth through conjugal union, and the debt of our first parents binding their whole posterity. . . . And therefore all men are originally under the prince of the power of the air. . . . But the way in which man was thus delivered into the power of the devil, ought not to be so understood as if God did this, or commanded it to be done; but that He only permitted it, yet that justly. For when He abandoned the sinner, the author of the sin immediately entered.[3]

The situation of Christians, in whom the power of concupiscence has been broken by baptism, has now changed to the extent that it is wrong to call the temptations they face 'sin':

> Now this concupiscence, this law of sin which dwells in our members, to which the law of righteousness forbids allegiance, saying in the words of the apostle, 'Let not sin, therefore, reign in your mortal body, that ye should obey it in the lusts thereof; neither yield ye your members as instruments of unrighteousness unto sin:' – this concupiscence, I say, which is cleansed only by the sacrament of regeneration, does undoubtedly, by means of natural

1. Augustine, *Against Lying*, 23.
2. Augustine, *Enchiridion*, 80.
3. Augustine, *On the Trinity*, 13.12.

> birth, pass on the bond of sin to a man's posterity, unless they are themselves loosed from it by regeneration. In the case, however, of the regenerate, concupiscence is not itself sin any longer, whenever they do not consent to it for illicit works, and when the members are not applied by the presiding mind to perpetrate such deeds. So that, if what is enjoined in one passage, 'Thou shalt not covet,' is not kept, that at any rate is observed which is commanded in another place, 'Thou shalt not go after thy concupiscences.' Inasmuch, however, as by a certain manner of speech it is called sin, since it arose from sin, and, when it has the upper hand, produces sin, the guilt of it prevails in the natural man; but this guilt, by Christ's grace through the remission of all sins, is not suffered to prevail in the regenerate man, if he does not yield obedience to it whenever it urges him to the commission of evil. As arising from sin, it is, I say, called sin, although in the regenerate it is not actually sin.[1]

Given the changed situation of creation and humankind, there remains the question of God's purpose in allowing sin. Augustine writes about both God's design in creation and the glory of his mercy that the fall of humanity allowed to shine:

> Thus, then, matters stood. The whole mass of the human race was under condemnation, was lying steeped and wallowing in misery, and was being tossed from one form of evil to another, and, having joined the faction of the fallen angels, was paying the well-merited penalty of that impious rebellion. For whatever the wicked freely do through blind and unbridled lust, and whatever they suffer against their will in the way of open punishment, this all evidently pertains to the just wrath of God. But the goodness of the Creator never fails either to supply life and vital power to the wicked angels (without which their existence would soon come to an end); or, in the case of mankind, who spring from a condemned and corrupt stock, to impart form and life to their seed, to fashion their members, and through the various seasons of their life, and in the different parts of the earth, to quicken their senses, and bestow upon them the nourishment they need. For He judged it better to bring good out of evil, than not to permit any evil to exist. And if He had determined that in the case of men, as in the case of the fallen angels, there should be no restoration to happiness, would it not have been quite just, that the being who rebelled against God, who in the abuse of his freedom spurned and transgressed the command of his Creator when he could so easily have kept it, who defaced in himself the image of his Creator by stubbornly turning away from His light, who by an evil use of his free-will broke away from his wholesome bondage to the Creator's

---

1. Augustine, *On Marriage*, 25.

laws – would it not have been just that such a being should have been wholly and to all eternity deserted by God, and left to suffer the everlasting punishment he had so richly earned? Certainly so God would have done, had He been only just and not also merciful, and had He not designed that His unmerited mercy should shine forth the more brightly in contrast with the unworthiness of its objects.[1]

The final issue that needs addressing in Augustine's later writing on sin concerns the question of whether a sinless life is possible. This was one of the main tenets of Pelagian teachings and thus receives due consideration by Augustine. Different answers can be found in Augustine's writings, although all tend ultimately towards the inability of achieving a sinless perfection. The closest Augustine comes to allowing a possibility is in *On Merit and the Forgiveness of Sins*:

> I should allow the possibility, through the grace of God and the man's own free will; not doubting that the free will itself is ascribable to God's grace, in other words, to the gifts of God – not only as to its existence, but also as to its being good, that is, to its conversion to doing the commandments of God. Thus it is that God's grace not only shows what ought to be done, but also helps to the possibility of doing what it shows.... [There follows examples of commandments to follow God's laws.] From these and many other like testimonies, I cannot doubt that God has laid no impossible command on man; and that, by God's aid and help, nothing is impossible, by which is wrought what He commands. In this way may a man, if he pleases, be without sin by the assistance of God.

Having allowed this theoretical possibility, Augustine goes on to state that this is not accomplished, and considers why this is so:

> Since by divine grace assisting the human will, man may possibly exist in this life without sin, why does he not? To this question I might very easily and truthfully answer: Because men are unwilling. But if I am asked why they are unwilling, we are drawn into a lengthy statement. And yet, without prejudice to a more careful examination, I may briefly say this much: Men are unwilling to do what is right, either because what is right is unknown to them, or because it is unpleasant to them. For we desire a thing more ardently in proportion to the certainty of our knowledge of its goodness, and the warmth of our delight in it. Ignorance, therefore, and infirmity are faults which impede the will from moving either for doing a good work, or for refraining from an evil one. But that what was hidden may come to light, and what was unpleasant may be made agreeable, is of the grace of God which helps the wills of men; and

1. Augustine, *Enchiridion*, 27.

> that they are not helped by it, has its cause likewise in themselves, not in God, whether they be predestinated to condemnation, on account of the iniquity of their pride, or whether they are to be judged and disciplined contrary to their very pride, if they are children of mercy.[1]

Elsewhere he states that a claim to perfection directly contradicts what we find in Scripture:

> He, moreover, who says that any man, after he has received remission of sins, has ever lived in this body, or still is living, so righteously as to have no sin at all, he contradicts the Apostle John, who declares that 'If we say we have no sin, we deceive ourselves, and the truth is not in us'.[2]

In *On Nature and Grace*, there is a more humble approach taken, whilst upholding the unlikelihood of someone achieving perfect righteousness:

> I do not much care about expressing a definite opinion on the question, whether in the present life there ever have been, or now are, or ever can be, any persons who have had, or are having, or are to have, the love of God so perfectly as to admit of no addition to it (for nothing short of this amounts to a most true, full, and perfect righteousness). For I ought not too sharply to contend as to when, or where, or in whom is done that which I confess and maintain can be done by the will of man, aided by the grace of God. Nor do I indeed contend about the actual possibility, forasmuch as the possibility under dispute advances with the realisation in the saints, their human will being healed and helped.[3]

There is one exception that Augustine provides in this work that relates to much of what we have read so far in this chapter, and this is Mary, the mother of Jesus:

> We must except the holy Virgin Mary, concerning whom I wish to raise no question when it touches the subject of sins, out of honour to the Lord; for from Him we know what abundance of grace for overcoming sin in every particular was conferred upon her who had the merit to conceive and bear Him who undoubtedly had no sin.[4]

In these later writings, Augustine produces a deep doctrine of sin, examining its effects on human nature from conception onwards and concluding that humankind is left in a more fundamentally corrupt state than we have seen in the previous writers. This changes and complicates the resulting doctrines of grace and free will, as we will now see.

1. Ibid., 2.26.
2. Augustine, *On Perfection in Righteousness*, Chapter 21.
3. Augustine, *On Nature and Grace*, 49.
4. Ibid., 42.

Grace and Free Will

Because these two themes are so closely connected in the later work of Augustine, they will not be completely separated here. This presentation will begin by looking at the nature of human free will that results from the changed condition of fallen humanity, with reference to the question of whether the will is so restrained as to be subject to some form of necessity. We then switch to the necessity of grace in salvation, with references to grace in the Old Testament and baptism. This sets up the situation of the Christian and the interaction of grace and will in Augustine's writings, which are complex in the way that the two are interwoven. Finally, aspects of the work of grace in sanctification will be presented. It is noticeable that there is less on the gifts of grace, the charismata, so it does not appear in this chapter. This is perhaps a result of grace being more closely linked with Christ than with Spirit in Augustine's writings, when previous theologians often directly equated grace with the work of the Spirit.

Nature of the Human Will

We start with a brief look at the free will that Adam had, unaffected by sin with the capacity to continue in an upright state:

> Thus also He made man with free will; and although ignorant of his future fall, yet therefore happy, because he thought it was in his own power both not to die and not to become miserable. And if he had willed by his own free will to continue in this state of uprightness and freedom from sin, assuredly without any experience of death and of unhappiness he would have received by the merit of that continuance the fulness of blessing with which the holy angels also are blessed; that is, the impossibility of falling any more, and the knowledge of this with absolute certainty.[1]

Associated with this state was a grace that would support Adam if he had continued to will that which was right:

> The first man had not that grace by which he should never will to be evil; but assuredly he had that in which if he willed to abide he would never be evil, and without which, moreover, he could not by free will be good, but which, nevertheless, by free will he could forsake. God, therefore, did not will even him to be without His grace, which He left in his free will; because free will is sufficient for evil, but is too little for good, unless it is aided by Omnipotent Good. . . . Nor

1. Augustine, *On Rebuke and Grace*, 28.

was that, indeed, a small grace by which was demonstrated even the power of free will, because man was so assisted that without this assistance he could not continue in good, but could forsake this assistance if he would.[1]

Augustine still recognises elements of freedom in the will post-Fall, primarily in the laws that are given by God, as the following quotes from *On Grace and Free Will* show:

> Now He has revealed to us, through His Holy Scriptures, that there is in a man a free choice of will. But how He has revealed this I do not recount in human language, but in divine. There is, to begin with, the fact that God's precepts themselves would be of no use to a man unless he had free choice of will, so that by performing them he might obtain the promised rewards.
>
> Now wherever it is said, 'Do not do this,' and 'Do not do that,' and wherever there is any requirement in the divine admonitions for the work of the will to do anything, or to refrain from doing anything, there is at once a sufficient proof of free will. No man, therefore, when he sins, can in his heart blame God for it, but every man must impute the fault to himself. Nor does it detract at all from a man's own will when he performs any act in accordance with God. Indeed, a work is then to be pronounced a good one when a person does it willingly; then, too, may the reward of a good work be hoped for from Him concerning whom it is written, 'He shall reward every man according to his works.'[2]

Augustine recognises an objection to this freedom of the will in the idea that everything received by humankind comes from God. To this, Augustine responds that the fact of the gift does not necessitate a particular use of that gift:

> To yield our consent, indeed, to God's summons, or to withhold it, is (as I have said) the function of our own will. And this not only does not invalidate what is said, 'For what hast thou that thou didst not receive?' but it really confirms it. For the soul cannot receive and possess these gifts, which are here referred to, except by yielding its consent. And thus whatever it possesses, and whatever it receives, is from God; and yet the act of receiving and having belongs, of course, to the receiver and possessor.[3]

While there is freedom in the will, Augustine stresses that in the sinful state this freedom is used to sin, and one needs grace in order to do good:

1. Ibid., 31.
2. Augustine, *On Grace and Free Will*, 2, 4.
3. Augustine, *Spirit and the Letter*, 60.

9. Late Augustine

> Through sin freedom indeed perished, but it was that freedom which was in Paradise, to have a full righteousness with immortality; and it is on this account that human nature needs divine grace, since the Lord says, 'If the Son shall make you free, then shall ye be free indeed' – free of course to live well and righteously. For free will in the sinner up to this extent did not perish – that by it all sin, especially they who sin with delight and with love of sin; what they are pleased to do gives them pleasure. . . . They are not, then, free from righteousness except by the choice of the will, but they do not become free from sin save by the grace of the Saviour.[1]

On the same lines, Augustine writes elsewhere:

> There is, however, always within us a free will – but it is not always good; for it is either free from righteousness when it serves sin – and then it is evil – or else it is free from sin when it serves righteousness – and then it is good. But the grace of God is always good; and by it it comes to pass that a man is of a good will, though he was before of an evil one.[2]

The condition of sinful (unbaptised) humanity can be summarised as having a free will that is directed by concupiscence towards that which is sinful.

A final teaching on the nature of the will concerns humanity after the resurrection, when there shall be a new freedom of will that does not contain the ability to sin. In *The City of God*, Augustine writes:

> Neither are we to suppose that because sin shall have no power to delight them, free will must be withdrawn. It will, on the contrary, be all the more truly free, because set free from delight in sinning to take unfailing delight in not sinning. For the first freedom of will which man received when he was created upright consisted in an ability not to sin, but also in an ability to sin; whereas this last freedom of will shall be superior, inasmuch as it shall not be able to sin. This, indeed, shall not be a natural ability, but the gift of God. . . . Are we to say that God Himself is not free because He cannot sin? In that city, then, there shall be free will, one in all the citizens, and indivisible in each, delivered from all ill, filled with all good, enjoying indefeasibly the delights of eternal joys, oblivious of sins, oblivious of sufferings, and yet not so oblivious of its deliverance as to be ungrateful to its Deliverer.[3]

Likewise, in *Enchiridion*:

1. Augustine, *Against Two Letters of Pelagius*, 1.5.
2. Augustine, *On Grace and Free Will*, 31.
3. Augustine, *City of God*, 22.30.

> Now it was expedient that man should be at first so created, as to have it in his power both to will what was right and to will what was wrong; not without reward if he willed the former, and not without punishment if he willed the latter. But in the future life it shall not be in his power to will evil; and yet this will constitute no restriction on the freedom of his will. On the contrary, his will shall be much freer when it shall be wholly impossible for him to be the slave of sin. We should never think of blaming the will, or saying that it was no will, or that it was not to be called free, when we so desire happiness, that not only do we shrink from misery, but find it utterly impossible to do otherwise. As, then, the soul even now finds it impossible to desire unhappiness, so in future it shall be wholly impossible for it to desire sin.[1]

Necessity of Sinning

Given the current condition of humanity and Augustine's doctrine of concupiscence that fundamentally affects the human will, there is a question raised whether there is a necessity of sinning that could absolve humanity from responsibility. Augustine confronts this at length in *The City of God*, working with the concept of God's foreknowledge but not allowing the involvement of any determinism on God's part in respect to sin. Here are three lengthy quotations that show the seriousness with which Augustine treats the issue:

> Now, against the sacrilegious and impious darings of reason, we assert both that God knows all things before they come to pass, and that we do by our free will whatsoever we know and feel to be done by us only because we will it. But that all things come to pass by fate, we do not say; nay we affirm that nothing comes to pass by fate; for we demonstrate that the name of fate, as it is wont to be used by those who speak of fate, meaning thereby the position of the stars at the time of each one's conception or birth, is an unmeaning word, for astrology itself is a delusion. But an order of causes in which the highest efficiency is attributed to the will of God, we neither deny nor do we designate it by the name of fate. . . . But it does not follow that, though there is for God a certain order of all causes, there must therefore be nothing depending on the free exercise of our own wills, for our wills themselves are included in that order of causes which is certain to God, and is embraced by His foreknowledge, for human wills are also causes of human actions; and He who foreknew all the causes of things would certainly among those causes not have

---

1. Augustine, *Enchiridion*, 105.

been ignorant of our wills.... How, then, does an order of causes which is certain to the foreknowledge of God necessitate that there should be nothing which is dependent on our wills, when our wills themselves have a very important place in the order of causes?... For one who is not prescient of all future things is not God. Wherefore our wills also have just so much power as God willed and foreknew that they should have; and therefore whatever power they have, they have it within most certain limits; and whatever they are to do, they are most assuredly to do, for He whose foreknowledge is infallible foreknew that they would have the power to do it, and would do it.....[1]

Among those things which they wished not to be subject to necessity they placed our wills, knowing that they would not be free if subjected to necessity. For if that is to be called our necessity which is not in our power, but even though we be unwilling effects what it can effect – as, for instance, the necessity of death – it is manifest that our wills by which we live up-rightly or wickedly are not under such a necessity; for we do many things which, if we were not willing, we should certainly not do. This is primarily true of the act of willing itself – for if we will, it is; if we will not, it is not – for we should not will if we were unwilling. But if we define necessity to be that according to which we say that it is necessary that anything be of such or such a nature, or be done in such and such a manner, I know not why we should have any dread of that necessity taking away the freedom of our will. For we do not put the life of God or the foreknowledge of God under necessity if we should say that it is necessary that God should live forever, and foreknow all things.... So also, when we say that it is necessary that, when we will, we will by free choice, in so saying we both affirm what is true beyond doubt, and do not still subject our wills thereby to a necessity which destroys liberty. Our wills, therefore, *exist as wills*, and do themselves whatever we do by willing, and which would not be done if we were unwilling.....[2]

Therefore, whatsoever a man suffers contrary to his own will, he ought not to attribute to the will of men, or of angels, or of any created spirit, but rather to His will who gives power to wills. It is not the case, therefore, that because God foreknew what would be in the power of our wills, there is for that reason nothing in the power of our wills. For he who foreknew this did not foreknow nothing. Moreover, if He who foreknew what would be in the power of our wills did not foreknow nothing, but something, assuredly, even though He did foreknow, there is something in the power of our wills. Therefore we are by no means compelled, either, retaining the

1. Augustine, *City of God*, 3.9.
2. Ibid., 3.10.

> prescience of God, to take away the freedom of the will, or, retaining the freedom of the will, to deny that He is prescient of future things, which is impious. But we embrace both. We faithfully and sincerely confess both. . . . For a man does not therefore sin because God foreknew that he would sin. Nay, it cannot be doubted but that it is the man himself who sins when he does sin, because He, whose foreknowledge is infallible, foreknew not that fate, or fortune, or something else would sin, but that the man himself would sin, who, if he wills not, sins not. But if he shall not will to sin, even this did God foreknow.[1]

Augustine acknowledges that there is an age before which one is able to use one's will, but once this has been reached, the will is free in its use, albeit not free for good until it is receives grace:

> It is not, therefore, true, as some affirm that we say, and as that correspondent of yours ventures moreover to write, that 'all are forced into sin,' as if they were unwilling, 'by the necessity of their flesh'; but if they are already of the age to use the choice of their own mind, they are both retained in sin by their own will, and by their own will are hurried along from sin to sin. For even he who persuades and deceives does not act in them, except that they may commit sin by their will, either by ignorance of the truth or by delight in iniquity, or by both evils – as well of blindness as of weakness. But this will, which is free in evil things because it takes pleasure in evil, is not free in good things, for the reason that it has not been made free.[2]

There is an awareness of scriptural passages that would seem to constrain people's will in sin, most notably God's hardening of Pharaoh's heart, but also the action of God in stirring up the enemies of Israel to conquer the country. In both cases, Augustine argues that while God was active in these cases, he was not active against the respective wills but instead in line with what Pharaoh and the nations desired:

> Here it is shown that God stirs up enemies to devastate the countries which He adjudges deserving of such chastisement. Still, did these Philistines and Arabians invade the land of Judah to waste it with no will of their own? Or were their movements so directed by their own will that the Scripture lies which tells us that 'the Lord stirred up their spirit' to do all this? Both statements to be sure are true, because they both came by their own will, and yet the Lord stirred up their spirit; and this may also with equal truth be stated the other way: The Lord both stirred up their spirit, and yet they came of their own will. For the Almighty sets in motion even in the innermost

---

1. Ibid.
2. Augustine, *Against Two Letters of Pelagius*, 1.7.

> hearts of men the movement of their will, so that He does through their agency whatsoever He wishes to perform through them – even He who knows not how to will anything in unrighteousness.
>
> Nor should you take away from Pharaoh free will, because in several passages God says, 'I have hardened Pharaoh;' or, 'I have hardened or I will harden Pharaoh's heart;' for it does not by any means follow that Pharaoh did not, on this account, harden his own heart. For this, too, is said of him, after the removal of the fly-plague from the Egyptians, in these words of the Scripture: 'And Pharaoh hardened his heart at this time also; neither would he let the people go.' Thus it was that both God hardened him by His just judgement, and Pharaoh by his own free will.[1]

Augustine recognises this potential attack against his doctrine of humanity in being affected by concupiscence from conception, but seeks to respond by upholding the concept of a free will acting from a damaged state.

Salvation by Grace

The dominant teaching on grace by Augustine in his later works is on salvation, responding to teachings from the Pelagians which argued that the will is key and grace is external to the human person. This develops what we have already seen of the human predicament. The effects of concupiscence mean that a person cannot turn to good without a work of grace.

There is a direct contrast of the roles of grace, will and law, all of which will be developed through this section in the work *Proceedings Against Pelagius*:

> This grace is not dying nature, nor the slaying letter, but the vivifying spirit; for already did he possess nature with freedom of will, because he said: 'To will is present with me.' Nature, however, in a healthy condition and without a flaw, he did not possess. . . . Therefore it is not from the liberty of the human will, nor from the precepts of the law, that there comes deliverance from the body of this death; for both of these he had already – the one in his nature, the other in his learning; but all he wanted was the help of the grace of God, through Jesus Christ our Lord.[2]

The idea of the bondage of the will that grace frees is also present in *Enchiridion*, as Augustine writes:

1. Augustine, *On Grace and Free Will*, 42, 45.
2. Augustine, *Proceedings Against Pelagius*, 21.

After the fall, however, a more abundant exercise of God's mercy was required, because the will itself had to be freed from the bondage in which it was held by sin and death. And the will owes its freedom in no degree to itself, but solely to the grace of God which comes by faith in Jesus Christ.[1]

In *On Grace and Free Will*, Augustine stresses the gifting element of this salvation grace:

> The eternal life which is the recompense of a good life is the grace of God; moreover it is given gratuitously, even as that is given gratuitously to which it is given. But that to which it is given is solely and simply grace; this therefore is also that which is given to it, because it is its reward – grace is for grace, as if remuneration for righteousness; in order that it may be true, because it is true, that God 'shall reward every man according to his works'.[2]

Unsurprisingly, this salvific grace is consistently linked into the person of Jesus Christ, including writing on the grace involved in the Christ event:

> Now here the grace of God is displayed with the greatest power and clearness. For what merit had the human nature in the man Christ earned, that it should in this unparalleled way be taken up into the unity of the person of the only Son of God? . . . . Now wherefore was this unheard of glory conferred on human nature – a glory which, as there was no antecedent merit, was of course wholly of grace – except that here those who looked at the matter soberly and honestly might behold a clear manifestation of the power of God's free grace, and might understand that they are justified from their sins by the same grace which made the man Christ Jesus free from the possibility of sin? . . . For the Truth Himself, who was the only-begotten of the Father, not by grace, but by nature, by grace took our humanity upon Him, and so united it with His own person that He Himself became also the Son of man.[3]

The grace found in Christ is contrasted with the sin that comes from Adam, following the teaching of Paul in the book of Romans:

> While Adam produced sinners from his one sin, Christ has by His grace procured free forgiveness even for the sins which men have of their own accord added by actual transgression to the original sin in which they were born . . . still, even that sin alone which was originally derived unto men not only excludes from the kingdom of

---

1. Augustine, *Enchiridion*, 106.
2. Augustine, *On Grace and Free Will*, 20.
3. Augustine, *Enchiridion*, 36.

God, which infants are unable to enter (as they themselves allow), unless they have received the grace of Christ before they die, but also alienates from salvation and everlasting life, which cannot be anything else than the kingdom of God, to which fellowship with Christ alone introduces us.[1]

There is also a Trinitarian element given to the grace given in the Son:

> We see that many come to the Son because we see that many believe on Christ, but when and how they have heard this from the Father, and have learned, we see not. It is true that that grace is exceedingly secret, but who doubts that it is grace? This grace, therefore, which is hiddenly bestowed in human hearts by the Divine gift, is rejected by no hard heart, because it is given for the sake of first taking away the hardness of the heart. When, therefore, the Father is heard within, and teaches, so that a man comes to the Son, He takes away the heart of stone and gives a heart of flesh, as in the declaration of the prophet He has promised. Because He thus makes them children and vessels of mercy which He has prepared for glory.[2]

The next stage in salvation by grace is to deal with the idea of salvation by works. Augustine takes time to show that human will has chosen sin and therefore cannot achieve salvation through a person's own merits:

> But this part of the human race to which God has promised pardon and a share in His eternal kingdom, can they be restored through the merit of their own works? God forbid. For what good work can a lost man perform, except so far as he has been delivered from perdition? Can they do anything by the free determination of their own will? Again I say, God forbid. For it was by the evil use of his free-will that man destroyed both it and himself. For, as a man who kills himself must, of course, be alive when he kills himself, but after he has killed himself ceases to live, and cannot restore himself to life; so, when man by his own free-will sinned, then sin being victorious over him, the freedom of his will was lost. . . . And as it is certainly true, what kind of liberty, I ask, can the bond-slave possess, except when it pleases him to sin? For he is freely in bondage who does with pleasure the will of his master. Accordingly, he who is the servant of sin is free to sin. And hence he will not be free to do right, until, being freed from sin, he shall begin to be the servant of righteousness. And this is true liberty, for he has pleasure in the righteous deed; and it is at the same time a holy bondage, for he is obedient to the will of God. But whence comes this liberty to do right to the man who is in bondage and sold under sin, except he

---

1. Augustine, *On Merit and Forgiveness of Sins*, 1.14-15.
2. Augustine, *Predestination of the Saints*, 13.

be redeemed by Him who has said, 'If the Son shall make you free, ye shall be free indeed?' And before this redemption is wrought in a man, when he is not yet free to do what is right, how can he talk of the freedom of his will and his good works, except he be inflated by that foolish pride of boasting which the apostle restrains when he says, 'By grace are ye saved, through faith.'[1]

To support this point, Augustine appeals to the example of Paul in two separate works:

> And lest men should arrogate to themselves the merit of their own faith at least, not understanding that this too is the gift of God, this same apostle, who says in another place that he had 'obtained mercy of the Lord to be faithful,' here also adds: 'and that not of yourselves; it is the gift of God: not of works, lest any man should boast.' And lest it should be thought that good works will be wanting in those who believe, he adds further: 'For we are His workmanship, created in Christ Jesus unto good works, which God hath before ordained that we should walk in them.' We shall be made truly free, then, when God fashions us, that is, forms and creates us anew, not as men – for He has done that already – but as good men, which His grace is now doing, that we may be a new creation in Christ Jesus.[2]

> Accordingly Paul, who, although he was formerly called Saul, chose this new designation, for no other reason, as it seems to me, than because he would show himself *little* – the 'least of the Apostles,' – contends with much courage and earnestness against the proud and arrogant, and such as plume themselves on their own works, in order that he may commend the grace of God. This grace, indeed, appeared more obvious and manifest in his case, inasmuch as, while he was pursuing such vehement measures of persecution against the Church of God as made him worthy of the greatest punishment, he found mercy instead of condemnation, and instead of punishment obtained grace. Very properly, therefore, does he lift voice and hand in defence of grace, and care not for the envy either of those who understood not a subject too profound and abstruse for them, or of those who perversely misinterpreted his own sound words; whilst at the same time he unfalteringly preaches that gift of God, whereby alone salvation accrues to those who are the children of the promise, children of the divine goodness, children of grace and mercy, children of the new covenant.[3]

1. Augustine, *Enchiridion*, 30
2. Ibid., 31.
3. Augustine, *Spirit and the Letter*, 12.

9. Late Augustine

Augustine highlights the point that he is making by moving the discussion from adults to infants, allowing that the baptised children of believers can fail to obtain saving grace if some obstacle causes them to stumble:

> Men, however, may suppose that there are certain good deserts which they think are precedent to justification through God's grace; all the while failing to see, when they express such an opinion, that they do nothing else than deny grace. But, as I have already remarked, let them suppose what they like respecting the case of adults, in the case of infants, at any rate, the Pelagians find no means of answering the difficulty. For these in receiving grace have no will; from the influence of which they can pretend to any precedent merit. We see, moreover, how they cry and struggle when they are baptised, and feel the divine sacraments. Such conduct would, of course, be charged against them as a great impiety, if they already had free will in use; and notwithstanding this, grace cleaves to them even in their resisting struggles. But most certainly there is no prevenient merit, otherwise the grace would be no longer grace. Sometimes, too, this grace is bestowed upon the children of unbelievers, when they happen by some means or other to fall, by reason of God's secret providence, into the hands of pious persons; but, on the other hand, the children of believers fail to obtain grace, some hindrance occurring to prevent the approach of help to rescue them in their danger.[1]

One important element of saving grace for Augustine is the accompanying grace of perseverance. This allows a person to remain in a state of grace until death. It is linked to his ideas on predestination, which he almost equates with grace:

> Further, between grace and predestination there is only this difference, that predestination is the preparation for grace, while grace is the donation itself. . . . God's predestination of good is, as I have said, the preparation of grace; which grace is the effect of that predestination.[2]

The grace that saves not only brings a person back to God but keeps them for the remainder of their lives. Interestingly, this does not necessarily create any assurance, since Augustine states that the calling is never a certainty in life:

> From all which it is shown with sufficient clearness that the grace of God, which both begins a man's faith and which enables it to persevere unto the end, is not given according to our merits, but is given according to His own most secret and at the same time

---

1. Augustine, *On Grace and Free Will*, 44.
2. Augustine, *Predestination of the Saints*, 19.

most righteous, wise, and beneficent will; since those whom He predestinated, them He also called, with that calling of which it is said, 'The gifts and calling of God are without repentance.' To which calling there is no man that can be said by men with any certainty of affirmation to belong, until he has departed from this world; but in this life of man, which is a state of trial upon the earth, he who seems to stand must take heed lest he fall.[1]

Augustine makes a similar point in *On Rebuke and Grace*, holding that those who have this grace of perseverance will amend their behaviour when corrected, but they may deviate from the straight path:

> Whosoever, then, are made to differ from that original condemnation by such bounty of divine grace, there is no doubt but that for such it is provided that they should hear the Gospel, and when they hear they believe, and in the faith which worketh by love they persevere unto the end; and if, perchance, they deviate from the way, when they are rebuked they are amended and some of them, although they may not be rebuked by men, return into the path which they had left; and some who have received grace in any age whatever are withdrawn from the perils of this life by swiftness of death. For He worketh all these things in them who made them vessels of mercy, who also elected them in His Son before the foundation of the world by the election of grace: 'And if by grace, then is it no more of works, otherwise grace is no more grace.' For they were not so called as not to be elected, in respect of which it is said, 'For many are called but few are elected;' but because they were called according to the purpose, they are of a certainty also elected by the election, as it is said, of grace, not of any precedent merits of theirs, because to them grace is all merit.[2]

One final quote on grace and salvation concerns the effect of actions of the living on those who have died. Augustine acknowledges that there are some who have no need of help after death, and others for whom no amount of help would change their punishment, but there is a group in the between these two extremes:[3]

> Nor can it be denied that the souls of the dead are benefited by the piety of their living friends, who offer the sacrifice of the Mediator, or give alms in the church on their behalf. But these services are of advantage only to those who during their lives have earned such merit, that services of this kind can help them. For there is a manner of life which is neither so good as not to require these services after

1. Augustine, *On the Gift of Perseverance*, 33.
2. Augustine, *On Rebuke and Grace*, 13.
3. Augustine, *Enchiridion*, 110.

death, nor so bad that such services are of no avail after death; there is, on the other hand, a kind of life so good as not to require them; and again, one so bad that when life is over they render no help. Therefore, it is in this life that all the merit or demerit is acquired, which can either relieve or aggravate a man's sufferings after this life.

Nature of Grace

There are two aspects of grace that come under this sub-heading: the Old Testament and Grace, and Baptismal Grace. For the former, the dominant work of Augustine is his *The Spirit and the Letter*, which repeatedly contrasts salvation in the Old and New Testaments. One of his most famous quotes comes in this context, highlighting different approaches to salvation depicted in the two covenants:

> Accordingly, by the law of works, God says to us, Do what I command thee; but by the law of faith we say to God, Give me what Thou commandest. Now this is the reason why the law gives its command – to admonish us what faith ought to do, that is, that he to whom the command is given, if he is as yet unable to perform it, may know what to ask for; but if he has at once the ability, and complies with the command, he ought also to be aware from whose gift the ability comes. . . . Now, having duly considered and weighed all these circumstances and testimonies, we conclude that a man is not justified by the precepts of a holy life, but by faith in Jesus Christ – in a word, not by the law of works, but by the law of faith; not by the letter, but by the spirit; not by the merits of deeds, but by free grace.

A key aspect of the transition between the Testaments is that the grace of the New Testament is present in the Old: '[I]t is evident that the grace of God was promised to the New Testament even by the prophet, and that this grace was definitively announced to take this shape – God's laws were to be written in men's hearts.'[1] It is not so clearly revealed, however:

> This grace hid itself under a veil in the Old Testament, but it has been revealed in the New Testament according to the most perfectly ordered dispensation of the ages, forasmuch as God knew how to dispose all things. And perhaps it is a part of this hiding of grace, that in the Decalogue, which was given on Mount Sinai, only the portion which relates to the Sabbath was hidden under a prefiguring precept. The Sabbath is a day of sanctification; and it is not without significance that, among all the works which God accomplished, the first sound of sanctification was heard on the day when He rested

---

1. Augustine, *Spirit and Letter*, 49.

from all His labours. On this, indeed, we must not now enlarge. But at the same time I deem it to be enough for the point now in question, that it was not for nothing that the nation was commanded on that day to abstain from all servile work, by which sin is signified; but because not to commit sin belongs to sanctification, that is, to God's gift through the Holy Spirit. And this precept alone among the others, was placed in the law, which was written on the two tables of stone, in a prefiguring shadow, under which the Jews observe the Sabbath, that by this very circumstance it might be signified that it was then the time for concealing the grace, which had to be revealed in the New Testament by the death of Christ – the rending, as it were, of the veil.[1]

The law is therefore not evil in itself, but law and will are not sufficient to create life – this needs the life-giving Spirit to be at work in a person:

> Let no Christian then stray from this faith, which alone is the Christian one; nor let any one, when he has been made to feel ashamed to say that we become righteous through our own selves, without the grace of God working this in us. . . .For there is no doubt that, without His assisting grace, the law is 'the letter which killeth;' but when the life-giving spirit is present, the law causes that to be loved as written within, which it once caused to be feared as written without.[2]

> Nevertheless, it is not by that law that the ungodly are made righteous, but by grace; and this change is effected by the life-giving Spirit, without whom the letter kills. . . . The law was therefore given, in order that grace might be sought; grace was given, in order that the law might be fulfilled. Now it was not through any fault of its own that the law was not fulfilled, but by the fault of the carnal mind; and this fault was to be demonstrated by the law, and healed by grace.[3]

The result of this grace, then, is not the removal of a person from the law but a restoration of nature that is in line with what the law teaches:

> Nor ought it to disturb us that the apostle described them as doing that which is contained in the law '*by nature*' – not by the Spirit of God, not by faith, not by grace. For it is the Spirit of grace that does it, in order to restore in us the image of God, in which we were naturally created. Sin, indeed, is contrary to nature, and it is grace that heals it – on which account the prayer is offered to God, 'Be merciful unto me: heal my soul; for I have sinned against Thee.'

1. Ibid., 27.
2. Ibid., 32.
3. Ibid., 34.

9. Late Augustine

> Therefore it is by nature that men do the things which are contained in the law; for they who do not, fail to do so by reason of their sinful defect. In consequence of this sinfulness, the law of God is erased out of their hearts; and therefore, when, the sin being healed, it is written there, the prescriptions of the law are done '*by nature*' – not that by nature grace is denied, but rather by grace nature is repaired.[1]

Augustine states that there were people in Old Testament times who were examples of this grace in action so that the law was not death to them:

> Yet, notwithstanding this, although not even the law which Moses gave was able to liberate any man from the dominion of death, there were even then, too, at the time of the law, men of God who were not living under the terror and conviction and punishment of the law, but under the delight and healing and liberation of grace. . . . The Apostle Peter says, 'Why tempt ye God to put a yoke upon the neck of the disciples, which neither our fathers nor we were able to bear? But we believe that through the grace of the Lord Jesus Christ we shall be saved, even as they.' Now on what principle does he make this statement, if it be not because even they were saved through the grace of the Lord Jesus Christ, and not the law of Moses, from which comes not the cure, but only the knowledge of sin?[2]

A further element of Augustine's teaching on grace over and above the law concerns those who were not part of the people of Israel in the Old Testament, yet who were able to receive grace, with Job being the prime example:

> Wherefore if we read of any foreigner – that is, one neither born of Israel nor received by that people into the canon of the sacred books – having prophesied something about Christ, if it has come or shall come to our knowledge, we can refer to it over and above; not that this is necessary, even if wanting, but because it is not incongruous to believe that even in other nations there may have been men to whom this mystery was revealed, and who were also impelled to proclaim it, whether they were partakers of the same grace or had no experience of it, but were taught by bad angels, who, as we know, even confessed the present Christ, whom the Jews did not acknowledge. Nor do I think the Jews themselves dare contend that no one has belonged to God except the Israelites, since the increase of Israel began on the rejection of his elder brother. For in very deed there was no other people who were specially called the people of God; but they cannot deny that there have been certain men even of other nations who

---

1. Ibid., 47.
2. Augustine, *On Grace and Original Sin*, 2.29.

belonged, not by earthly but heavenly fellowship, to the true Israelites, the citizens of the country that is above. Because, if they deny this, they can be most easily confuted by the case of the holy and wonderful man Job.... And I doubt not it was divinely provided, that from this one case we might know that among other nations also there might be men pertaining to the spiritual Jerusalem who have lived according to God and have pleased Him. And it is not to be supposed that this was granted to any one, unless the one Mediator between God and men, the Man Christ Jesus, was divinely revealed to him; who was pre-announced to the saints of old as yet to come in the flesh, even as He is announced to us as having come, that the self-same faith through Him may lead all to God who are predestinated to be the city of God, the house of God, and the temple of God. But whatever prophecies concerning the grace of God through Christ Jesus are quoted, they may be thought to have been forged by the Christians.[1]

The second aspect in this section is Baptismal Grace, which was highlighted above in the section on sin. The life-giving power of this sacrament for Augustine is clear:

> Whence they, who are not liberated through grace ... because they did not receive, at the time when they were unable on account of youth to hear, that bath of regeneration, which they might have received and through which they might have been saved, are indeed justly condemned; because they are not without sin, either that which they have derived from their birth, or that which they have added from their own misconduct.[2]

We have focused so far on Augustine's two primary opponents in the context of sin, grace and free will: the Manicheans and the Pelagians. Augustine also confronted another group, the Donatists, who separated themselves from the mainline Catholic church during and after the great persecutions in the church in the late third and early fourth centuries. The main issue of division was how the church should treat those who renounced their faith in the persecutions and then sought to come back to the church when peace was established. While the Catholic church allowed for forgiveness and restoration, even allowing such people to become priests, the Donatists refused them re-entry into the church. This led to discussions about the nature of the sacraments and how they gain their efficacy.

Augustine's teaching, in line with the Catholic church's position, is that the grace of the sacraments is a work of God, with the priests acting as instruments. A sacrament received at the hands of a sinful man is thus

1. Augustine, *City of God*, 18.47.
2. Augustine, *On Nature and Grace*, 4.

9. Late Augustine

still effective because it is the Spirit that is at work: 'Wherefore God gives the sacrament of grace even through the hands of wicked men, but the grace itself only by Himself or through His saints.'[1] This works not only for those priests within the church who are wicked, but also for those who receive Christian baptism outside the church:

> It has already been said that the grace of baptism can be conferred outside the Catholic communion, just as it can be also there retained. But no one of the Donatists themselves denies that even apostates retain the grace of baptism; for when they return within the pale of the Church, and are converted through repentance, it is never given to them a second time, and so it is ruled that it never could have been lost. So those, too, who in the sacrilege of schism depart from the communion of the Church, certainly retain the grace of baptism, which they received before their departure, seeing that, in case of their return, it is not again conferred on them whence it is proved, that what they had received while within the unity of the Church, they could not have lost in their separation. But if it can be retained outside, why may it not also be given there?[2]

There is one group who are exempt from this need for baptism as a foundational step in their Christian faith: the martyrs for the faith who were not baptised, because they were killed before they had a chance to undergo this sacrament:

> For whatever unbaptised persons die confessing Christ, this confession is of the same efficacy for the remission of sins as if they were washed in the sacred font of baptism. . . . For those who have been baptised when they could no longer escape death, and have departed this life with all their sins blotted out have not equal merit with those who did not defer death, though it was in their power to do so, but preferred to end their life by confessing Christ, rather than by denying Him to secure an opportunity of baptism. And even had they denied Him under pressure of the fear of death, this too would have been forgiven them in that baptism, in which was remitted even the enormous wickedness of those who had slain Christ. But how abundant in these men must have been the grace of the Spirit, who breathes where He listeth, seeing that they so dearly loved Christ as to be unable to deny Him even in so sore an emergency, and with so sure a hope of pardon! Precious, therefore, is the death of the saints, to whom the grace of Christ has been applied with such gracious effects, that they do not hesitate to meet death themselves, if so be they might meet Him.[3]

1. Augustine, *On Baptism*, 5.21.
2. Ibid., 1.1.
3. Augustine, *City of God*, 13.7.

Grace and Free Will

It is slightly strange to have a subtitle with the same wording as the main title but we come now to the direct interaction of grace and will, and 'Free Will and Grace' seemed a rather awkward way of avoiding this repetition. There is a clarifying structure to the place of this thought provided in response to Pelagius in Augustine's work, *On Grace and Original Sin*, in which Augustine highlights Pelagius' teaching that while God gives the ability (*posse*) for an action, the will (*velle*) and deed (*esse*) are the responsibility of the person.

> In his system, he posits and distinguishes three faculties, by which he says God's commandments are fulfilled – *capacity, volition*, and *action*: meaning by 'capacity,' that by which a man is able to be righteous; by 'volition' that by which he wills to be righteous; by 'action,' that by which he actually is righteous. The first of these, the capacity, he allows to have been bestowed on us by the Creator of our nature; it is not in our power, and we possess it even against our will. The other two, however, the volition and the action, he asserts to be our own; and he assigns them to us so strictly as to contend that they proceed simply from ourselves. In short, according to his view, God's grace has nothing to do with assisting those two faculties which he will have to be altogether our own, the volition and the action, but that only which is not in our own power and comes to us from God, namely the capacity; as if the faculties which are our own, that is, the volition and the action, have such avail for declining evil and doing good, that they require no divine help, whereas that faculty which we have of God, that is to say, the capacity, is so weak, that it is always assisted by the aid of grace.[1]

The Pelagians allow for some assistance to the human will, but only through external instruction that teaches a person how to use the will rightly:

> They, however, must be resisted with the utmost ardor and vigor who suppose that without God's help, the mere power of the human will in itself, can either perfect righteousness, or advance steadily towards it; and when they begin to be hard pressed about their presumption in asserting that this result can be reached without the divine assistance, they check themselves, and do not venture to utter such an opinion, because they see how impious and insufferable it is. But they allege that such attainments are not made without God's help on this account, namely, because God both created man with the free choice of his will, and, by giving him commandments, teaches him, Himself,

1. Augustine, *On Grace and Original Sin*, 1.4.

> how man ought to live; and indeed assists him, in that He takes away his ignorance by instructing him in the knowledge of what he ought to avoid and to desire in his actions: and thus, by means of the free-will naturally implanted within him, he enters on the way which is pointed out to him, and by persevering in a just and pious course of life, deserves to attain to the blessedness of eternal life.[1]

In response to this, Augustine's later work allows the deed to remain a person's responsibility, but argues that the nature and intent of the will are fundamentally affected by sin and grace. Augustine shows the weakness he perceives in Pelagius' construct of will and grace in a direct response:

> Again, in the first book of his *Defence of the Freedom of the Will*, he says: 'But while we have within us a free will so strong and so stedfast against sinning, which our Maker has implanted in human nature generally, still, by His unspeakable goodness, we are further defended by His own daily help.' What need is there of such help, if free will is so strong and so stedfast against sinning? But here, as before, he would have it understood that the purpose of the alleged assistance is, that that may be more easily accomplished by grace which he nevertheless supposes may be effected, less easily, no doubt, but yet actually, without grace.[2]

The basis of Augustine's teachings against this view arise from his concept of the effect of sin and the resultant nature of the human will as that which tends only to evil:

> If, however, this help [sufficient grace to avoid sin] had been wanting, either to angel or to man when they were first made, since their nature was not made such that without the divine help it could abide if it would, they certainly would not have fallen by their own fault, because the help would have been wanting without which they could not continue. At the present time, however, to those to whom such assistance is wanting, it is the penalty of sin; but to those to whom it is given, it is given of grace, not of debt; and by so much the more is given through Jesus Christ our Lord to those to whom it has pleased God to give it, that not only we have that help without which we cannot continue even if we will, but, moreover, we have so great and such a help as to *will*. Because by this grace of God there is caused in us, in the reception of good and in the persevering hold of it, not only to be able to do what we will, but even to will to do what we are able.[3]

1. Augustine, *Spirit and the Letter*, 4.
2. Augustine, *On Grace and Original Sin*, 1.29.
3. Augustine, *Rebuke and Grace*, 32.

There is thus a flaw in humanity that makes it unable to avoid sin: '[N]ature (especially in that corrupt state from which we have become by nature "children of wrath") has too little determination of will to avoid sin, unless assisted and healed by God's grace through Jesus Christ our Lord.'[1] The work of grace is thus to allow the will to act as it ought, and Augustine thus is determined that his teaching incorporates the action of both grace and free will, in line with Scripture:

> Therefore, my dearly beloved, as we have now proved by our former testimonies from Holy Scripture that there is in man a free determination of will for living rightly and acting rightly; so now let us see what are the divine testimonies concerning the grace of God, without which we are not able to do any good thing . . . was it not to Timothy's free will that the apostle appealed, when he exhorted him in these words: 'Keep thyself continent'? He also explained the power of the will in this matter when He said, 'Having no necessity, but possessing power over his own will, to keep his virgin.' And yet 'all men do not receive this saying, except those to whom the power is given.' Now they to whom this is not given either are unwilling or do not fulfil what they will; whereas they to whom it is given so will as to accomplish what they will. In order, therefore, that this saying, which is not received by all men, may yet be received by some, there are both the gift of God and free will.[2]

There is thus an active role that a person takes, but not one that allows for boasting:

> And further, should any one be inclined to boast, not indeed of his works, but of the freedom of his will, as if the first merit belonged to him, this very liberty of good action being given to him as a reward he had earned, let him listen to this same preacher of grace, when he says: 'For it is God which worketh in you, both to will and to do of His own good pleasure;' and in another place: 'So, then, it is not of him that willeth, nor of him that runneth, but of God that showeth mercy.' Now as, undoubtedly, if a man is of the age to use his reason, he cannot believe, hope, love, unless he will to do so, nor obtain the prize of the high calling of God unless he voluntarily run for it. . . . Surely, if no Christian will dare to say this, 'It is not of God that showeth mercy, but of man that willeth,' lest he should openly contradict the apostle, it follows that the true interpretation of the saying, 'It is not of him that willeth, nor of him that runneth, but of God that showeth mercy,' is that the whole work belongs to God, who both makes the will of man

---

1. Augustine, *On Perfection*, 3.
2. Augustine, *On Grace and Free Will*, 7.

righteous, and thus prepares it for assistance, and assists it when it is prepared. For the man's righteousness of will precedes many of God's gifts, but not all; and it must itself be included among those which it does not precede.[1]

The first movements in the restoration of will are thus by the grace of God by the power of the Holy Spirit:

> We, however, on our side affirm that the human will is so divinely aided in the pursuit of righteousness, that (in addition to man's being created with a free-will, and in addition to the teaching by which he is instructed how he ought to live) he receives the Holy Ghost, by whom there is formed in his mind a delight in, and a love of, that supreme and unchangeable good which is God, even now while he is still 'walking by faith' and not yet 'by sight;' in order that by this gift to him of the earnest, as it were, of the free gift, he may conceive an ardent desire to cleave to his Maker, and may burn to enter upon the participation in that true light, that it may go well with him from Him to whom he owes his existence. A man's free-will, indeed, avails for nothing except to sin, if he knows not the way of truth; and even after his duty and his proper aim shall begin to become known to him, unless he also take delight in and feel a love for it, he neither does his duty, nor sets about it, nor lives rightly.[2]

This operative grace works on a will that is dead, then leads to a cooperative grace with the awakened will, allowing a person to grow the strength of their will:

> He, therefore, who wishes to do God's commandment, but is unable, already possesses a good will, but as yet a small and weak one; he will, however, become able when he shall have acquired a great and robust will. When the martyrs did the great commandments which they obeyed, they acted by a great will – that is, with great love. . . . Forasmuch as in beginning He works in us that we may have the will, and in perfecting works with us when we have the will. On which account the apostle says, 'I am confident of this very thing, that He which hath begun a good work in you will perform it until the day of Jesus Christ.' He operates, therefore, without us, in order that we may will; but when we will, and so will that we may act, He co-operates with us. We can, however, ourselves do nothing to effect good works of piety without Him either working that we may will, or co-working when we will. Now, concerning His working that we may will, it is said: 'It is God which worketh

1. Augustine, *Enchiridion*, 32.
2. Augustine, *Spirit and the Letter*, 5.

in you, even to will.' While of His co-working with us, when we will and act by willing, the apostle says, 'We know that in all things there is co-working for good to them that love God.'

When these concepts are understood, a person is able to assess whether they have yet received grace, since it is this gift that makes the task of following God's commandments enjoyable, rather than seeming difficult:

> In order, however, that this love may be possessed, even as far as it can possibly be possessed in the body of this death, the determination of will avails but little, unless it be helped by God's grace through our Lord Jesus Christ. For as it must again and again be stated, it is 'shed abroad in our hearts,' not by our own selves, but 'by the Holy Ghost which is given unto us.' And for no other reason does Holy Scripture insist on the truth that God's commandments are not grievous, than this, that the soul which finds them grievous may understand that it has not yet received those resources which make the Lord's commandments to be such as they are commended to us as being, even gentle and pleasant; and that it may pray with groaning of the will to obtain the gift of facility. . . .Neither, indeed, on the one hand, would any injunctions be laid upon us to keep them, if our own will had nothing to do in the matter; nor, on the other hand, would there be any room for prayer, if our will were alone sufficient. God's commandments, therefore, are commended to us as being not grievous, in order that he to whom they are grievous may understand that he has not as yet received the gift which removes their grievousness; and that he may not think that he is really performing them, when he so keeps them that they are grievous to him.[1]

At times, Augustine writes of the power of grace in ways that seem to override the human will: 'Now it is by this Spirit, and not by the strength of their own will, that they who are God's children are governed and led.'[2] In the section on sin, we saw Augustine argue that in Scriptural instances of God using evil deeds for good purposes, God was using their evil free decisions that were in line with his will. Elsewhere, similar texts are given a slightly different stress, creating a picture of a more controlling will of God:

> And, moreover, who will be so foolish and blasphemous as to say that God cannot change the evil wills of men, whichever, whenever, and wheresoever He chooses, and direct them to what is good? But

1. Augustine, *On Perfection*, Chapter 10.
2. Augustine, *Proceedings Against Pelagius*, 6.

> when He does this He does it of mercy; when He does it not, it is of justice that He does it not for 'He hath mercy on whom He will have mercy, and whom He will He hardeneth.'[1]

> From these statements of the inspired word, and from similar passages which it would take too long to quote in full, it is, I think, sufficiently clear that God works in the hearts of men to incline their wills whithersoever He wills, whether to good deeds according to His mercy, or to evil after their own deserts; His own judgement being sometimes manifest, sometimes secret, but always righteous.[2]

In commenting on the proceedings against Pelagius for heresy, Augustine is keen to encourage his readers towards a stronger view of God's action as a comfort for them in gaining a right will:

> For, unquestionably to be led is something more compulsory than to be ruled. He who is ruled at the same time does something himself – indeed, when ruled by God, it is with the express view that he should also act rightly; whereas the man who is led can hardly be understood to do any thing himself at all. And yet the Saviour's helpful grace is so much better than our own wills and desires, that the apostle does not hesitate to say: 'As many as are led by the Spirit of God, they are the sons of God.' And our free will can do nothing better for us than to submit itself to be led by Him who can do nothing amiss; and after doing this, not to doubt that it was helped to do it by Him of whom it is said in the psalm, 'He is my God, His mercy shall go before me.'[3]

Augustine frequently confronts the idea that his doctrines of sin and grace lead to the vanquishing of human free will:

> Do you not see how he does not say that God's grace is necessary to prevent us from sinning, but because we have sinned? . . . Now we do not, when we make mention of these things, take away freedom of will, but we preach the grace of God.[4]

And:

> If I were to propose to you the question how God the Father draws men to the Son, when He has left them to themselves in freedom of action, you would perhaps find it difficult of solution. For how does He draw them to Him if He leaves them to themselves, so that each should choose what he pleases? And yet both these facts are true;

1. Augustine, *Enchiridion*, 98.
2. Augustine, *On Grace and Free Will*, 43.
3. Augustine, *Proceedings Against Pelagius*, 5.
4. Augustine, *On Nature and Grace*, 36.

> but this is a truth which few have intellect enough to penetrate. As therefore it is possible that, after leaving men to themselves in free will, the Father should yet draw them to the Son, so is it also possible that those warnings which are given by the correction of the laws do not take away free will. . . . No one, therefore, takes away from you your free will. But I would urge you diligently to consider which you would rather choose – whether to live corrected in peace, or, by persevering in malice, to undergo real punishment under the false name of martyrdom.[1]

If Augustine is successful in conveying his thought, he establishes that humans with the aid of grace have their will freed rather than constrained:

> Do we then by grace make void free will? God forbid! Nay, rather we establish free will. For even as the law by faith, so free will by grace, is not made void, but established. For neither is the law fulfilled except by free will; but by the law is the knowledge of sin, by faith the acquisition of grace against sin, by grace the healing of the soul from the disease of sin, by the health of the soul freedom of will, by free will the love of righteousness, by love of righteousness the accomplishment of the law. Accordingly, as the law is not made void, but is established through faith, since faith procures grace whereby the law is fulfilled; so free will is not made void through grace, but is established, since grace cures the will whereby righteousness is freely loved. . . . If, therefore, they are the slaves of sin, why do they boast of free will? For by what a man is overcome, to the same is he delivered as a slave. But if they have been freed, why do they vaunt themselves as if it were by their own doing, and boast, as if they had not received?[2]

This is true even when God's action is recognised not only in the initial conversion of the will, but also in ongoing grace to direct a person to good:

> I think I have now discussed the point fully enough in opposition to those who vehemently oppose the grace of God, by which, however, the human will is not taken away, but changed from bad to good, and assisted when it is good. I think, too, that I have so discussed the subject, that it is not so much I myself as the inspired Scripture which has spoken to you, in the clearest testimonies of truth; and if this divine record be looked into carefully, it shows us that not only men's good wills, which God Himself converts from bad ones, and, when converted by Him, directs to good actions and to eternal life, but also those which follow the world are so entirely at the

1. Augustine, *Answer to Petilian*, 2.85.
2. Augustine, *Spirit and the Letter*, 52.

disposal of God, that He turns them whithersoever He wills, and whensoever He wills – to bestow kindness on some, and to heap punishment on others, as He Himself judges right by a counsel most secret to Himself, indeed, but beyond all doubt most righteous.[1]

Grace and Sanctification

Given how the human will is transformed from the limitations of concupiscence and sin into the freedom of following God through the operation of grace, it is unsurprising that grace is the key element in the Christian life and the process of sanctification. The freed human will is thus not left to itself once it has been awakened, but receives ongoing grace in life:

> Now the Lord Himself not only shows us what evil we should shun, and what good we should do, which is all that the letter of the law is able to effect; but He moreover helps us that we may shun evil and do good, which none can do without the Spirit of grace; and if this be wanting, the law comes in merely to make us guilty and to slay us. It is on this account that the apostle says, 'The letter killeth, but the Spirit giveth life.' He, then, who lawfully uses the law learns therein evil and good, and, not trusting in his own strength, flees to grace, by the help of which he may shun evil and do good. But who is there who flees to grace except when 'the steps of a man are ordered by the Lord, and He shall determine his way'? And thus also to desire the help of grace is the beginning of grace; of which, says he, 'And I said, Now I have begun; this is the change of the right hand of the Most High.' It is to be confessed, therefore, that we have free choice to do both evil and good; but in doing evil every one is free from righteousness and a servant of sin, while in doing good no one can be free, unless he have been made free by Him who said, 'If the Son shall make you free, then you shall be free indeed.'[2]

This grace comes from Christ through the Spirit:

> But besides this imitation, His grace works within us our illumination and justification, by that operation concerning which the same preacher of His [name] says: 'Neither is he that planteth anything, nor he that watereth, but God that giveth the increase.' For by this grace He engrafts into His body even baptised infants, who certainly have not yet become able to imitate any one. As therefore He, in whom all are made alive, besides offering Himself

1. Augustine, *On Grace and Free Will*, 41.
2. Augustine, *On Rebuke and Grace*, 2.

as an example of righteousness to those who imitate Him, gives also to those who believe on Him the hidden grace of His Spirit, which He secretly infuses even into infants.[1]

This could be misunderstood as the transformation into a purely passive person in the restored life, but Augustine writes more of a humble dependence in seeking a unity of spirit:

> Inasmuch, then, as strength is made perfect in weakness, whoever does not own himself to be weak, is not in the way to be perfected. This grace, however, by which strength is perfected in weakness, conducts all who are predestinated and called according to the divine purpose to the state of the highest perfection and glory. By such grace it is effected, not only that we discover what ought to be done, but also that we do what we have discovered – not only that we believe what ought to be loved, but also that we love what we have believed.
>
> Great indeed is the help of the grace of God, so that He turns our heart in whatever direction He pleases. But according to this writer's foolish opinion, however great the help may be, we deserve it all at the moment when, without any assistance beyond the liberty of our will, we hasten to the Lord, desire His guidance and direction, suspend our own will entirely on His, and by close adherence to Him become one spirit with Him.[2]

Augustine pictures a circle that starts with grace inspiring a Christian to pray for grace to accomplish God's will:

> But when we pray Him to give us His help to do and accomplish righteousness, what else do we pray for than that He would open what was hidden, and impart sweetness to that which gave no pleasure? For even this very duty of praying to Him we have learned by His grace, whereas before it was hidden; and by His grace have come to love it, whereas before it gave us no pleasure. . . . There ensued, however, out of the penalty which was justly due such a defect, that henceforth it became difficult to be obedient unto righteousness; and unless this defect were overcome by assisting grace, no one would turn to holiness; nor unless it were healed by efficient grace would any one enjoy the peace of righteousness. But whose grace is it that conquers and heals, but His to whom the prayer is directed.[3]

This ongoing grace of perseverance is necessary for a Christian to reach salvation, and Augustine is careful to warn against any presumption that would prevent a person from continuing to work through their salvation.

1. Augustine, *On Merit and Forgiveness of Sins*, 1.10.
2. Augustine, *On Grace and Original Sin*, 1.13, 1.24.
3. Augustine, *On Merit and Forgiveness of Sins*, 2.33.

The receipt of the grace of salvation is thus no guarantee for Augustine. He cites examples of some who lived in the faith without persevering grace, who therefore fell away from the faith, and thus a right fear is necessary to encourage the believer to continue seeking grace throughout the trials of life:

> For on account of the usefulness of this secrecy, lest, perchance, any one should be lifted up, but that all, even although they are running well, should fear, in that it is not known who may attain – on account of the usefulness of this secrecy, it must be believed that some of the children of perdition, who have not received the gift of perseverance to the end, begin to live in the faith which worketh by love, and live for some time faithfully and righteously, and afterwards fall away, and are not taken away from this life before this happens to them. If this had happened to none of these, men would have that very wholesome fear, by which the sin of presumption is kept down, only so long as until they should attain to the grace of Christ by which to live piously, and afterwards would for time to come be secure that they would never fall away from Him. And such presumption in this condition of trials is not fitting, where there is so great weakness, that security may engender pride. Finally, this also shall be the case; but it shall be at that time, in men also as it already is in the angels, when there cannot be any pride. Therefore the number of the saints, by God's grace predestinated to God's kingdom, with the gift of perseverance to the end bestowed on them, shall be guided thither in its completeness, and there shall be at length without end preserved in its fullest completeness, most blessed, the mercy of their Saviour still cleaving to them, whether in their conversion, in their conflict, or in their crown![1]

In addition to this, there are factors that help a Christian to trust the grace that they have received:

> Without God's grace no man can live rightly. But then, again, there are other helps, which render us assistance in such a way that we might in some other way effect the object to which they are ordinarily auxiliary in their absence.... The mass of the members of Christ, who are scattered abroad everywhere, being ignorant of the very profound and complicated contents of the law, are commended by the piety of simple faith and unfailing hope in God, and sincere love. Endowed with such gifts, they trust that by the grace of God they may be purged from their sins through our Lord Jesus Christ.[2]

1. Augustine, *On Rebuke and Grace*, 40.
2. Augustine, *Proceedings Against Pelagius*, 3.

Conclusion

The later works of Augustine, written in the context of different challenges and primarily influenced by the Pelagians, have a different approach to sin, grace compared to his earlier books. The developed doctrine of sin is key in this, working through what he sees as the ongoing effects of Adam's sin on human nature and particularly on free will. With a concept of concupiscence that allows free will to lead to sin without divine assistance, the doctrine of grace becomes far more influential in later Augustine than it had been in any of the earlier writers. This last phase of Augustine's work is the foundation for Western thought going forward.

Chadwick's biography mentioned in the previous chapter is again recommended as a background to Augustine's life and work. For access to the primary sources presented in this chapter, visit www.ccel.org, where you can access them for free in volumes 2-5 of the Nicene and Post-Nicene Fathers series.

Epilogue
After Augustine

It is not the purpose of this work to draw conclusions for the reader, but to encourage readers to engage with the range of sources that have been influential in the history of the church in the areas of sin, grace and free will. This is in order to broaden their approach to these themes, confirming the strength of traditions that have been passed on and expanding beyond these in recognising views that add to or even challenge what has been received. As such, this concluding chapter does not seek to synthesise that which has come before, but rather to add on thoughts from two later sources that show the continuance of thought in the Western tradition after Augustine.[1]

The two texts that will be briefly presented here are the Canons of the Second Council of Orange and John Erigena's *On Divine Predestination*. Both are indicative of the importance of Augustine's teachings for the church in its thought on grace and free will, but also show that succeeding generations were not wholly restricted by what they received from Augustine.

The Canons of the Council of Orange

The Second Council of Orange met in 529 CE on the occasion of the dedication of a new church built in the Gallic town. Fourteen bishops attended and the decisions that were made there sought to help the church respond to a teaching that was a revised version of that put forward by the Pelagians, and which was therefore called Semipelagianism.

The roots of Semipelagianism began during Augustine's lifetime. The essence of the movement was the attempt to find a middle ground between the perceived extremes of Pelagianism, in its absolute

1. The continuity of the Eastern tradition from the Greek Fathers was shown in those chapters in the voice of John of Damascus, a later writer with little discernible variance of thought from the earlier writers in the areas of sin, grace and free will.

affirmation of the role of the will, and developing Augustinianism, which was seen as denying any role to the will in its emphasis on grace. Original sin and the necessity of grace were upheld by adherents of this movement, but the first movement of grace and absolute predestination are questioned in terms of their universal application. At least two of Augustine's later works, *On Grace and Free Will* and *On Rebuke and Grace*, were written with an awareness of the development of this new teaching in mind, while *On the Predestination of the Saints* and *On the Grace of Perseverance* were more conciliatory, recognising that Augustine had taught similar ideas in these respects in his early writings.

The centre of Semipelagianism was in Southern France and its foremost proponent was Abbot John Cassian at St Victor in Marseilles. Cassian was educated in the East, and the influence of this tradition meant that he resisted the absolute corruption of the human will that Augustine put forward. Cassian and his followers were known as Massilians and were the most notable group of those arguing for a Semipelagian position. Despite Augustine's engagement with these ideas in his later works, Semipelagianism continued to influence the church throughout the fifth century – it is difficult to see that it was ever completely overcome – and the bishops meeting at Orange resolved on statements that responded to this more nuanced challenge to the teachings of the church.

The first two canons affirm the doctrine of Original Sin, which was not at the heart of the new controversy, although the first does refute the important belief 'that the freedom of the soul remains unimpaired',[1] which is foundational for all that follows. The changed condition of the human person is then stressed in a denial that the first movement can come from a person rather than from God, which was one of the key tenets of Semipelagianism:

> If anyone says that the grace of God can be conferred as a result of human prayer, but that it is not grace itself which makes us pray to God, he contradicts the prophet Isaiah, or the Apostle who says the same thing. . . .[2]

> If anyone maintains that God awaits our will to be cleansed from sin, but does not confess that even our will to be cleansed comes to us through the infusion and working of the Holy Spirit, he resists the Holy Spirit himself.[3]

1. Council of Orange, Canon 1.
2. Ibid., Canon 3.
3. Ibid., Canon 4.

Canons 5-8 continue to stress the initiative of God in salvation and baptism and the inability of the human will to turn of its own inclination to God in its sinful condition:

> If anyone says that not only the increase of faith but also its beginning and the very desire for faith, by which we believe in Him who justifies the ungodly and comes to the regeneration of holy baptism – if anyone says that this belongs to us by nature and not by a gift of grace, that is, by the inspiration of the Holy Spirit amending our will and turning it from unbelief to faith and from godlessness to godliness, it is proof that he is opposed to the teaching of the Apostles.[1]

> If anyone says that God has mercy upon us when, apart from his grace, we believe, will, desire, strive, labour, pray, watch, study, seek, ask, or knock, but does not confess that it is by the infusion and inspiration of the Holy Spirit within us that we have the faith, the will, or the strength to do all these things as we ought; or if anyone makes the assistance of grace depend on the humility or obedience of man and does not agree that it is a gift of grace itself that we are obedient and humble, he contradicts the Apostle.[2]

> If anyone affirms that we can form any right opinion or make any right choice which relates to the salvation of eternal life, as is expedient for us, or that we can be saved, that is, assent to the preaching of the Gospel through our natural powers without the illumination and inspiration of the Holy Spirit, who makes all men gladly assent to and believe in the truth, he is led astray by a heretical spirit.[3]

> If anyone maintains that some are able to come to the grace of baptism by mercy but others through free will, which has manifestly been corrupted in all those who have been born after the transgression of the first man, it is proof that he has no place in the true faith. For he denies that the free will of all men has been weakened through the sin of the first man, or at least holds that it has been affected in such a way that they have still the ability to seek the mystery of eternal salvation by themselves without the revelation of God.[4]

One can see in these affirmations the influence of Augustine in the effects of sin on the will of man and the necessity, not only for grace, but for a first movement of grace from God in salvation.

1. Ibid., Canon 5.
2. Ibid., Canon 6.
3. Ibid., Canon 7.
4. Ibid., Canon 8.

The following Canons go on to discuss the support that God gives with his grace, which 'is to be ever sought by the regenerate and converted also, so that they may be able to come to a successful end or persevere in good works'.[1] The key event in this regeneration is the work of grace in baptism, following Augustine's extensive teaching on that sacrament:

> The freedom of will that was destroyed in the first man can be restored only by the grace of baptism, for what is lost can be returned only by the one who was able to give it. . . . [2]

The Canons continue to emphasise the importance of grace in salvation and works, recognising that, 'Recompense is due to good works if they are performed; but grace, to which we have no claim, precedes them, to enable them to be done',[3] and affirming that

> a man can do no good without God. God does much that is good in a man that the man does not do; but a man does nothing good for which God is not responsible, so as to let him do it.[4]

The conclusion to the Council's statements reflects Augustine's stress on grace in salvation:

> And thus according to the passages of Holy Scripture quoted above or the interpretations of the ancient Fathers we must, under the blessing of God, preach and believe as follows. The sin of the first man has so impaired and weakened free will that no one thereafter can either love God as he ought or believe in God or do good for God's sake, unless the grace of divine mercy has preceded him. We therefore believe that the glorious faith which was given to Abel the righteous, and Noah, and Abraham, and Isaac, and Jacob, and to all the saints of old, and which the Apostle Paul commends in extolling them (Heb. 11), was not given through natural goodness as it was before to Adam, but was bestowed by the grace of God. And we know and also believe that even after the coming of our Lord this grace is not to be found in the free will of all who desire to be baptised, but is bestowed by the kindness of Christ.[5]

This conclusion also affirms Augustine's teaching concerning ongoing cooperative grace and the absolute removal of God from any responsibility for evil:

1. Ibid., Canon 10.
2. Ibid., Canon 13.
3. Ibid., Canon 18.
4. Ibid., Canon 20.
5. Ibid., Conclusion.

> According to the catholic faith we also believe that after grace has been received through baptism, all baptised persons have the ability and responsibility, if they desire to labour faithfully, to perform with the aid and cooperation of Christ what is of essential importance in regard to the salvation of their soul. We not only do not believe that any are foreordained to evil by the power of God, but even state with utter abhorrence that if there are those who want to believe so evil a thing, they are anathema.[1]

What would become known as Double Predestination – that God predestines both who will be saved and who will be damned – is therefore clearly rejected by the Council of Orange. The first movement of grace in both salvation and good works, however, is strongly affirmed against a view that seemed to allow for the impetus in these areas to be allowed in the human will.

The Council of Orange does not quote Augustine, but the influence of his teachings clearly comes through in the construction of these Canons in the refutation of Semipelagianism.

John Scottus Erigena

John the Scot is a rather veiled figure in terms of his personal life. He came from Ireland to France with a knowledge of the Greek language at least (possibly other Eastern languages as well) and was highly affected by Greek systems of thought as evidenced by his most notable work, *On the Division of Nature*. He arrived in the court of Charles the Bald, the grandson of Charlemagne, around 845 CE. Charlemagne's empire had allowed a minor renaissance in the ninth century, although Erigena's own education seems to have taken place before his arrival in Gaul.

The work presented here is Erigena's *On Divine Predestination*, a book he was commissioned to write in response to teachings by Gottschalk, a Saxon monk who had taught, based on Augustine, that God predestined people both for good and for bad, for which he was condemned by succeeding synods in 848 and 849. Although Erigena's book was written at the request of a senior churchman, Hincmar, to defend orthodox teaching, the work was itself condemned in 853 and 855. Its style in particular came in for attack, described as 'Irish porridge'.

Central to Erigena's argument in *On Divine Predestination* is a sense that Gottschalk misinterpreted Augustine in making God a part of time in the way that he teaches about predestination, since God is essentially

1. Ibid.

eternal. In addition, agreeing with Augustine's definition of sin as the absence of being, Erigena argues that God cannot predestine sin or punishment since no evil actually exists – it is the opposite of existence.

Erigena begins by stating the case against which he is working:

> As he [Gottschalk] states, the inevitable and effective cause of all the just is constituted in one predestination; similarly that of the impious in the other. Certainly one, as he says, is of the just, the other of the impious; this is so much the case that no one, unless by the immutable necessity of the one predestination, either comes to merit justice or his end, which is eternal life; neither is anyone, unless by a necessity of the other, compelled to fall into the punishment merited by his impiety, or into end of eternal torment.[1]

The response begins in the will of God, that is free in creating and therefore under no compulsion. That which is created is therefore completely good in the image of its maker, and its intention is likewise good: 'And whatever is clearly understood about the divine will, that also must necessarily be understood in the same way about his predestination.'[2]

This absolute, unchanging nature of God is contrasted with humanity, with a telling reference to Augustine's concept of grace in support: 'For a person who has used his own free choice for evil is not able to return to that which he deserted without labour unless he works diligently and with the gift of cooperating grace.'[3] Again, the perfection of God is stressed against any involvement with evil, which occurs when a rational creature, 'making use of his free will for evil, deserting his maker, is ruined by wanton desires for lower things, which are however from the creator.'[4] This same point is made in the next chapter:

> But God is the highest essence. Therefore he is the cause of all those things which are from him. Sin, death and misery are not from God. Therefore God is not the cause of them.... Therefore, neither God nor his predestination, which is that which he is, is able to be the cause of them.[5]

Erigena concludes that there can only be one predestination of God, since there can be no conflict in his absolute perfection. He then moves on to examine what this predestination means for salvation, highlighting the

1. Erigena, *On Divine Predestination*, 1.4.
2. Ibid., 2.1.
3. Ibid., 2.3.
4. Ibid., 2.4.
5. Ibid., 3.3.

Epilogue: After Augustine

two extreme positions that have come down to him from the Pelagians. He also discusses what might be termed a hyper-Augustinian position, although Erigena is not willing to allow that Augustine himself taught the doctrine that he is taking issue with:

> The Pelagian sect, indeed, commend freedom of choice in the rational nature so much that it is sufficient to achieve the perfect justification of humankind without the gift of grace. Those of the contrary sect confirm the gratuitous gift of grace so that, in operating alone in humans in contempt of all effort of free choice, it reaches to the height of justification in all the faithful. As it has been said, one therefore has contempt for the gift of grace, the other for the gift of free choice; both are equal in their impiety, but different in their thought.[1]

Using the language of Augustine, Erigena questions how grace that is necessary because of predestination can be considered a gift:

> For they are not gifts which are not of the will but of necessity, as is most noted by all who are wise and foolish; everything which is given is bestowed by the will of the giver and is received by the will of the one who accepting.[2]

Against the first extreme, Erigena argues strongly in defence of grace:

> For it is not possible that at the same time that there is the salvation of the world and not the grace of God. For if the world is not liberated by the grace of God, in what way will its salvation follow? But at the same time there is the possibility for the salvation of the world and the grace of God. If therefore there is the salvation of the world, it is necessary that there will be the grace of God.[3]

Against the second, Erigena appeals to the concept of justice:

> For there cannot be both a judgement of the world in the future and no free choice now. For by what justice is there future judgement if there is no free choice? At the same time, however, it is possible that there is both future judgement and free choice. If therefore there is future judgement of the world, it is necessary that there is free choice of the will. But it is impious to deny the just future judgement of the world. Therefore it is impious not to believe that free choice is a gift to humankind from God.[4]

1. Ibid., 4.1.
2. Ibid., 4.2.
3. Ibid., 4.3.
4. Ibid.

Erigena identifies his opponent Gottschalk creating a third position, equally problematic, that states the necessity of freedom for those predestined to evil and a necessity of grace in those who will be saved. Against this, Erigena constructs his own position:

> Indeed freedom is given to all people generally as a property of the will, but it is not in all but as much as, through the predestined gift of grace, they are prepared, helped, guarded, completed and crowned. But in none is it generally forced or captured by divine predestination, but it is impeded by both original and individual sin by the secret but right justice of God.[1]

There is a great deal of tension in this statement. Erigena works through the root of these quandaries in looking at the sin of Adam and its results:

> For although by sinning he lost the blessed life, he did not lose his substance, which is to be, to will, to know. . . . What therefore did the first man have before sin that he lost after sin? . . . If we say free will, therefore he lost his nature. But if reason teaches that that no nature can perish, we are prohibited from saying that free will was lost, which without doubt is substantial. For God did not create in man a captive will but a free will, which freedom remained after sin. . . . Or perhaps the strength and power of free will, by which alone he was able to keep the commands, if he had wanted, was lost by sin? And from this the strength and power of free will was not in the first man in his substance, but from the grace of the creator, which great gift he lost by an evil use of the free choice of the will. For he did not want to do what he could, which is to keep the commands; after sin he is not able to do this, even if we wants, if grace does not help.[2]

Erigena brings in the concept of foreknowledge at various points to clarify his views on predestination. He believes that all that is predestined is foreknown, but not all that is foreknown is predestined. In the latter category clearly comes the concept of sin:

> God by his foreknowledge foresees the future evil works of men, however he is not the one who does them. It is not believed that by his predestination he has predestined the future evil deeds of people, therefore in what way could he be thought to do them?[3]

It is interesting in terms of the legacy of Augustine that at this point Erigena quotes from *On Free Choice of the Will*, one of Augustine's early

1. Ibid., 4.4.
2. Ibid., 4.6.
3. Ibid., 5.1.

works, when it would be his later works that would ultimately be far more influential in the history of Christian thought.[1]

In chapter nine, Erigena takes up a new task regarding predestination and foreknowledge in God's relationship to time, which allows for a human that is not controlled by decisions made before by God since 'before' has no meaning in relation to God: 'Therefore it is concluded that foreknowledge and predestination are applied to God through a similitude to temporal things.'[2]

Erigena adds to this querying of predestination a question concerning the nature of evil, taking as his basis Augustine's definition of evil as the opposite of good, and therefore the opposite of being. From this, Erigena argues that any language of God predestining to evil must be understood 'from the contrary', a phrase that indicates that since sins do not actually have existence (being essentially non-existent), they are not things that God could know or predestine:

> Therefore everything that is evil is either sin or the punishment of sin. If no true reason allows God to foreknow these two, how great would one be who dares to say they are predestined, unless from a contrary perspective?[3] Why? Surely we can have no right thought about God, who alone is true essence, who made all things that exist to the amount that they exist, that he has foreknowledge or predestination of those things which are not himself nor are from him because they are nothing? For if there is no right knowledge unless of things that are, by what reason is there said to be knowledge or foreknowledge of these things that are not? In the same way, if predestination is nothing else, unless the preparation of those things which God foresaw would be made: in what way can God be said to predestine those things that he neither made nor prepared to be made?[4]

It is noticeable throughout Erigena's work how authoritative he considers Augustine for the faith of the church, yet because of his very different audience to either early or late Augustine, there is consequently a very different line of thought produced. Erigena's task is to refute

1. Erigena makes more use of Augustine's early works, particularly *On Free Choice of the Will*, than he does his later writings as the book progresses; more than half of chapter seven is taken up with quotations from this work.
2. Ibid., 9.7.
3. The idea of a contrary perspective is that in making and intending all things for good, God creates the conditions for the abuse of this goodness, which he does not cause.
4. Ibid., 10.3.

Gottschalk's idea of the predestination of the damned, which is seen as a theological novelty and the foundational points that he uses to build his case are the nature of evil as nothing (which is very similar to the line taken by Augustine) and the essential timelessness of God. This latter is also a concept found in Augustine, but Erigena proposes an alternative approach. He suggests that scriptural references to the predestination of evil must be understood metaphorically, since the non-existence of sin means it cannot have any relation to the being or knowledge of God.

Conclusion

These two texts show the fundamental significance of Augustine for the Western church as it developed in the medieval period. Erigena's work is particularly significant in this regard; written over four hundred years after Augustine's death, only Pope Gregory the Great and Isadore of Seville still receive minor recognition as authorities for Erigena's arguments. The different feats that the two works were trying to accomplish in taking on Semipelagianism and Gottschalk meant that the writers could not and did not simply repeat the same lines of thought that were found in Augustine but moulded the same principles to answer the issues they were addressing. In the second volume of this work, we will see the extent to which later writers felt able to follow the same approach in their new contexts.

The canons of the Council of Orange are available on many websites, one of which is www.ewtn.com/library/councils/orange.htm. The quotations here from John Erigena are my own translation from the Latin in the *Patrologia Latina*, while there is an excellent recent translation of the whole by Mary Brennan, published by the University of Notre Dame Press (Notre Dame, Indiana, 1998).

Final Thoughts

Growing up in any church tradition, one gets used to a culture that informs all that happens – worship, teaching, prayer, architecture – that can easily form a bubble around the believer that informs their faith and life. These practices are not 'wrong', but it is often hard to perceive where development has been driven by scriptural teachings (even in the case of this book, what scriptures have been the focus and which interpretive paradigm was used?) and what has been subtly informed by external cultural or philosophical trends. This is as true in the use of theological terms as in any other area of church life. Groups of Christians have become comfortable with certain meanings of sin, grace and free will without recognising that others, from the same biblical basis, understand these concepts very differently. This is particularly true of those living in very distant times or cultural settings.

Unfortunately, it has been my experience that discussions of sin, grace and free will can cause divisions between Christians and even judgement by one Christian of another in ways that are destructive both to the individual and to the church as a body. As I listen to such talk, my reaction now is to recognise strengths on both sides in their motivation, their use of certain parts of Scripture and their application in a given context. At the same time, there seem to be certain facets of scriptural teaching and Christian thought left unconsidered that might enrich each position.

This first part of the survey takes us back to the earliest Christian teachers who wrestled with the complex revelation of God in Scripture, Christ, Spirit and church, seeking to discern ways of communicating the Gospel and helping Christians to live well, in many cases before the canon of the New Testament or key Christian doctrines were agreed. At this time, the great desire of the writers was to be faithful to the Apostolic Tradition that they had received and to live an honourable Christian life in light of this.

One of the results of this that comes through in many of the writers looked at in this volume is the dynamism to their theology, while modern books often feel constrained in their use of language and in the faith experience to which people are called. It became apparent during my research how widely each of these areas can be comprehended and applied, which shows how limited my understanding has been and that there is much more to learn from the experience of the church through history.

In discussing sin, it is interesting to see how the writers engage with the theme across multiple dimensions – physical, spiritual, mental – whilst seeking to maintain a unity to the human person and their experience. Grace before Augustine is not treated systematically to any great extent, which means that research into its usage consistently challenges the reader by taking them into a range of areas of Christian thought. Where thought on these two subjects is often driven by direct references in Scripture, free will is more naturally a philosophical discussion, and yet it is integral to many aspects of theology. Coming from a twenty-first century perspective, when it has become apparent how easily this topic can lead to determinist or libertarian extremes, the subtlety and nuance of the presentations by many early sources are greatly appreciated.

Volume II will pick up the history of thought after several centuries during which it is difficult to discern much novelty or progress in these areas of thought. Starting with Anselm of Canterbury, that book will look through some of the foundational thinkers of the medieval period before moving on to the reformations and writings of the sixteenth century which have become foundational for many Christian denominations since. The aim again will be to acquaint readers with more of the treasures of the church with an encouragement to investigate these sources directly and gain an appreciation for the breadth and depth of thought in these key areas of the Christian faith.

Bibliography of Editions Used for This Book

'1 Clement' in A. Roberts and J. Donaldson (eds.), *Ante-Nicene Christian Library: Volume 1* (tr. A. Roberts, J. Donaldson and F. Crombie). Edinburgh: T&T Clark, 1867.
'2 Clement' in A. Roberts and J. Donaldson (eds.), *Ante-Nicene Christian Library: Volume 1* (tr. A. Roberts, J. Donaldson and F. Crombie). Edinburgh: T&T Clark, 1867.
'Epistle of Barnabas' in A. Roberts and J. Donaldson (eds.), *Ante-Nicene Christian Library: Volume 1* (tr. A. Roberts, J. Donaldson and F. Crombie). Edinburgh: T&T Clark, 1867.
'Martyrdom of Polycarp' in A. Roberts and J. Donaldson (eds.), *Ante-Nicene Christian Library: Volume 1* (tr. A. Roberts, J. Donaldson and F. Crombie). Edinburgh: T&T Clark, 1867.
'Pastor of Hermas' in A. Roberts and J. Donaldson (eds.), *Ante-Nicene Christian Library: Volume 1* (tr. A. Roberts, J. Donaldson and F. Crombie). Edinburgh: T&T Clark, 1867.
'The Didache' (tr. M. Riddle) in A. Roberts, J. Donaldson and A. Coxe (eds.), *Ante-Nicene Fathers Volume 7*. New York: Christian Literature Publishing Co., 1886.
Athanasius, 'On the Incarnation' in P. Schaff and H. Wace (eds.) *Nicene and Post-Nicene Fathers Second Series: Volume 4* (tr. A. Robertson). New York: Christian Literature Company, 1891.
——, 'Against the Heathen' in P. Schaff and H. Wace (eds.) *Nicene and Post-Nicene Fathers Second Series: Volume 4* (tr. A. Robertson). New York: Christian Literature Company, 1891.
——, 'Against the Arians' in P. Schaff and H. Wace (eds.) *Nicene and Post-Nicene Fathers Second Series: Volume 4* (tr. A. Robertson). New York: Christian Literature Company, 1891.
——, 'Circular to Bishops of Egypt and Libya' in P. Schaff and H. Wace (eds.) *Nicene and Post-Nicene Fathers Second Series: Volume 4* (tr. A. Robertson). New York: Christian Literature Company, 1891.
Augustine of Hippo, 'Reply to Faustus the Manichaean' in P. Schaff (ed.) *Nicene and Post-Nicene Fathers First Series: Volume 4* (tr. R. Stothert). New York: Christian Literature Company, 1887.

——, 'Concerning the Nature of Good, Against the Manichaeans' in P. Schaff (ed.) *Nicene and Post-Nicene Fathers First Series: Volume 4* (tr. A. Newman). New York: Christian Literature Company, 1887.

——, 'On the Morals of the Manicheans' in P. Schaff (ed.) *Nicene and Post-Nicene Fathers First Series: Volume 4* (tr. R. Stothert). New York: Christian Literature Company, 1887.

——, 'On Two Souls, Against the Manichaeans' in P. Schaff (ed.) *Nicene and Post-Nicene Fathers First Series: Volume 4* (tr. A. Newman). New York: Christian Literature Company, 1887.

——, 'Acts or Disputation Against Fortunatus the Manichaean' in P. Schaff (ed.) *Nicene and Post-Nicene Fathers First Series: Volume 4* (tr. A. Newman). New York: Christian Literature Company, 1887.

——, 'On the Free Choice of the Will' in J. Migne (ed.) *Patrologia Latina: Volume 44* (tr. M. Knell). Paris: Imprimerie Catholique, 1865.

——, 'Enchiridion' in P. Schaff (ed.) *Nicene and Post-Nicene Fathers First Series: Volume 3* (tr. J. Shaw). New York: Christian Literature Company, 1887.

——, 'On Nature and Grace' in P. Schaff (ed.) *Nicene and Post-Nicene Fathers First Series: Volume 5* (tr. P. Holmes and R. Wallis). New York: Christian Literature Company, 1887.

——, 'Confessions' in P. Schaff (ed.) *Nicene and Post-Nicene Fathers First Series: Volume 1* (tr. J. Pilkington). New York: Christian Literature Company, 1886.

——, 'On Grace and Free Will' in P. Schaff (ed.) *Nicene and Post-Nicene Fathers First Series: Volume 5* (tr. P. Holmes and R. Wallis). New York: Christian Literature Company, 1887.

——, 'On Lying' in P. Schaff (ed.) *Nicene and Post-Nicene Fathers First Series: Volume 3* (tr. H. Browne). New York: Christian Literature Company, 1887.

——, 'On Rebuke and Grace' in P. Schaff (ed.) *Nicene and Post-Nicene Fathers First Series: Volume 5* (tr. P. Holmes and R. Wallis). New York: Christian Literature Company, 1887.

——, 'City of God' in P. Schaff (ed.) *Nicene and Post-Nicene Fathers First Series: Volume 2* (tr. M. Dods). New York: Christian Literature Company, 1886.

——, 'On the Catechising of the Uninstructed' in P. Schaff (ed.) *Nicene and Post-Nicene Fathers First Series: Volume 3* (tr. S. Salmond). New York: Christian Literature Company, 1887.

——, 'On Continence' in P. Schaff (ed.) *Nicene and Post-Nicene Fathers First Series: Volume 3* (tr. C. Cornish). New York: Christian Literature Company, 1887.

——, 'On the Merits and Remission of Sins, and on the Baptism of Infants' in P. Schaff (ed.) *Nicene and Post-Nicene Fathers First Series: Volume 5* (tr. P. Holmes and R. Wallis). New York: Christian Literature Company, 1887.

——, 'The Creed' in P. Schaff (ed.) *Nicene and Post-Nicene Fathers First Series: Volume 3* (tr. C. Cornish). New York: Christian Literature Company, 1887.

——, 'On the Spirit and the Letter' in P. Schaff (ed.) *Nicene and Post-Nicene Fathers First Series: Volume 5* (tr. P. Holmes and R. Wallis). New York: Christian Literature Company, 1887.

——, 'To Consentius: Against Lying' in P. Schaff (ed.) *Nicene and Post-Nicene Fathers First Series: Volume 3* (tr. H. Browne). New York: Christian Literature Company, 1887.

——, 'On the Holy Trinity' in P. Schaff (ed.) *Nicene and Post-Nicene Fathers First Series: Volume 3* (tr. A. Haddan). New York: Christian Literature Company, 1887.

——, 'On the Good of Marriage' in P. Schaff (ed.) *Nicene and Post-Nicene Fathers First Series: Volume 3* (tr. C. Cornish). New York: Christian Literature Company, 1887.

——, 'Against Two Letters of the Pelagians' in P. Schaff (ed.) *Nicene and Post-Nicene Fathers First Series: Volume 5* (tr. P. Holmes and R. Wallis). New York: Christian Literature Company, 1887.

——, 'On the Proceedings of Pelagius' in P. Schaff (ed.) *Nicene and Post-Nicene Fathers First Series: Volume 5* (tr. P. Holmes and R. Wallis). New York: Christian Literature Company, 1887.

——, 'On the Predestination of the Saints' in P. Schaff (ed.) *Nicene and Post-Nicene Fathers First Series: Volume 5* (tr. P. Holmes and R. Wallis). New York: Christian Literature Company, 1887.

——, 'On the Gift of Perseverance' in P. Schaff (ed.) *Nicene and Post-Nicene Fathers First Series: Volume 5* (tr. P. Holmes and R. Wallis). New York: Christian Literature Company, 1887.

——, 'On the Grace of Christ, and on Original Sin' in P. Schaff (ed.) *Nicene and Post-Nicene Fathers First Series: Volume 5* (tr. P. Holmes and R. Wallis). New York: Christian Literature Company, 1887.

——, 'On Baptism, Against the Donatists' in P. Schaff (ed.) *Nicene and Post-Nicene Fathers First Series: Volume 4* (tr. J. King). New York: Christian Literature Company, 1887.

——, 'On Man's Perfection in Righteousness' in P. Schaff (ed.) *Nicene and Post-Nicene Fathers First Series: Volume 5* (tr. P. Holmes and R. Wallis). New York: Christian Literature Company, 1887.

——, 'Answer to Letters of Petilian' in P. Schaff (ed.) *Nicene and Post-Nicene Fathers First Series: Volume 4* (tr. J. King). New York: Christian Literature Company, 1887.

Basil of Caesarea, 'Hexaemeron' in P. Schaff and H. Wace (eds.) *Nicene and Post-Nicene Fathers Second Series: Volume 8* (tr. B. Jackson). New York: Christian Literature Company, 1894.

——, *Against Eunomius* (tr. M. DelCogliano and A. Radde-Gallwitz). Washington, D.C.: Catholic University of America Press, 2011.

——, 'On the Holy Spirit' in P. Schaff and H. Wace (eds.) *Nicene and

Post-Nicene Fathers Second Series: Volume 8 (tr. B. Jackson). New York: Christian Literature Company, 1894.
Cyril of Alexandria, 'Against Nestorius' (tr. P. Pusey) in *LFC 47*. Oxford: James Parker & Co., 1881.
——, 'Christ is One' (tr. P. Pusey) in *LFC 47*. Oxford: James Parker & Co., 1881.
Cyril of Jerusalem, 'Catechetical Lectures' in P. Schaff and H. Wace (eds.) *Nicene and Post-Nicene Fathers Second Series: Volume 7* (tr. E. Gifford). New York: Christian Literature Company, 1893.
Gregory of Nazianzus, 'Oration 2' in P. Schaff and H. Wace (eds.) *Nicene and Post-Nicene Fathers Second Series: Volume 7* (tr. C. Browne). New York: Christian Literature Company, 1893.
——, 'Oration 16' in P. Schaff and H. Wace (eds.) *Nicene and Post-Nicene Fathers Second Series: Volume 7* (tr. C. Browne). New York: Christian Literature Company, 1893.
——, 'Oration 37' in P. Schaff and H. Wace (eds.) *Nicene and Post-Nicene Fathers Second Series: Volume 7* (tr. C. Browne). New York: Christian Literature Company, 1893.
——, 'Oration 38' in P. Schaff and H. Wace (eds.) *Nicene and Post-Nicene Fathers Second Series: Volume 7* (tr. C. Browne). New York: Christian Literature Company, 1893.
——, 'Oration 39' in P. Schaff and H. Wace (eds.) *Nicene and Post-Nicene Fathers Second Series: Volume 7* (tr. C. Browne). New York: Christian Literature Company, 1893.
——, 'Oration 40' in P. Schaff and H. Wace (eds.) *Nicene and Post-Nicene Fathers Second Series: Volume 7* (tr. C. Browne). New York: Christian Literature Company, 1893.
Gregory of Nyssa, 'Against Eunomius' in P. Schaff and H. Wace (eds.) *Nicene and Post-Nicene Fathers Second Series: Volume 5* (tr. W. Moore and H. Wilson). New York: Christian Literature Company, 1892.
——, 'On Virginity' in P. Schaff and H. Wace (eds.) *Nicene and Post-Nicene Fathers Second Series: Volume 5* (tr. W. Moore and H. Wilson). New York: Christian Literature Company, 1892.
——, 'On the Making of Man' in P. Schaff and H. Wace (eds.) *Nicene and Post-Nicene Fathers Second Series: Volume 5* (tr. W. Moore and H. Wilson). New York: Christian Literature Company, 1892.
——, 'On Infants' Early Deaths' in P. Schaff and H. Wace (eds.) *Nicene and Post-Nicene Fathers Second Series: Volume 5* (tr. W. Moore and H. Wilson). New York: Christian Literature Company, 1892.
——, 'On the Soul and the Resurrection' in P. Schaff and H. Wace (eds.) *Nicene and Post-Nicene Fathers Second Series: Volume 5* (tr. W. Moore and H. Wilson). New York: Christian Literature Company, 1892.
——, 'On the Holy Trinity' in P. Schaff and H. Wace (eds.) *Nicene and Post-Nicene Fathers Second Series: Volume 5* (tr. W. Moore and H. Wilson). New York: Christian Literature Company, 1892.

Bibliography

——, 'On the Holy Spirit Against Macedonius' in P. Schaff and H. Wace (eds.) *Nicene and Post-Nicene Fathers Second Series: Volume 5* (tr. W. Moore and H. Wilson). New York: Christian Literature Company, 1892.

——, 'The Great Catechism' in P. Schaff and H. Wace (eds.) *Nicene and Post-Nicene Fathers Second Series: Volume 5* (tr. W. Moore and H. Wilson). New York: Christian Literature Company, 1892.

Ignatius of Antioch, 'Letter to the Smyrnaeans' in A. Roberts and J. Donaldson (eds.), *Ante-Nicene Christian Library: Volume 1* (tr. A. Roberts, J. Donaldson and F. Crombie). Edinburgh: T&T Clark, 1867.

——, 'Letter to the Ephesians' in A. Roberts and J. Donaldson (eds.), *Ante-Nicene Christian Library: Volume 1* (tr. A. Roberts, J. Donaldson and F. Crombie). Edinburgh: T&T Clark, 1867.

——, 'Letter to the Magnesians' in A. Roberts and J. Donaldson (eds.), *Ante-Nicene Christian Library: Volume 1* (tr. A. Roberts, J. Donaldson and F. Crombie). Edinburgh: T&T Clark, 1867.

Irenaeus of Lyons, 'Against Heresies', in A. Roberts and J. Donaldson (eds.), *Ante-Nicene Christian Library: Volumes 5, 9* (tr. A. Roberts and W. Rambaut). Edinburgh: T&T Clark, 1868, 1869.

John Chrysostom, 'Three Homilies' in P. Schaff (ed.) *Nicene and Post-Nicene Fathers First Series: Volume 9* (tr. T. Bandram). New York: Christian Literature Company, 1889.

——, 'Two Instructions to Candidates for Baptism' in P. Schaff (ed.) *Nicene and Post-Nicene Fathers First Series: Volume 9* (tr. T. Bandram). New York: Christian Literature Company, 1887.

——, 'Two Letters to Theodore after His Fall' in P. Schaff (ed.) *Nicene and Post-Nicene Fathers First Series: Volume 9* (tr. W. Stephens). New York: Christian Literature Company, 1887.

——, 'Six Books on the Priesthood' in P. Schaff (ed.) *Nicene and Post-Nicene Fathers First Series: Volume 9* (tr. W. Stephens). New York: Christian Literature Company, 1887.

John Erigena, 'On Divine Predestination' in J. Migne (ed.) *Patrologia Latina: Volume 122* (tr. M. Knell). Paris: Imprimerie Catholique, 1865.

John of Damascus, 'Exposition of the Christian Faith' in P. Schaff and H. Wace (eds.) *Nicene and Post-Nicene Fathers Second Series: Volume 9* (tr. E. Watson and L. Pullan). New York: Christian Literature Company, 1898.

Justin Martyr, 'Dialogue with Trypho' in A. Roberts and J. Donaldson (eds.), *Ante-Nicene Christian Library: Volume 1* (tr. A. Roberts, J. Donaldson and F. Crombie). Edinburgh: T&T Clark, 1867.

——, 'On the Resurrection' in A. Roberts and J. Donaldson (eds.), *Ante-Nicene Christian Library: Volume 1* (tr. A. Roberts, J. Donaldson and F. Crombie). Edinburgh: T&T Clark, 1867.

——, 'Hortatory Address to the Greeks' in A. Roberts and J. Donaldson (eds.), *Ante-Nicene Christian Library: Volume 1* (tr. A. Roberts, J. Donaldson and F. Crombie). Edinburgh: T&T Clark, 1867.

——, 'First Apology' in A. Roberts and J. Donaldson (eds.), *Ante-Nicene Christian Library: Volume 1* (tr. A. Roberts, J. Donaldson and F. Crombie). Edinburgh: T&T Clark, 1867.

——, 'Second Apology' in A. Roberts and J. Donaldson (eds.), *Ante-Nicene Christian Library: Volume 1* (tr. A. Roberts, J. Donaldson and F. Crombie). Edinburgh: T&T Clark, 1867.

Origen of Alexandria, 'Against Celsus' in A. Roberts and J. Donaldson (eds.), *Ante-Nicene Christian Library: Volume 10, 23* (tr. F. Crombie). Edinburgh: T&T Clark, 1869, 1872.

——, 'De Principiis' in A. Roberts and J. Donaldson (eds.), *Ante-Nicene Christian Library: Volume 10* (tr. F. Crombie). Edinburgh: T&T Clark, 1869.

Polycarp of Smyrna, 'Letter to the Philippians' in A. Roberts and J. Donaldson (eds.), *Ante-Nicene Christian Library: Volume 1* (tr. A. Roberts, J. Donaldson and F. Crombie). Edinburgh: T&T Clark, 1867.

Tertullian of Carthage, 'On the Prescription of Heretics' in A. Roberts and J. Donaldson (eds.), *Ante-Nicene Christian Library: Volume 15* (tr. P. Holmes). Edinburgh: T&T Clark, 1870.

——, 'Against Marcion' in A. Roberts and J. Donaldson (eds.), *Ante-Nicene Christian Library: Volume 7* (tr. P. Holmes). Edinburgh: T&T Clark, 1870.

——, 'Against Hermogenes' in A. Roberts and J. Donaldson (eds.), *Ante-Nicene Christian Library: Volume 15* (tr. P. Holmes). Edinburgh: T&T Clark, 1870.

——, 'Apology' in A. Roberts and J. Donaldson (eds.), *Ante-Nicene Christian Library: Volume 11* (tr. S. Thelwall). Edinburgh: T&T Clark, 1869.

——, 'On the Testimony of the Soul' in A. Roberts and J. Donaldson (eds.), *Ante-Nicene Christian Library: Volume 11* (tr. S. Thelwall). Edinburgh: T&T Clark, 1869.

——, 'On Exhortation to Chastity' in A. Roberts and J. Donaldson (eds.), *Ante-Nicene Christian Library: Volume 13* (tr. S. Thelwall). Edinburgh: T&T Clark, 1870.

——, 'Treatise on the Soul' in A. Roberts and J. Donaldson (eds.), *Ante-Nicene Christian Library: Volume 15* (tr. P. Holmes). Edinburgh: T&T Clark, 1870.

——, 'On Idolatry' in A. Roberts and J. Donaldson (eds.), *Ante-Nicene Christian Library: Volume 11* (tr. S. Thelwall). Edinburgh: T&T Clark, 1869.

——, 'On Repentance' in A. Roberts and J. Donaldson (eds.), *Ante-Nicene Christian Library: Volume 11* (tr. S. Thelwall). Edinburgh: T&T Clark, 1869.

——, 'On the Spectacles' in A. Roberts and J. Donaldson (eds.), *Ante-Nicene Christian Library: Volume 11* (tr. S. Thelwall). Edinburgh: T&T Clark, 1869.

———, 'Antidote to the Scorpion's Sting' in A. Roberts and J. Donaldson (eds.), *Ante-Nicene Christian Library: Volume 11*. Edinburgh: T&T Clark, 1869.

———, 'On Baptism' in A. Roberts and J. Donaldson (eds.), *Ante-Nicene Christian Library: Volume 11* (tr. S. Thelwall). Edinburgh: T&T Clark, 1869.

F. Woods (ed.), *Canons of the Second Council of Orange, A.D. 529*. London, 1882.

Index

1 Clement: 5-26
2 Clement: 5-26
Abraham: 19, 32, 65, 242
Adam: 10, 22, 33, 34, 37, 48, 51, 52, 53, 55, 61, 64, 74-75, 89, 99, 105, 106, 116, 123, 124, 133, 182, 189, 190, 195, 196, 199, 201, 202, 203, 204, 211, 218, 238, 242, 246
Angel of Repentance: 6, 11, 12, 14
Angels: 6, 11, 12, 13, 20, 22, 23, 31, 32, 40, 42, 49, 50, 55, 60, 68, 75, 85, 86, 88, 111, 115, 118, 119, 122, 129, 130, 132, 138, 144, 145, 147, 148, 159-60, 166, 179, 211, 215, 229, 237
Arianism: 70, 99, 132, 134, 141, 153
Assurance: 67, 127, 144, 211, 221-22
Astrology: 72, 87, 101, 102, 160-61, 169, 201, 214
St Athanasius: 98-176

St Augustine: 2, 48, 177-238, 239, 240, 241, 242, 243, 244, 245, 246, 247, 248, 250
Baptism: 22, 63, 64, 66-68, 91, 96, 136, 140, 143, 144-149, 150, 152, 157, 196, 203-05, 207, 211, 221, 223, 226, 227, 235, 241, 242-43
St Basil of Caesarea: 98-176
Blasphemy: 32, 138
Blessing: 9, 36, 110, 124, 153, 164, 166, 211, 242
Celsus: 71, 72, 74, 75, 88, 89-90, 93, 94
Charismata: 17, 91, 95, 96, 153-56, 211
Concupiscence: 39, 204-05, 207-08, 213, 214, 217, 235, 238
Council of Orange: 239-243
Covenant: 19, 23, 37, 39, 76, 145, 156, 220, 223
St Cyril of Alexandria: 98-176
St Cyril of Jerusalem: 98-176

Demiurge: 31, 35
Demons: 10, 11, 12-14, 25, 31, 49-51, 55, 74-76, 85, 87, 88, 99, 105, 112-19, 152-53, 160, 168-69, 172, 199, 203, 208, 225,
Determinism: 23, 61, 160, 169, 195, 214
Devil/Satan: 10-11, 12, 14, 15, 22, 24, 25, 31, 33, 34, 35, 48, 49-51, 52, 60, 61, 62-63, 73, 74, 83-84, 86, 87, 99, 105, 106, 111, 112-19, 121, 123, 127, 153, 155, 160, 166, 175, 179, 188-89, 199, 200-01, 207
Didache, The: 5-26
Donatism: 191, 226, 227
Epistle of Barnabas, The: 5-26
Eve: 33, 34, 89, 106, 116
Fall: 11, 12, 22, 33, 34, 35, 39, 42, 46, 53, 55, 57, 59, 61, 62, 63, 64, 116, 118, 126, 131, 159, 171, 201, 204, 208, 218
Fasting: 16

Index

Foreknowledge: 12, 21-24, 36, 37, 38, 57, 59-60, 83, 89-90, 126, 173, 174, 186-88, 200, 214-16, 246-47
St Gregory of Nazianzus: 98-176
St Gregory of Nyssa: 98-176
Gnosticism: 5, 28, 29, 31, 32, 35, 36, 45, 47, 48, 49, 70, 71
Hermogenes: 49
Idolatry: 11, 36, 50, 52, 65, 118, 119, 141, 146
Ignatius: 5-26
Imago Dei: 29-30, 35, 37, 46, 48, 55, 57-58, 60, 64, 72, 86, 102, 109-10, 118, 120-21, 123, 131, 161-62, 164, 166, 175, 204, 208, 224, 244
Immortality: 29-30, 35, 43, 62, 92, 102, 121, 130, 138, 147, 159, 161, 199, 213
Incarnation: 27, 44, 54, 87, 124
Infants: 67, 91, 124-26, 196, 203, 204, 205, 219, 221, 235-36
St Irenaeus of Lyon: 27-46, 48, 55, 56, 70, 72, 77, 86, 90, 97
St John Chrysostom: 98-176
St John of Damascus: 98-176
John Scottus Erigena: 239-248
Joy: 17, 18, 59, 71, 110, 139, 186, 213

Justice: 36, 54, 56, 59, 76, 77, 79, 93, 125, 126, 174-75, 180, 186, 188, 190, 192, 207, 233, 244-46
Justin Martyr: 5-26
Law: 19, 23, 30, 37, 39, 59, 61, 64, 65, 74, 96, 106, 109, 132, 140, 156, 166, 173, 191-92, 198, 212, 217, 223-25, 234, 235
Manicheanism: 100, 178, 179, 191, 195, 226
Marcion: 36, 38, 47, 48-49, 53, 57, 60, 61, 64, 66, 68
Mary: 34, 37, 73, 210
Mercy: 10, 16, 30, 64, 79, 80, 82, 186, 190, 208, 209, 210, 218, 219, 220, 222, 230, 233, 241, 242
Miracles: 37, 45, 142, 148, 154-55
Montanism: 47
Moses: 20, 30, 37, 38, 74, 80, 85, 95-96, 142, 156, 192, 225
Necessity: 13, 24, 28, 29-30, 42, 58-59, 67, 75, 87, 89, 104, 106, 109, 113, 116, 118, 123, 161, 163-65, 168-70, 173, 182, 186-87, 190, 211, 214-17, 230, 244, 245-46
Nestorius: 99, 135, 153
Omnipotence: 57, 72, 211
Origen of Alexandria: 70-97

Original sin: 48, 195, 203, 204, 205, 218, 228, 240
Pelagianism: 178, 191, 195, 196, 209, 217, 221, 226, 228, 229, 233, 238, 239, 240, 243, 245, 248
Perfection (Divine): 27, 48, 49, 59, 71, 168, 244
Perfection (Human): 15, 28-29, 33, 35, 39, 40, 45, 75, 82, 91, 93, 95, 106, 122, 124, 130, 147, 150, 206, 209, 210, 228, 236
Perseverance: 33, 41, 43, 65, 66, 189, 199, 221-22, 229, 236-37, 242
Pharaoh: 38, 39, 80, 145, 216-17
Plato: 6, 36, 50, 70, 71, 95, 97
St Polycarp of Smyrna: 5-26
Praxeas: 47
Prayer: 8-9, 16, 19, 20, 107, 113, 133, 142, 147, 154, 157, 205-06, 224, 232, 236, 240, 241, 249
Predestination: 23, 36-37, 174, 210, 221-22, 226, 236, 237, 240, 243-48
Prophecy: 19, 20, 24, 41, 44-45, 56, 64, 80, 93, 95-97, 134-35, 147, 155-56, 192, 225-26
Providence: 36, 56, 66, 76, 93, 113, 119, 124, 159, 169, 171, 173-76, 183, 201, 221, 226

Punishment: 7, 11, 13, 22, 23, 24, 36, 71, 76, 86, 104-05, 106, 120, 123, 157, 161, 163, 166, 171-72, 179, 180, 181, 182, 183, 185, 186, 187-88, 189, 190, 198, 202-03, 208-09, 214, 220, 222, 225, 234, 235, 244, 247

Redemption: 31, 34, 37, 43, 139, 154, 220

Responsibility: 10, 12, 15, 21, 23, 25, 29, 30, 31, 33, 35, 38-41, 49, 60, 61, 62, 63, 70, 71, 74, 75, 78, 97, 99, 102, 105-08, 112, 162, 166, 174, 178, 184, 186, 199, 200, 207, 214, 228-29, 242-43

Resurrection: 127, 137, 139, 146, 147, 149, 203, 213

Righteousness: 7-9, 12, 13, 15-23, 45, 53, 87, 102, 106, 114, 117, 124, 145-46, 151-52, 155, 200, 206, 210, 213, 218, 224, 228, 231, 234-37, 242

Salvation: 7, 11, 16-19, 33, 38, 41, 45, 64-65, 67, 79, 82, 87, 90-91, 93-94, 117, 119, 122, 126, 127, 129, 139-46, 159, 171-73, 174, 190, 191, 192, 195, 205, 211, 217-23, 236-37, 241-45

Sanctification: 17, 19, 68, 73, 92, 94-95, 102, 130, 138, 148, 150-152, 153, 211, 223-24, 235-237

Serpent: 10-11, 22, 33-34, 36, 51, 59, 106, 116, 152, 173

Shepherd of Hermas, The: 5-26

Sovereignty: 23, 25, 36, 37, 56, 57, 112, 175

Temptation: 10-12, 15, 33, 34, 52, 60, 68, 77-78, 84-85, 116-17, 119, 122, 143, 145, 200-201, 204, 207

Tertullian of Carthage: 47-69, 70, 72, 77, 86, 90, 97

Virginity: 65, 151

Wisdom: 15, 18, 65, 74, 94-95, 96, 104, 153, 155, 157, 185, 201

Works: 7, 16, 18, 42, 43, 45, 63, 65, 66, 107, 114, 141, 142, 170, 174, 209, 212, 218-20, 222, 223, 230, 231, 236, 242, 243